A MAN NAMED JOHN

A MAN NAMED JOHN

THE LIFE OF POPE JOHN XXIII

By

ALDEN HATCH

Illustrated with drawings by Allene Gaty Hatch

HAWTHORN BOOKS, INC. / *Publishers*

NEW YORK

First Edition, July, 1963

NIHIL OBSTAT

Robert E. Hunt, S.T.D.

CENSOR LIBRORUM

IMPRIMATUR

✠ Thomas A. Boland, S.T.D.

ARCHBISHOP OF NEWARK

Newark, New Jersey, June 6, 1963

The Nihil obstat and the Imprimatur are official declarations that a book or pamphlet is free of doctrinal or moral error. No implication is contained therein that those who have granted the Nihil obstat and Imprimatur agree with the contents, opinions or statements expressed.

H-5640

CONTENTS

5

ILLUSTRATIONS

Pope John in the Sedia Gestatoria

CHAPTER ONE

ONCE IN A HUNDRED YEARS

The greatest day of Angelo Roncalli's life began on Thursday, October 11, 1962 as he awoke at 4:50 A.M. from a brief sleep of less than four hours. Opening his eyes in the dimness of the high-ceilinged bedroom of his apartment in the Vatican he must have remembered instantly what day it was, and through the flood-gates of consciousness poured a torrent of thought, of anxiety and hope, of fear and faith, the pressure of awful responsibility relieved by confidence in the guidance of our Lord. This was the day he had anticipated, planned for and prayed for during all the forty-five months since the Holy Spirit had inspired him to summon the first Ecumenical Council of the World-Wide Church in nearly one hundred years. Indeed, looking backward at fifty-eight years of priesthood, Pope John may well have felt that his entire life had been an unplanned but divinely guided preparation for its climactic moment—the opening of the Ecumenical Council.

As a young priest, Angelo Roncalli's first position as secretary to Bishop Radini-Tedeschi of Bergamo, brought him under the influence of that warm, wise, courageous and highly intelligent gentleman who not only showed him by example how a bishop should be a pastor to his flock, but also took him on many pilgrimages from which he learned how the Universal Church can adapt itself to the ways of people of other lands and even other races.

Service as an army chaplain on the blasted battlefields and in the stinking, agony-filled hospitals of World War I, taught young Roncalli to hate war and to love the warriors who fought so bravely for the things in which they believed.

And from his service as trouble-shooter for Popes Benedict XV and Pius XI in bringing the jealous national societies for the Propagation of the Faith together under one head in Rome, he learned how to handle devout but proudly nationalistic prelates.

Most important of all from the ecumenical point of view was the twenty years Roncalli spent as papal representative in the Balkans and the Near East, which gave him so deep an understanding of the Orthodox churches and fired his great ambition to unite them once more with Rome. As Papal Nuncio to faction-torn, post-war France, he polished his abilities as a diplomat and learned how to win over a Catholic but basically anti-clerical people.

Finally, during his wonderful years as Patriarch of Venice, that ancient "bridge between West and East," he not only savored at last the exaltation of service as a priest and a pastor, but also gained the knowledge of the functions of an executive and administrator without which he would not have been so well equipped to deal with the enormously complex problems of the Papacy and of setting up such a vast undertaking as an ecumenical council—and making it work.

Above all, Pope John could recall having seen thousands of Christian men and women, of many lands and different sects, serving God with selfless devotion and ardent faith and hoping eagerly for the far-off millennium when all Christians might be united in one brotherhood under God.

In all humility John might feel that his long and arduous novitiate had a divine purpose, and that, with God's help, he might bring that unification, which in his informed judgment was now more ardently desired than at any time since the Reformation and the final break between Rome and the Orthodox Churches, at least one step nearer.

Even though John's belief was that his calling of the Council had been divinely inspired to renew Holy Church and adapt her to modern times, and, above all, to open the road for the unity of all Christians, human fears and doubts must have entered his mind. Many fine prelates, especially the older cardinals of the Roman Curia, had warned him of the dangers. They feared the Council might run wild, imperiling true dogma and doctrine, or that it might degenerate into ecclesiastical squabbles that could undermine true faith.

Though his faith was strong that the Holy Spirit would enter the hearts of the assembled bishops and guide them to great decisions, as on the famous day of Pentecost, there were, inevitably, moments when John XXIII, successor to St. Peter as Vicar of Christ on Earth, knew doubts, even as Peter had on a certain dark morning in Jerusalem.

Pope John would have been less than human—he was far from that—if he had not quickly jumped out of bed and gone to the window to see what sort of a day this was. It was a horrible day. Sheets of rain blew past the street lights in the desolate expanse of St. Peter's Square as the wind howled down from the Alban Hills. There, he thought sadly, was an end to the outdoor pageantry which should mark and symbolize to the watching world the importance of this tremendous occasion.

Disappointed, but submissive to God's Will, he turned from the window and knelt before the little altar in his room. When his secretary, Monsignor Capovilla, came to call him at six o'clock he was still kneeling there.

The Pope said Mass. He had a little breakfast which it was a wonder he could swallow, and soon after seven he was standing being vested in the white and gold-embroidered ceremonial robes of the Pontifex Maximus by the attendant monsignori, a process that took nearly an hour. The traditional vestments were enormously heavy, so heavy that frail Pope Pius XII had barely been able to stagger under them. Even at eighty years of age, and undermined by a recent illness, Pope John's strong peasant body could support them more easily; but their weight was a reminder, if he needed one, of the heavier burden he must bear that day.

At a little after eight he joined all the cardinals at one end of the great Hall of Benedictions. On this high occasion, instead of scarlet, they wore white copes and tall white miters like the great crowd of 2500 bishops that overflowed the Hall of Benedictions and the vast stately rooms leading from it to the Scala Regia, the "Royal Stairway," which descends to the Gate of Bronze.

As Pope John came into the hall a blaze of sunlight almost blinded him, and through the high windows he saw the pure blue, rain-washed sky, like Noah's rainbow, a symbol and a promise.

On the stroke of eight-thirty the distant fringe of the white-robed crowd eddied as the first of the bishops began descending the broad, marble steps of the Scala Regia four and five abreast, preceded by monsignori in purple bearing the golden miter and the triple tiara of the Pope. The bishops wound around under Bernini's colonnade and started across St. Peter's Square in the channel held open for them through the enormous crowd. A detachment of the Palatine Guard in their blue and gold Napoleonic uniforms and Roman helmets marched ahead of them. On either side military bands played rousing hymns in march tempo. The bishops, however, did not march. The column flowed, a torrent of white, a forest of miters, sparkling in the strong sunlight.

Now came a burst of brilliant color like a rainbow in the clouds as the bishops of the Catholic Eastern Rite appeared in robes of purple and gold, stemming from the days of Byzantium. Around their shoulders were broad white stoles emblazoned with Greek crosses and on their heads instead of pointed miters were fat, round golden crowns set with great gleaming jewels and surmounted by small golden crosses. A few bishops of the Syrian Rite, somber in black with veiled headdresses followed.

Then the tide of white copes and pointed miters was flowing again as though it would never end. Here and there an individual would be noticed because he wore the name of some far, tragic place—the Bishop of Algiers, the Bishop of Hiroshima. Later the crowd cheered Cardinal Wyzinsky from enslaved Poland and smiling he put his finger to his lips to quiet them.

African bishops walked proudly, their faces brilliant black against the brilliant white. Then came Chinese, Japanese, Indonesians, all the colors of the human race wearing the same white livery of the World-Wide Church.

After almost an hour the crowd of bishops thinned a little, and the eighty-two cardinals began to descend the Royal Stairs. Flanked by Swiss Guards and helped by purple-clad monsignori they strode or tottered according to their age. After them in purple and gold came the nine patriarchs of the Eastern Rite wearing titles straight out of the Old Testament, like the Patriarch of Babylon of the Chaldeans . . .

At last came Pope John walking very slowly, weighted down by his gold-encrusted vestments, his jeweled white and gold miter, and his awful cares. His face was deeply lined and torn by emotion. He seemed almost in tears and yet exalted. Slowly, he walked down the stairs and around the colonnade. Then he took his place in the Sedia Gestatoria, the throne-like litter of the Popes. He had wanted to walk across the Square, the Bishop of Rome among his bishops, but he had been persuaded to ride so that the faithful could see him.

As the Pope started across the Square high above the crowd, the golden canopy carried above him was whipped by the strong wind into strange shapes a little like the tents of Genghis Khan. The bands played triumphantly; the people

cheered like a great wind; all the bells of Rome began to
peal and thunder, and the bells of every Catholic Church
throughout the world echoed them. Riding that storm of sound,
his face held in rigid control lest it break under the more fearful storm within him, Pope John came to the great doors of
the Basilica, and the climax of his life.

Within St. Peter's they had built a hall larger than most
public buildings. This Council hall enclosed the nave. Its decor
was extremely rich: crimson and gold were the dominant colors,
although the seats for the bishops, rising tier on tier on either
side, were moss green. Each tier of seats was about two hundred
and seventy-five feet long and seventy-five feet deep rising steeply
from the floor. On the shelf-desk in front of each bishop's chair
were buttons labeled *placet* and *non placet* (yes and no) to
record the votes on an electronic computor. Every second aisle
had a microphone. Closer to the Papal throne, which stood on
a dais between the enormously high, twisted bronze columns
that support Bernini's baldachin over the main altar, were tiers
of crimson armchairs for the cardinals.

Above the bishops' seats were long boxes, or galleries,
faced with dark red velvet and ropes of gold, and behind them
were splendid tapestries of the Raphael School. The theologians
and other experts were seated in these galleries. One stood
empty. It had originally been planned for the delegate observers
from the non-Catholic Christian churches, but when Pope John
had inspected the arrangements a few days before, he said,
"That won't do! Put our separated brothers close to me."

Armchairs then were placed in front of the Diplomatic
Tribune as close as possible to the Papal throne. As one pleased
Anglican prelate put it, "So there we were—bang in the front
row."

The last of the cardinals were still filing into their seats
when Pope John was carried through the great doors of St.
Peter's and slowly up the nave. On either side of him the

mitered bishops rose and stood in their endless ranks, like snowy conifers on a steep hillside. Ahead, the Pope could see the great altar gleaming with newly polished gold, and on either side of it the tribunes filled with the brilliantly-uniformed diplomats and special envoys, sent by almost all the nations of the western world to honor the occasion, and the special guests like Princes Albert of Belgium and Charles of Luxembourg. Enthroned in a large armchair in the center of this tribune was Antonio Segni.

In the armchairs in front of it, somber black in that colorful scene, sat the observers representing most of the non-Catholic Christian churches. The Anglicans and Episcopalians wore vestments stemming from their Catholic heritage; others wore academic robes or plain, dark business suits.

Whatever they wore, the Pope was delighted to see them there. He was especially happy to note the two black-veiled observers from the Russian Orthodox Church behind the Iron Curtain, who by a miracle of sorts had unexpectedly arrived the night before.

A little more than halfway up the nave, the purple-clad bearers of the Sedia Gestatoria slid it expertly to the ground. The Pope stepped out and walked the rest of the way. He knelt to pray, and then took his place on the gold and crimson throne on the dais above the crypt where the body of St. Peter lay. High above his head, a single guard, no bigger than an ant, patrolled the balcony at the base of the great dome.

A beautiful white and gold altar with six tall candles burning on it was wheeled into the nave in front of the dais, and, as the Sistine Choir invoked the Holy Spirit with the incredible sweetness of *Veni Creator Spiritus,* the enormous Basilica was filled with sound and exaltation.

Then the Service began. White-bearded Cardinal Tisserant, Dean of the Sacred College, celebrated the Mass. Reading from a huge ancient Bible he spoke the Latin words with a delicate French accent that somehow made them seem new.

From his crimson and gold throne on the dais Pope John

looked down the immensely long nave at a scene of Renaissance splendor. So might it have looked to Michelangelo or Bernini four hundred years ago when St. Peter's Basilica was being built. Mitered bishops, Swiss Guards in doublets and hose, the papal chamberlains and the purple-robed choir were all in key. There were but two intrusions of modernity and Pope John delighted in them both—the Protestant observers in business suits, and the brilliance of television lights and a huge camera crane at the far end swinging restlessly up and down, across and back, to bring this religious scene to millions of people in Europe, Africa, and even, by Telstar, to America.

Sitting there in that searching glare of light, the Holy Father's face looked immensely sad and fragile. Every ravine of care and gully of age was sharply shadowed by that brilliance. People's hearts yearned toward him and their thoughts were summarized in the words of one Italian peasant girl watching a television set who sobbed, *"Il povero Papa; troppo lavoro!"* (The poor Pope; too much work).

But later when the moment came for Pope John to read the Confession of Faith, his voice rang through Christendom's greatest church with the resonance of youthful fervor. A Protestant observer said in wonder, "He read it as though he were saying it for the first time!" That was true; Pope John's heart and soul and simple love of God made eloquent those ancient time-worn words.

And again, when the Pope knelt to invoke the Holy Spirit to inspire, guide and transcend the human frailities of the men of the Council, the pure passion of his soul lighted his words.

Now a cardinal approached the throne and knelt to kiss the Fisherman's Ring. As the Pope raised him and embraced him, his face lighted with his familiar, warm, happy smile and he gave the cardinal's shoulders an extra little pat of affection. When he smiled, he suddenly looked twenty years younger, and all over the Basilica, and in fact throughout the world, people gave a great sigh of relief and pleasure. Again the little

peasant girl put it into words as she said radiantly, *"Ecco!
Adesso è felice!"* (Now he is happy!)

The cardinal left the throne and went to the tribune where
the other cardinals sat. He climbed up the aisle between them,
embracing the aisle men on each side, who gravely and ceremonially embraced the cardinals next to them, who in turn
passed on the touch of the Pope's hands to their colleagues.

Then came another moment of high emotion as Pope
John stood in the great light to give his blessing to the people
in the Basilica and to all the millions into whose view he was
brought by the wonder of electronics. As he spoke the holy
words, twenty thousand people in St. Peter's sank to their knees;
so did millions more in homes and apartments, in chapels, in
theatres and other gathering places, in offices and stores. Even
in the taverns people dropped to their knees on the barroom
floors.

Now the actual opening ceremonies of the Council began.
Pope John took off the white cope, and his white and gold
miter was replaced by one of pure gold. Led by Archbishop
Pericle Felice, the Secretary General of the Council, the Fathers
read the Document of Obedience. Then all the cardinals, one
by one, mounted the dais to make their submission and kiss the
Pontiff's hand. Litanies were sung in Latin and Greek.

As the final act before the allocution, the Golden Book
of the Council was presented to the Pope. On its first page in
illuminated letters were the words: *Incipit Joannes* (Invoked
by John).

Pope John put on his old-fashioned gold spectacles and
began to read his address. As he spoke the precise Latin phrases,
the Pope gestured with his free right hand, emphasizing each
point emphatically. Speaking first of the glorious work of the
twenty other Ecumenical Councils which had preceded this
one and of the unnumbered smaller councils in shaping
the teaching of the Church for two thousand years, he told the

"Venerable Fathers," of his hopes for this Council. It had been called, he said, by "the latest and humble successor to the Prince of the Apostles to assert once again the *magisterium* (the teaching authority) of the Church in order that this *magisterium,* taking into account the errors, the requirements and the opportunities of our time, might be presented in exceptional form to all men throughout the world. . . .

"Illuminated by the light of this Council the Church, we confidently trust, will become greater in spiritual riches, gaining the strength of new energies from it. She will look to the future without fear. In fact, bringing herself up to date where required . . . the Church will make men, families and peoples really turn their minds to heavenly things."

With typical wit the Pope then spoke of being frequently obliged to listen to people, who though burning with zeal, "are not endowed with much sense of discretion or proportion"— people who think the world is getting steadily worse and "who behave as though they had learned nothing from history. . . . They behave as though at the time of former councils everything was a full triumph for the Christian ideal and for proper religious liberty."

With emphatic optimism Pope John said, "We feel we must disagree with these prophets of doom . . . In the present order of things, Divine Providence is leading us to a new kind of human relations which by men's own efforts, and even beyond their expectations, are directed toward the fulfillment of God's superior and inscrutable designs . . ."

The Pope then spoke of the Council's principal duty of advancing and defending the truth. He added that while not departing from it, the Church must always take note of the present, of "the new conditions and new ways of life introduced into the modern world which have opened new avenues to the Catholic apostolate . . ."

Pope John then pointed out that the business of the Fathers was not to discuss one or another fundamental doctrine of the Church—"for this a council was not necessary." Instead,

"The whole world expects a step forward . . . toward doctrinal penetration . . . studied and expounded through the methods of research and through the literary forms of modern thought . . . The substance of the Doctrine of Faith is one thing, and the way it is presented quite another . . ."

Finally the Holy Father came to his great hope—that the Council would promote Christian unity, which was his main reason for calling it. "Unfortunately, the entire Christian family has not yet fully attained . . . unity in truth," he said. "The Catholic Church, therefore, considers it her duty to work actively toward the fulfillment of the great mystery of that unity which Jesus invoked with fervent prayer from his heavenly Father on the eve of His sacrifice . . . (The Church) exults greatly at seeing that invocation extended . . . even among those who are outside her fold.

"Indeed . . . this same unity . . . seems to shine, as it were, with a triple ray of beneficent, supernal light; in the unity of Catholics among themselves; in the unity of prayers and ardent desires with which those Christians, separated from this Apostolic See, aspire to be united with us; and the unity in esteem and respect for the Catholic Church which animates those who follow non-Christian religions. . . .

"Venerable brothers, such is the aim of the second Vatican Council, which, bringing together the Church's best energies . . . prepares and consolidates the path toward that unity of mankind which is required as a necessary foundation in order that the earthly city may be brought to resemble that heavenly city where truth reigns, charity is the law and whose extent is eternity.

"Now our voice is directed to you, venerable brothers in the episcopate," the Pope continued exultantly. "The Council now beginning rises in the Church like daybreak, a forerunner of most splendid light. . . . The Church is confided to you. . . . we might say heaven and earth are united in the holding of this Council, the saints of heaven to protect your work, the faithful by continuing prayer to the Lord, and you seconding

the inspiration of the Holy Spirit in order that the work of all
may correspond to the modern expectations and the needs of
the various peoples of the world . . .

"God grant that your labors and your work, toward which
the eyes of all peoples and the hope of the whole world are
turned, may abundantly fulfill the aspirations of them all . . ."

It had been a long, long day. Pope John was very tired, yet
happily so, as a man is who rests after work well done. The
morning's doubts and fears were gone; it seemed to him that
the Holy Spirit had in truth inspired and animated that divine
outpouring of hope, homage, and devotion to God in St. Peter's.
Now it would be good to have a tranquil evening with time
for a prayer of thanksgiving and then the quiet that would
ease the small nagging pain that lately had bothered him.

Pope John knew that this was an illusory dream. He must
make one more great effort. Already St. Peter's Square, brilliantly illuminated by flood lights so that each lovely detail of
the great Basilica and the classic colonnades embracing the
Square was more clearly defined than by day, was jammed by
another great crowd. Thousands of young men carried flaming
torches. Looking down from the window of his room, the Pope
saw that the torch-bearers had arranged themselves in one, long,
straight line from the Via della Conciliazione to the steps of
St. Peter's. This was intersected by another torch-lit line stretch-
ing across the Square so that against the black crowd they made
a huge pulsing cross of golden light in celebration of the Council's opening.

When it seemed impossible that one more person could
wedge his way into that enormous throng, Pope John ordered
the window opened and a microphone connected to the loud-
speaker system. As he appeared in the open window, a great
roar of affectionate greeting went up. The torches seemed to
dance with joy, and the fountains tossed cascades of sparkling
water.

The tide of love flowing up to Pope John and from him

down to those thousands of people, his people, washed all weariness away. The strength of youthful happiness flooded through him, and he humbly wondered at God's munificence to him. Pope John held up his hand, and the noise of cheering stopped as instantly as an orchestra stops when the conductor lowers his baton. So eager were they to hear him that the people hardly seemed to breathe. Then he began to speak in a voice that was strong and warm with happiness.

"We are ending a day of peace and glory to God," he said. "Today has seen a spectacle that not even St. Peter's Basilica with its four centuries of history, has ever witnessed. It has been a scene that will remain forever in my memory and yours."

Then he talked to them for a little while of his high hopes for the Council. He did not speak in formal phrases or use the pontifical "We," but in the colloquial, almost slangy, idiom of the people. And he ended with no peroration but the kind of fatherly words straight from his heart which has made him, perhaps, the best loved man on earth.

"Now go back to your homes," Pope John said. "Give your tiny children a fond caress, and tell them that it is a caress from the Pope."

Birthplace of Pope John—Sotto il Monte

CHAPTER TWO

UNDER THE MOUNTAIN

The little town was called Under The Mountain. Looking at its clustering earth-gray buildings on the rising ground in front of Monte Canto it is possible to imagine its christening in some distant medieval day, with a wandering peddler asking a scythe-swinging peasant where the nearest shelter was, and the peasant replying *"Ecco, sotto il monte!"* (There, under the mountain.)

So, possibly, many peddlers and peasants came. Later, the small collection of buildings in front of that craggy back drop of Alpine foothills became officially Sotto il Monte. The name became it; it was an inconspicuous place destined to almost certain oblivion except for the accident of a birth.

Most of those who have written of Sotto il Monte since its sudden fame have preferred to describe it in the summer, when it is indeed lovely. Situated on the first swelling rise to the north of the Lombard plane, it overlooks the long, gentle slope of the Isola d' Adda with its two winding rivers and many-toned greens and golds of agricultural abundance, interrupted by little clusters of stone houses and the square *campanili* of churches and shrines. Behind it the foothills rise steeply like a guardian rampart, and, with the gray and ocher of its ancient stones and plaster and the faded-rose tiles of its roofs, it seems

23

to spring from the soil rather than be artificially imposed upon
nature by the work of men.

So it stands today in the imagination of almost everyone
in the world who can read, forever drenched in golden Italian
sunshine, while the sweet or aromatic odors of clover and
grain and laden vineyards, of fresh turned earth, and sweating
beasts and men tinge the fresh breeze flowing down from Lake
Como hidden in its cup among the hills.

Sotto il Monte was not a bit like that on November 25,
1881. That day the mountains were draped in ragged clouds
and sudden veils of rain. The vicious *tramontano,* that cutting,
cross-mountain wind, was blowing hard, slamming doors, rat-
tling wooden shutters, and forcing rain into the damp, frigid
houses of the hill town.

In the small, cold room with peeling plaster walls and red
brick floor of an ancient four-family house on the Via Brusicio,
Maria Anna Mazzola Roncalli lay in bed covered by every
blanket, quilt, and rug the household owned. Beside her, in
that nest made warm by her big-framed body, lay her son, born
that morning. He was a fine, solid baby who gave audible evidence of splendid lungs and a strong appetite.

Signora Roncalli was only resting to regain her strength.
After eating her midday meal of soup, bread, and cheese, she
got out of bed and dressed herself in her best clothes, a dress,
coat, and shawl of black wool, all somewhat gray with age. Then
she bundled the baby in a mass of ancient blankets and called
to her husband Giovanni Battista Roncalli that it was time to
take their son to be baptized.

In those days because of the high death rate of infants,
the Church strongly emphasized the necessity of baptizing
babies within hours after their birth, and the Roncallis were
far too devout to let bad weather interfere with the instruction
of their pastor.

Carrying her child—men never carried babies—she made
her way along the balcony outside her room, down the narrow
stone stairs to the cobbled courtyard in which chickens huddled

and a cow mooed mournfully, then through a tunnel under the house to the round-arched door that opened on a street just wide enough for a two-wheeled cart.

Giovanni and his bearded Uncle Saverio, whom the whole family called "Barba," accompanied her. Through slashing rain they trudged around the corner and across the square to the bleak parish church of San Giovanni with stucco flaking from its walls and its tall, thin bell tower. It was quite a walk for a mother a few hours after childbirth, but Maria Anna was a strong young woman who already had two daughters, and she did not mind.

They were all very disappointed, however, to find that the priest, Don Francesco Rebuzzini, had gone to visit a sick parishioner in the neighboring hamlet of Terno. There was nothing to do but to wait for him; they sat stiffly on wooden benches in the vesting room while Maria Anna nursed her child.

Don Francesco arrived four hours later, very wet and tired, looking forward to his fire and a cup of hot wine. It is easy to imagine his dismay when he saw the Roncallis sitting there stolidly. Very gently he suggested that perhaps the good Lord would not mind if they put the baptism off until tomorrow. Giovanni Roncalli was too humble to argue with a priest, but Don Francesco sensing his disappointment changed his mind. "All right," he said, "we'll do it now."

The little procession then went into the cold, bare church. The priest opened the wrought iron gates in front of the small marble font, and Saverio Roncalli took his godson in his arms. Don Francesco began the service, which could hardly be heard above the howling wind and banging doors. The good Lord surely would not blame him if he said the prayers rather rapidly.

So at lightning speed, but nonetheless devoutly, Giuseppe Angelo Roncalli—as it is written in the baptismal certificate, though later the names were reversed—was received into the Church he was to serve wholeheartedly for many, many years. When the ceremony was over Barba carried him to the altar of the Madonna, and, kneeling there, placed his godson under the protection of the Holy Virgin. There were no unusual signs, and no one even thought, much less prophesied, that one day he would hold the Keys of Saint Peter.

From the moment John XXIII mounted the Papal Throne numerous genealogists have been busy searching for an aristocratic link in the humble chain of his ancestry. They have proven, at least, his descent from Pietro Martino de Roncalli who came from the Valle Imagna to Sotto il Monte in 1429, and who could be called "landed gentry," but that thin strain of blue blood has been swamped by the rich red blood of hundreds of strong peasant strains. The Pope himself laughs at such pretense. When asked if, according to custom, his brothers should be given the title of "Excellency," he chuckled at the thought, and said, "No. Let's just call them kin of John XXIII."

Angelo Roncalli's father was a small man with a dark toothbrush mustache under a slightly crooked nose and piercing dark eyes. His slight body was wiry and tough. His wife looked more powerful than he with her big, amply padded bones, deep breasts and strong legs. She wore her dark hair parted in the middle and coiled in back which emphasized her large, regular features. Her mouth and eyes were made for smiling.

In fact, the Roncallis, in spite of their poverty, were a merry family. They did not have much to eat. Although their fare of bread, cheese, pasta, fruits and vegetables in season, and an occasional garlic-spiced sausage would make a gourmet turn pale, they thrived and grew strong on it. Of the thirteen Roncalli children ten survived infancy and most of them passed the Biblical three score years and ten. Of course, clothes were a problem, and amusement in the modern sense was nonexistent. Undoubtedly they were very cold all winter and suffocatingly hot in the summer when they all, at one time or another, worked in the fields under the blazing Italian sun. Their quarters, part of the musty second floor of that poor house, were bare, ugly, and extremely uncomfortable. The rooms all opened on the sagging balcony with doors that leaked cold air. There were no fireplaces; there was no running water. The smells from animals in the fortress-like courtyard permeated everything.

But they really were merry. As Pope John once said, "I grew up in an atmosphere of self-sufficient, blessed poverty, which makes few demands." If the Roncallis were poor, so was everyone else. There were no Joneses to keep up with in Sotto il Monte. If the food was plain, they seasoned it with enormous appetites, the result of hard work; they did not even notice the smells of their domicile. As long as they were modest, clothes did not matter. And if the climate was harsh at times, it was wonderful at others when the soft, scented air was luxurious and the sunlight touched the beauty of the valley with a golden clarity not seen in any other land.

But the true source of the Roncalli's serenity and happiness was their unquestioning faith. They had no great worries because they had the only satisfactory security known to men —confidence in God's love. Each morning they went to Mass —twice on Sunday—in San Giovanni where Don Francesco not only ministered to their souls, but in his sermons gave them the news of the town and the world. He was their only newspaper. And every evening when the Angelus boomed from many hilltop *campanili* they gathered around the kitchen table to say the Rosary.

Giovanni Roncalli has been called a share-cropper on the estate of Count Ottavio Morlani. That is not an exact translation of the Italian phrase, but "share-cropper" is close enough if you remember that it does not have the derogatory connotation in Italy that it does in America. Since the Count's lands were hilly and hard to farm, Roncalli made very little money. But, by frugality that might have shamed a Scot, most of what he made he saved. In fact, he saved enough to buy twenty-seven acres of land and a rambling old house from his patron, Count Morlani. It was the year Angelo was six. This house on the lip of the hill at the edge of town is the one in which Pope John grew up, the one he thinks of as home.

It was called Colombara Farm. Built in the seventeenth

century, it must have seemed very imposing after the apartment in town. This two-storied house, built of stone covered by drab yellow stucco, formed two sides of a courtyard. The third side consisted of sheds for animals; a low, red brick wall facing the valley completed the court. The house itself rambled around covered by old tile roofs at different levels and angles. There were eighteen rooms. Of course, the Roncallis, used to the happy congestion of their apartment, could not live in all of them. The spare rooms were used to store farm produce and precious tools.

Even before Angelo went to school, his education began. Uncle Barba liked to come in after work and read to his brother's children who enjoyed his stories of the wonderful world—and heaven, too. His taste ran to sacred literature and the stories of the saints, which were as thrilling as television to the Roncalli children.

Angelo probably began to work even before he went to school. Certainly he went down to the fields with his parents, brothers, and sisters; everyone had to lend a hand. It was not all hard work, because at noon they all gathered happily to munch their bread and cheese, and, on very special days, a small sweet. In the late afternoon they trudged up the hill toward home, with the father mounted on the donkey in the lordly custom of Italian peasants. It probably never occurred to Giovanni to let Maria Anna ride.

Sotto il Monte had no school; when he was six, Angelo and his father walked to Carvico about a mile and a half away where there was a one-room school house. Giovanni Roncalli handed his son over to the local pastor, young Don Pietro Nolis, who was also the teacher, saying, "He is bright, so if he won't study beat him." The harassed Don Pietro, prowling between the wooden benches trying to keep order in his three classes of boys ranging in age from six to eleven, must have taken that remark seriously. The Pope says, "Grammar was pounded into my head with many a box on the ears."

Giovanni Roncalli was right about his son's intelligence. Angelo's schoolmate, Battista Ogazzi, who still has a blacksmith shop in Sotto il Monte says, "Even in the first grade Angelo was smarter than any of us." And, he adds, "We all knew he would be great some day." This seemed questionable at the time. Angelo was a carefree boy who learned quickly, but who also liked to play. The mile and a half walk did not seem much to a sturdy boy who was used to working in the fields. Except in the worst weather, he probably enjoyed frolicking along barefoot with his friend, "Battistrel," more than he liked school. Certainly it helped to give him a magnificent constitution. Except for a vague mention of childhood diseases no record exists of young Roncalli having been ill.

If formal education did not enchant him, however, reading soon did. As soon as he was proficient he began to read voraciously. There was a little room off the courtyard of Colombara where he loved to hole up with a book, lying on his stomach or, when it got exciting, kneeling. His father began to fear that he was not raising a farmer as he had hoped, but an intellectual.

In three years, Angelo had exhausted the resources of the little primary school at Carvico. It was not so much his application to his studies as his almost photographic memory which got him through so fast. His younger brother Giuseppe says, "He was a keen one. For example, he never forgets a face even if he sees it in a crowd of people. He was like that as a boy. What he saw once, he always remembered."

Maria Anna was very proud of her son. Though she was a loving mother to all her ten living children, Angelo evidently was her favorite. She began to dream of his becoming a priest. So did the boy. Pope John says, "I cannot remember a time when I did not want to serve God as a priest."

The Sanctuario della Caneva, a tiny, square chapel with a classic, pillared portico was quite close to Colombara. Angelo often would slip in there for a few moments of happy devotions. On holy days, when no one worked, the Roncallis took their children on family pilgrimages to one of the numerous shrines that dotted the valley. From the rising ground of Colombara you could see six shrines which were dedicated to the Blessed

Virgin under such lovely names as Our Lady of the Woods, Our Lady of the Fields, and Our Lady of the Rose. Angelo knew and loved them all. One of his happiest days was in 1954, when, as Patriarch of Venice, he officiated at the crowning of Our Lady of the Woods. Another famous shrine which they visited was dedicated to St. Jerome Emiliani to whom the Pope has a special devotion.

Even though he wanted Angelo to be a farmer, Giovanni Roncalli was not a man to stand in his son's way. In fact, he was prepared to break himself to secure an education for Angelo. The secondary school nearest to Sotto il Monte was the Catholic "College" at Celano in the San Marino Valley beyond the hill called Monte San Giovanni. Angelo was sent there in October, 1890, at the age of nine. The first winter he stayed with a family in the neighborhood, but when spring came the lady of the house became involved in a scandal, and Maria Anna yanked her little angel out from under that hospitable but compromised roof. From that day on he walked the three miles over the mountain.

Zealous writers like to draw a comparison with St. Pius X who also walked barefoot to school and put on his shoes when he got there. Of course, Angelo went barefoot. He could not afford to wear out shoe leather, and he was undoubtedly more comfortable without shoes.

He had a good companion on his walks, another boy from Sotto il Monte who was also on his way to learning. He was Pierino Donezetti who later became mayor of Sotto il Monte, and, which was more important in the eyes of his townspeople, a professor. Donezetti says that Angelo usually walked with his nose buried in a book trying to keep up with his homework.

The boys had a convenient half-way house. Angelo's great aunt worked for Don Martinelli, the parish priest of the village of San Gregorio. On chilly days the two boys could stop at the rectory to warm up at the stove. Don Martinelli, who was hospitable and kind, never grudged them a bite to fortify their ever-empty stomachs. But even so, the four-hour climb over the mountain on the cart-track roads took fortitude. In winter Angelo never got home before sunset, and that last mile in icy darkness at the end of a weary day seemed terribly long.

Possibly because of sheer exhaustion, Angelo's marks at Celano were definitely mediocre. One report card showed him getting the equivalent of C— in four subjects and a failing D in arithmetic. In addition to his academic troubles, Angelo was once falsely accused by another boy of obtaining certain things forbidden by the rules of the school. He denied it, but the teacher, who did not believe him, gave him a letter complaining about it to carry to good Don Francesco. The future Pope sensibly solved his problem by not delivering it, as he said later, "with a tranquil conscience."

Despite his poor grades, Angelo was accepted in the seminary at Bergamo, the big city of the district, when he was eleven years old. Attending the seminary did not mean that he was committed to the priesthood because at the time the seminaries were virtually the only schools of higher education, and boys destined for all the professions went to them. However, to Angelo it was a giant step toward the service of God for which he felt an ever-stronger vocation. Giovanni Roncalli remained unconvinced. "He's a poor farmer's son," he said. "He'll be a poor priest."

There were fees to be paid for which Monsignor Morlani, who had watched the boy growing closer to God, made himself responsible. But his proud mother felt that her son should have a little money for unexpected contingencies. Although the Roncallis had food to eat and a house to live in, they had literally no cash at all. In this emergency, Maria Anna consulted Don Francesco, who suggested that she call on the members of her family to ask for contributions. On the day before Angelo was to set out in the world, Maria Anna made the rounds of the family. In the late afternoon when she came home, she broke down for the only time in Angelo's memory. In a storm of weeping, she flung the coppers and tiny silver pieces on the kitchen table. The sum total was two lire—about forty cents.

The Cathedral—Bergamo

CHAPTER THREE

"THOSE BELLS OF BERGAMO"

Bergamo is a two-in-one city on a steep hillside. The upper town looks down on the lower, socially as well as geographically. The minor seminary to which Angelo Roncalli went was in the upper town, but Angelo gave little thought to its location; he was just supremely, humbly happy to be where he was.

His life as a seminarian was rigorous. After the clanging bells at 6 o'clock every morning—5:30 in summer—there were prayers, studies, Mass, and then a brief breakfast. The whole morning was given to further study and some chores. Dinner at noon was filling, although it consisted of extremely dull food which was usually badly cooked. Dinner was followed by brief relaxation, four hours of classes and studies, a meager supper, devotions, and bed.

Boys who had been brought up in aristocratic and middle class families found this Spartan round hard to bear. The health of young Eugenio Pacelli (later Pius XII) broke under the strain when he was a student. But strong, young Roncalli was accustomed to far greater privations than seminary life imposed.

Stocky and tough, with brown hair, and fair, ruddy skin, Angelo had laughing grey eyes that changing light could turn

to blue or green. Never in his life did Roncalli confuse piety
with gloom. If a man who served God was living the best
of all possible lives, why should he be gloomy? From the day
he entered the seminary and put on a cassock, as all the seminarians did whether destined for the priesthood or not, he wore
it joyously. He lived by the maxim, "A sad priest is a bad
priest."

Incidentally, the first time he went home wearing clerical
clothes, his parents and his brothers and sisters with touching
humility dropped the familiar *tu* (thou) and addressed him by
the more formal *voi*. Even Giovanni Roncalli was inspired to
a rare flight of imagination by the sight of his son so clothed.
Sticking a new spade in the ground so that it gleamed in the
sun like a bishop's silver miter, he said, "Oh, if I could some
day see you with that spade on your head."

Bergamo was a provincial city only about eight miles from
Sotto il Monte, but it was a metropolis to young Roncalli; it
was another world where the windows of his mind were flung
wide open. Although the city was small and isolated, it was, in
fact, rich in music and other arts. It was perhaps the intellectual
center of Catholicism at that time.

Many of the Italian intellectuals of the nineties were members of the anti-clerical, socialistic parties which, about twenty
years before had wrested the Papal States from Pope Pius IX,
"the Prisoner of the Vatican." These intellectuals denied that
freedom of thought could co-exist with religion, and sneered
at simple faith—it was not "modern." Catholics were persecuted
and imprisoned for their faith.

Pius IX, in his bitter seclusion, had then ordered Cath-
lics to take no part in the political life of newly united Italy.
But his successor, Leo XIII, partially lifted this interdiction in
his great Encyclical *Rerum Novarum*. So Italian Catholics were
beginning again to be active in the life of the nation. Bergamo,
among its sheltering mountains, had always remained profoundly loyal to the Church. *L'Osservatore Romano* called it
"the most Catholic land." For this reason it attracted some of

the most profound Catholic thinkers, and was the center from which the great revival of religious thinking and Catholic action flowed over all Italy.

The man who led this movement was Monsignor Camillo Guindani, Bishop of Bergamo. At a time when government hostility toward the church was near its peak, Guindani by sheer moral force and courage kept the minds, loyalty and faith of his people free and uncorrupted by Marxist materialism. He did this, not simply by preaching, but in highly practical ways —notably by encouraging the organization of 366 Parish Councils in his diocese, as well as workmen's Catholic unions or federations, agricultural cooperatives, farmers' credit banks, and other associations of Catholic laymen. These organizations had a total of over forty thousand members, the precursors of the great Italian Catholic Action movement. Also sparking this movement were two brilliant and devoted Catholic laymen, Count Stanislao Medolago Albani and Nicolo Rezzara who worked closely with the Bishop, supplying practical organization and inspiration for the laity.

Though only a young seminarian, Angelo Roncalli was thrilled to feel himself part of a great spiritual renaissance. As a youth he saw the great leaders only from a distance, though, of course, he often heard Bishop Guindani preach in the richly ornamented, Byzantine-style church of Santa Maria Maggiore. However, just seeing and hearing them from afar was enough to give him a conception of priestly duties according to their ideas, and he has since sought the cooperation of laymen in the affairs of the Church.

The life of the city stimulated Roncalli's mind as well as his spirit. No longer was he dull at his studies; now the subjects gripped his interest—philosophy, liturgy, world history, and, more particularly, the long, colorful, inspiring history of Christianity and the Roman Catholic Church. However, he improved little at scientific subjects such as mathematics, geology, and so forth. Theology interested him—and the humanities, in the most human connotation of the word.

But not all of Roncalli's reading was theological. He began to read the writings of Alessandro Manzoni, the great, eighteenth century Catholic author. The moving, religious style of Manzoni's poetry and novels influenced the faithful in Bergamo more than a decade of sermons. His writings certainly had more influence than the outpouring of religious pedantry in many formal theological works of the times. Roncalli's favorite is said to have been Manzoni's novel, "The Betrothed," part of which takes place around Bergamo, the countryside he knew so well.

In Bergamo, too, Roncalli learned to love good music. Though Milan, about thirty miles away, was in the throes of the fashionable vogue of Verdi's romantic operas, the people of Bergamo preferred the "old fashioned" music of their native son, Gaetano Donizetti, and the great works of Ponchielli, Mozart, Bach, and the seventeenth century Italians. These composers, whose music he plays on his hi-fi set in the Vatican, are still Pope John's favorites.

However, despite this intellectual stimulation, Angelo Roncalli did not change. In his heart, he remained a peasant boy from Sotto il Monte, and on every possible occasion he hiked the eight miles over the mountains to spend a night or a brief vacation with his family. At Colombara Farm he easily slipped back into the regular routine of hard work in the fields and homey family evenings, although he was undoubtedly slightly embarrassed by the respect that his kinsfolk accorded to his cassock.

After three years in the seminary there was no longer much doubt that Angelo Roncalli would become a priest. The steps were taken slowly but regularly. On June 28, 1895, at the age of thirteen and a half, he was given his first tonsure. In another three years he received minor orders. And in 1900, he graduated with honors.

By this time, the mediocre student of Celano had such a brilliant scholastic record and generous personality that instead of allowing him to complete his education in his native diocese, Bishop Guindani gave him one of the seven scholarships of the Cerasoli Institute to the famous Seminario Romano —at that time usually called the Apollinare. This was certainly a mark of distinction. The administrators of the Church are careful to choose for this seminary only those students whose brilliance and high character suggest them as "officer material" for the Apollinare, which might be described as the West Point of the Holy See from which many of its highest officials emerge.

Roncalli came then to the center of the Catholic world where new and more complex influences joined in forming his mind—though not in changing the simplicity of his character.

On January 3, 1901, Angelo arrived in Rome with two other young students from Bergamo. His high anticipations of the famous Apollinare were at first considerably dashed by the reality. At that time it was housed in a gloomy old building in a rabbit warren of twisting streets between Via della Scrofa and Piazza Sant' Agostino. The great stone structure was joined by an enclosed arched bridge to an equally ancient building across the narrow street that contained the Church of Sant' Apollinare, from which the university took its familiar name.

Roncalli's cell-like room had an enormously high ceiling and one small, square, barred window high above his head. The penetrating, damp chill of the building had been accumulating for five centuries. The country boy felt as though he were in jail.

However, he soon recovered his exuberant spirits. Outside the grim walls was the wonderful city with its thousand churches, adorned in beauty by the greatest artists of mankind. In his hours of leisure, Roncalli roamed its streets with fellow seminarians, encountering flocks of other young men from all the countries of the world who had come to Rome to study for the priesthood. Most of them wore plain black cassocks like his, but the Germans were dressed in bright red. He learned that this custom stemmed from the Middle Ages, when the boys from Germany were such a boisterous lot that the authorities decreed they should wear their colorful cassocks to make them easier to spot and apprehend.

To a youth who loved history as Roncalli did, just walking around in Rome was exciting. The very ground beneath his feet was stratified history, layer upon layer, city piled on city. Where the archeological excavations were being dug you could see the different strata containing virtually the whole record of western civilization from the little pagan village on the Capitoline Hill through the days of the Roman Republic and the Empire, from the relics of the early Christians to the Romanesque churches of the great conversion, and from the elaborate beauty of the Renaissance building to the modern shops on the Piazza di Spagna lit by those dazzling new electric lights.

But if it was the city beyond the seminary walls that first enthralled Roncalli, it was not long before its forbidding interior became a place of even greater wonder to him as he absorbed its inspiring atmosphere of selfless devotion to God combined with intellectual brilliance. Great as his love of God, of Jesus, and of His mother had always been, it was deepened as the theology taught at the Apollinare enriched his understanding; with knowledge came more fervent devotion.

Roncalli's spiritual director in the seminary was a gentle, saintly man named Father Francesco Pitocchi, who combined great ability and great piety with warm affection for his pupils. Later Pope John said of him, "Ah Padre Francesco! If later we managed to make something of our lives we must say it came from him."

Other teachers who made a great impression on the young Roncalli were the Rector, Monsignor Spolverini, who frightened the pupils although they loved him, austere Monsignor Bugarini and Monsignor Benigni, Professor of Church History, who talked very fast with a slight stutter but had a fine ringing voice. Benigni was also editor of the *Voce della Verità* which was published in the great dank basement of the Apollinare; he used to correct the proofs in the classroom. The rigid rules of the seminary forbade the students to read any newspapers, even the Vatican's *L'Osservatore Romano,* but Monsignor Benigni kept them up with the news—like Don Francesco in Sotto il Monte—by apparently spontaneous ejaculations such as, "Oh my! This is very serious! King Alexander and Queen Draga of Serbia have been assassinated."

The students used to gather in the chapel of the Madonna della Fiducia to hear eminent preachers who came to talk to them. One summer evening when the windows were all open, an impassioned young Jesuit was talking of hell and eternal damnation. In his spirited peroration he shouted at the top of his voice, "Fire! Fire! Fire!" Out of the shops, taverns and tenements around the Piazza Sant' Apollinare tumbled butchers, bartenders, and housewives to mill around the chapel yelling, "Where's the fire?"

Another man who amused Roncalli was the bursar, a worried little fellow named Garroni. Almost every day as the students sat in the echoing refectory eating their plain midday meal, Garroni would move rapidly up and down between the long tables saying loudly, "Don't eat too much! Please, don't eat too much." "One would have thought," says Pope John, "that the responsibility for provisioning all Rome weighed on his shoulders."

Of the subjects taught at the Apollinare, Canon Law was a specialty. An assistant lecturer on this subject attracted the attention of all the students, and it was whispered that the Holy Father himself had taken note of him. Almost exactly the opposite of Roncalli, he was very tall and so thin that his body seemed too frail to support his exertions. When he lectured the clarity of his mind made his complex subject seem simple. He was friendly and gentle, but seemed somehow aloof as though his attention was half distracted by unworldly meditations. His name was Don Eugenio Pacelli.

After less than a year in Rome the impersonal hand of the State plucked Roncalli from the cloisters for his military service. Though the anti-clerical Government did not grant deferment to seminarians, they at least allowed them the same privilege that other university students had—"volunteering." This enabled them to choose their branch of the service, in which they served for one year, emerging with the rank of sergeant. Then they were put in the active reserve which meant two weeks of field training every year, very much as in the United States today.

Roncalli volunteered with the 73rd Infantry Regiment stationed at Bergamo. The abrupt transition from monastic life to the rough fellowship of the army did not faze him. He adapted to army life as easily as he did to any environment— he even grew a very becoming military mustache—and he got along well with his comrades.

This was probably the most luxurious period of Roncalli's youth. After the rigorous confinement of his monastic schooling, army discipline must have seemed lax. Good food was plentiful, and there was even a ration of wine! Marching was nothing to the youth who had traveled over Monte San Giovanni every day in his boyhood. The barracks were not as bare as his cell in Rome, and though he did not realize it, his own gay, affectionate nature and his own goodness brought out the very best in his comrades, many of whom became his lifelong friends.

On his frequent holidays he could walk to Sotto il Monte and enjoy a get-together with his family and the wonderful warm feeling of being home. It was all so much fun that a devout young man might have felt it was almost sinful, but Angelo Roncalli knew that it was never a sin to be truly happy.

When Roncalli returned to the Apollinare after his military service, he got down to serious work. In the course of his studies he read the *Annales Ecclesiastici*, the great history of the Church by Cesare Cardinal Baronio. It stirred his imagination and, though he always pictured his priestly role as that of the simple shepherd of a pastoral flock, he wondered if he might some day make a similar contribution to ecclesiastical history. The first historical work he ever published (in 1908) was a monograph on the life of Cardinal Baronio whose method and philosophy greatly influenced his youth.

In July, 1903, when Pope Leo XIII died at the age of ninety, twenty-two-year-old Roncalli underwent the tremendous emotional experience of the death and funeral of a great Pope with all its solemn ritual and somber splendor. It was, of course, followed by the exciting conclave to elect a new Pope.

This was a long business in 1903. Day after day, Roncalli with his fellows seminarians stood in the great colonnaded Square of St. Peter's watching the iron stove pipe that stuck out of a frosted window of the Vatican to see whether the first puff of smoke would be white, meaning that a new Pope had been elected, and groaning with the crowd as time after time the smoke was the black signal that no agreement had been reached.

Finally the white smoke rose thinly on the hot summer air, and a cardinal appeared to announce the joyous news: "We have a Pope!"

Roncalli was as surprised as everyone else to learn that it was Giuseppe Sarto, the Cardinal-Patriarch of Venice, who chose to be named Pius X. Roncalli knew that Cardinal Sarto had also been a barefoot peasant boy. Naturally, he carried the comparison no further in his mind. The new Pope came out on the balcony of St. Peter's, a tiny, white and scarlet figure against the immensity of the dome, and, faintly in the breathless silence of that great crowd, Angelo heard the first blessing to "the city and the world" of the man whom he would live to see be canonized a saint.

Graduated from the Apollinare in 1904, Angelo Roncalli was ordained a deacon on June 18, and according to custom asked for his ordination as a priest. After a month of waiting the date was set.

On one side of the Piazza del Popolo in Rome two lovely

little baroque churches stand side by side, separated only by a narrow street. With small golden domes and pillared doorways they are exactly alike. As you face them the one on your right is Santa Maria in Monte Santo, where on August 10, 1904, Angelo Roncalli was ordained.

In what seems a sign of the future the bishop who performed the rite was Monsignor Cappetelli, Patriarch of Constantinople and Vice-Gerent of Rome. As Roncalli lay in symbolic prostration before the altar no one may have known what his thoughts were, but it is certain that incredulous gratitude mingled with utter submission to the Will of God.

The next day Roncalli celebrated his first Mass in St. Peter's at the altar which is immediately above the tomb of the first Bishop of Rome. How small and yet how great he must have felt in that huge, splendid Basilica, as he offered the Church's greatest sacrifice. In the exaltation of his spirit no higher plane seemed attainable, yet one more thing was given him. An incident occurred that appeared like a mark of divine favor.

As Roncalli and the monsignor who accompanied him moved down a passage crowded with pilgrims, the Holy Father himself unexpectedly appeared. Dropping to his knees Roncalli looked up at the round, serene face with its gentle blue eyes behind gold-rimmed spectacles. Then his companion spoke to the Holy Father, saying, "Your Holiness, this is a young priest of Bergamo who has celebrated his first Mass this morning."

The Pope's face became very serious, and he knelt facing Roncalli in the corridor while the awed pilgrims drew back. The Pope seemed to recall the vivid emotion and joy of his own first Mass. Kneeling face to face the young priest repeated to the Vicar of Christ the vows of his priesthood. When he had finished, the Pope said, "Bravo!" with paternal approval. Then rising he placed his hands on Roncalli's head and gave him his blessing, adding "Go in grace and go with courage to do honor to your calling."

The Pope moved away to greet the other pilgrims, then changed his mind and turned back. "When will you say your first Mass in your own country?" he asked.

"On the Feast of the Assumption, Holy Father," Roncalli managed to say.

The Pontiff smiled gently and his eyes seemed far away in memory of the little villages of Lombardy and Veneto that he would never see again. He repeated, "On the Assumption. What a beautiful occasion! And those bells of Bergamo. How they ring! How they ring . . ."

Church of San Giovanni—Sotto il Monte

CHAPTER FOUR

THE BISHOP OF BERGAMO

Don Angelo Roncalli went to celebrate the Mass of the Assumption at Sotto il Monte on August 15, 1904. The bare little church on the hill to which Maria Anna had carried him to be baptized was crowded that day by friends and fellow townsmen smiling their good wishes. The two front pews were taken up by the Roncalli family, bursting with pride in their best black clothes.

With as great emotion as in St. Peter's, Don Angelo celebrated the Mass. Then, trembling with the stage fright of any young person making his public debut before his family and friends, he preached his first sermon. Its subject, suggested by old Father Francesco, was the theological significance of the Assumption of the Blessed Virgin. It was said to be an adequate performance, although it was a little over the heads of his audience.

After the Mass everyone crowded up to congratulate Don Angelo. The family physician, Doctor Cesare Mingazzi, shook his hand warmly and made the conventional compliment to young priests, "Now you must go on to become Pope." Both he and Roncalli laughed heartily at the absurdity of it.

After a brief stay at Colombara Farm, Roncalli went back

45

to Rome to join the faculty of the Apollinare as an assistant instructor, and to study for a doctorate in Canon Law. While there he was saddened to hear of the death of his sponsor at the Seminary, Bishop Guindani.

To replace the Bishop of Bergamo, Pope Pius X chose one of the most brilliant members of the Roman Curia, Monsignor Giacomo Maria Radini-Tedeschi. Before he entered the priesthood he had been Count Radini-Tedeschi, and had given up the privileges of his rank to serve God.

Radini-Tedeschi was overdue for the episcopate. For fifteen years he had served the Holy See directly as a combination ambassador, trouble shooter and public relations man. In that capacity his courtesy and charm, combined with extraordinary zeal, had made him so valuable that Pope Leo XIII had deferred his elevation to a bishopric. Now there was trouble in Bergamo, and Pope Pius felt that Radini-Tedeschi was the man to tackle it. So highly did the Pope regard him that he decided to perform the rite of consecration himself. Because they were from Bergamo, Gugliemo Carozzi and Angelo Roncalli were chosen to assist at the Mass.

This was the first consecration performed by Pius X. He chose January 29, 1905, for the ceremony because it was the feast day of St. Francis de Sales for whom the bishop-elect had a particular devotion. It was both a moving and brilliant occasion, one that Pope John can recall in detail today.

The candles burning on the altar of the Sistine Chapel seemed pale in the clear light which poured through the high windows illuminating the superb paintings of the Renaissance masters that lined the chapel walls and the sombre magnificence of Michelangelo's "Last Judgment," behind the altar, and his famous ceiling. Except for the cleared space before the canopied papal throne and the altar, the long narrow chapel was crowded by cardinals in their splendid robes, mitered bishops in purple, diplomats in sparkling full dress uniforms, and the Roman aristocracy in somber black relieved by the flash of the great jewels worn by their lace-veiled ladies.

The ceremony had moments of high religious drama. At the very instant of consecration, when the Pope laid his hands upon the kneeling bishop's head, it was young Roncalli who placed the Book of the Gospels on his bowed neck in token of his acceptance of the Yoke of Christ. Then, when the Holy Father raised the newly consecrated bishop and embraced him, he whispered something in his ear which brought a look of ineffable spiritual exaltation to Radini's face. No one heard that message then, but many years later Roncalli learned it from Radini-Tedeschi's dying lips.

Soon after his consecration Bishop Radini-Tedeschi paid a call on Monsignor Spolverini, Rector of the Apollinare. "I have come to ask you to recommend some young priest of Bergamo to act as my secretary," he said.

The Rector rapidly ran over the possibilities in his mind and came to a quick decision. "I suggest Roncalli," he said. "He is intelligent and conscientious. You will get on with him well—everyone does—and though he is of Bergamo to the core, he has so completely absorbed the spirit of the Seminary that he is the most *Romanized* of them all."

"Send him to me," said Radini.

Thus, instead of becoming a simple country priest as he had expected, Roncalli was propelled into a life of special responsibility under the guidance of the man who became the model he always sought to emulate. Pope John calls him, "My spiritual father," and "The Pole Star of my priesthood."

Before taking up his residence in the Episcopal Palace at Bergamo, the young secretary went with his bishop on a pilgrimage to Lourdes. This was the first time Roncalli had left his native land, and he enjoyed the experience with all the ebullience of his nature.

The Grotto at Lourdes, where the Blessed Virgin had appeared so often to Bernadette, her little peasant friend, made so deep an impression on Angelo that ever after he made frequent pilgrimages there. Indeed, when he became Pope he expressed the desire to break the precedent that chains the Pontiff to Rome and go once more to that sacred place. But the rigid traditions of the Vatican discouraged his pious wish.

On that trip the Bishop also took Father Roncalli to Ars to pay homage to the saintly curé, John Mary Vianney, patron of parish priests, and to Paray-le-Monial where St. Margaret Mary Alacoque had the vision of the Sacred Heart.

However, the journey was not entirely devoted to pilgrimages. One of Radini-Tedeschi's purposes was to study the workings of French Catholic Action for innovations that might be applied to the problems of Bergamo. This was the first awakening of Angelo's interest in the French people and their problems which enabled him to serve the Holy See so well in a still distant future.

Then they returned to Bergamo and got to work. How they worked!

It would be difficult to imagine two less similar people than the Bishop of Bergamo and his young secretary. The Bishop was a patrician with all the elegance birth and environment had given him. "So tall and noble in person and manner," Pope John once said. He was vibrant, authoritative and filled with nervous energy and anxiety. The secretary was still a stocky, earthy peasant who spoke Italian with the harsh accent of the north country folk and whose sunny disposition was not disposed to worry. For this very reason they made a splendid team.

They had two things in common: their gaiety and their enormous energy. The Bishop has been described as a perfect whirlwind who spared neither himself nor his subordinates. Angelo could take it. There were never enough hours in the day for all that needed to be done so he formed the habit of sleeping only four hours a night. Pope John's splendid constitution has enabled him to maintain this Spartan existence almost until the present time.

When Bishop Radini-Tedeschi first entered the Episcopal Palace at Bergamo he was appalled. It was like a tenement house owned by an avaricious landlord. Even a peasant boy was shocked by its dilapidated condition and unsavory odors. In his life of the Bishop, Roncalli wrote, "The Episcopal Palace was in an ugly, uncomfortable and unhealthy state . . . the condition of the Chancery was even worse. . . ."

Even the fine seventeenth century cathedral, with its huge cupola, octagonal baptistery walled by sheets of precious red marble, and its religious masterpieces was falling apart. Characteristically, putting the dignity of the dead before the comfort of the living, Radini-Tedeschi first restored the tombs of the Bishops of Bergamo in the crypt, and then tackled his own housing. He built a brand new episcopal palace. Such was his drive that in the land of *"dolce far niente"* (sweetness of doing nothing), he had it completed within a year.

At the same time he was building churches, monasteries and educational institutions all over his diocese. To Roncalli's admiring eyes he was like "those splendid prelates of the Renaissance who displayed their magnificence by the superb edifices they built," and he thought that a worthy memorial to his Bishop would be the quotation, "Stones will speak of thee."

Men would speak of this Bishop, too. He came to Bergamo at a time when the Catholic Action movement, which had its wellsprings there, had been thrown into confusion by an internal quarrel between the progressives or "modernists" and the conservatives. He saved the best of its social institutions and helped mightily to restore its unity.

As the Bishop's secretary, Roncalli was in the thick of the socio-ecclesiastical politics, which eventually led to the founding of the Italian Christian-Democratic Party. Thus he came to know the grand old man of the movement, Professor Nicolo Rezzara, whom he had once admired from afar. When Rezzara met with the disfavor of the conservative element of Bergamo, who complained to the Holy See, Roncalli accompanied Radini-Tedeschi to an audience with Pope Pius X at which the Bishop of Bergamo successfully pleaded the cause of the old humanitarian whose zeal occasionally exceeded his prudence.

From his Bishop, Don Angelo learned a new definition of that word which is so stressed in the behavior of the Catholic clergy. Said the Bishop of Bergamo, "Prudence does not consist of doing nothing. It means to act, and act well."

He might have added courageously, for Radini-Tedeschi was no man to shirk a fight for the right. At times his free-swinging, knightly blade made him extremely unpopular with his more conservative parishioners. The trouble at Ranica was an example. In 1909, the workers of the factory in that suburb of Bergamo went on strike. Roncalli wrote, "The question was not a simple one of wages or personalities, but one of principle: the fundamental right of Christian labor to organize against the powerful organization of capital."

The Bishop was one of the first to put his name down for a generous contribution to the strikers' relief fund. Both he and his secretary visited the strikers' homes bringing food, necessities, and moral support. The gratitude of the strikers to the handsome prelate and the jolly young priest was touching.

But the conservative industrialists and aristocracy of Bergamo turned as purple with rage as the Bishop's robe at what they considered his scandalous conduct. With witty understatement Roncalli wrote, "Less than benevolent reports were dispatched to his superiors (in Rome) . . . (However) taking the side of the strikers was for him a highly Christian duty . . . and one of justice, charity and social peace. So he let them scream and calmly continued (to support the strikers)."

When it was all over and the precedent-setting strike was finally won, the Bishop received a vote of confidence from the highest possible source. "We cannot disapprove of what you have thought prudent to do," wrote Pope Pius X, "because you are fully acquainted with the place, the persons involved and with the circumstances."

This was another lesson for Don Angelo: how a great bishop and a great Pope can take care of the material needs of their flock.

Bishop Radini-Tedeschi and his ubiquitous secretary were involved in many other activities. The Bishop visited every one of the 352 parishes of his diocese. In addition they organized a travel service of sorts to help tens of thousands of laborers who, because of unemployment at home, were emigrating to other countries of Europe and America. The Bishop also created the League of Women Workers to help those unfortunate females who at that time had practically no legal rights in a man's world. Other projects were the Association for the Protection of Young Women, and the *Casa di Maternita* to give financial help to expectant mothers and those with children newly born —in or out of wedlock.

Nor did these things end their far-ranging activities. The Bishop was a great man for pilgrimages to foreign places, both to worship at the famous shrines and confer with foreign prelates about the world-wide problems of the Church. During these years Roncalli went with him to France again and also to Spain and Palestine. Don Angelo loved to travel. Because of his open mind and open heart, he profited by these opportunities, and learned how the Universal Church adapts itself to the ways and customs of her children in different countries. More especially, he gained a deep understanding of the peoples of foreign lands.

However, busy as his Bishop was, he did not take up all of Roncalli's time. If only four hours a night are given to sleep, twenty hours are left for work and prayer. During his years in Bergamo, the young priest had an active career of his own. He often took the place of some local pastor celebrating Mass in one of the lovely old churches of the diocese. He spent much time hearing confessions and comforting the sick, and he taught the children catechism every Sunday at the Church of San Michale del Arco.

Of course, at any Roncalli family occasion, such as a wedding or a Baptism, at Sotto il Monte, he was on hand to officiate. In addition, he frequently hiked the five miles over the mountains to visit his family at Colombara Farm and sit through long golden evenings talking with his father about religion, politics or farming, thus learning the needs of the people and renewing his own contact with the land.

In 1906, he was asked to teach at the seminary in Bergamo, from which he had gone on to Rome. He lectured on Church History, and the lives of the Fathers of the Church as well as Apologetics. His former students, among them the present rector, Monsignor Giuseppe Angiolini, still recall him dashing into the classroom a little late and puffing hard from having run up the long flight of steps that led to the seminary. They remember, too, how exciting he made the subjects he taught because he was excited by them himself. He never talked down to them, but rather carried them away with him, spicing his lectures with interesting anecdotes, bubbling with unexpected humor and enthusiasm, or moving them deeply by the real emotion with which he described the sufferings of the martyrs in his deep, resonant voice. Don Angelo left with his students in Apologetics a message that they never forgot: "Always be prepared to answer anyone who demands a reason for your faith."

It was also in 1906 that Roncalli made an important historical discovery of his own. The Bishop had to make numerous trips to Milan to confer with the Cardinal-Archbishop. While the prelates talked, Roncalli liked to browse in the grimy archives of the Archdiocese. One day he climbed a ladder to see what a set of thirty-nine tall volumes of manuscript was. As he opened one and carefully turned its parchment pages, brittle with age, he almost fell off his high perch with excitement. They were the original documents relating to the pastoral visits of St. Charles Borromeo, sixteenth-century Cardinal-Archbishop of Milan, to Don Angelo's beloved Bergamo.

On the way home in the train to Bergamo he told Bishop Radini-Tedeschi about his discovery and his inspiration to collate, annotate and publish these records of a saint whom both he and the Bishop revered. Laughing at his eagerness and yet caught up in his enthusiasm, the Bishop promised help.

After that, every time he went to Milan Roncalli went straight to the high shelf of books, and each time he told the Bishop about his further discoveries. The Bishop advised his young secretary to consult his old friend, Monsignor Achille Ratti, who was prefect of the Ambrosiana Library in Milan.

Pope John well remembers his first meeting with the man who became Pope Pius XI. Awed by the librarian's towering reputation for scholarship and fearful that he would throw cold water on his project, Don Angelo tiptoed through the great stone reading room of the Ambrosiana, conscious of his slightly squeaking shoes and an occasional irritated glance from a student bent over a pile of books. Monsignor Ratti was sitting behind a big table-desk piled high with manuscripts at the right end of the hall. As Roncalli approached, he looked up from his work and welcomed his visitor with "cordial amiability." While the young priest poured out the news of his discovery and his great project, Monsignor Ratti regarded him through rimless spectacles with amused but kindly interest. "I can still see him," Pope John says, "with his broad, open-browed head bent toward me as he listened to my plan and formed his first impression of me."

Ratti's interest was aroused by Don Angelo's glowing exposition. "I can't advise you until I examine the papers myself," he said. "Come back in a few days."

The prefect of the Ambrosiana was that rare sort of librarian who gets things done. When Roncalli returned he found that Monsignor Ratti had gone through the whole collection of manuscripts and had chosen the sixth and seventh volumes as the most important. Documents from them were actually spread on the librarian's desk ready to be photostated for Roncalli's convenience. This was done under Ratti's supervision, and he himself arranged the negatives in chronological order.

Spurred by the interest of a scholar for whom he had great respect, Bishop Radini-Tedeschi became really enthusiastic. He gave Roncalli a little money for expenses and appointed one committee of professors and another committee from the diocese to work with him. However, the only person who really helped much was Monsignor Ratti. In the preface to the first volume of his monumental work on St. Charles Borromeo's Apostolic Visits to Bergamo, Roncalli slyly noted, "What so often happens occurred in this case, too: a project begins with the naming of a committee, but it ends with one person doing all the work."

As the ten years of their association flew by, Don Angelo's relationship with "my bishop" deepened from that of disciple and master to that of a son to his beloved father. His love and admiration for the Bishop overflowed. He wrote, "This man, this bishop, with his martial spirit, his energetic and robust will was truly good, profoundly good. What long-suffering patience he displayed! Others less ardent would have given up long before. He never gave up . . .

"I shall never forget the delicate inspiration that flowed from the affectionate soul of Monsignor Radini; the respect with which he always treated his young priests, the patience with which he regarded their faults, the force with which he inspired them to work and sacrifice. For all of them working with him was a great schooling in ecclesiastical activities and virtues . . . because his unfailing sweetness and gaiety ever encouraged them in work and study . . ."

In Bergamo they called Roncalli, "the shadow of the bishop." The last four years of their association were made more poignant by the Bishop's failing health. Though he valiantly continued his active life, anyone could see that the

Bishop, though only in his fifties, was failing fast. Each morning when he saw him, Roncalli's heart was torn by suffering. He wrote: "Radini sensed a terrible menace hanging over his head."

In the early summer of 1914, the Bishop was confined to his bed in a villa in the mountainous country outside of Bergamo. He was in terrible pain, and there was no longer any doubt that he had cancer. As the pain grew worse the doctors decided that they must take him back to Bergamo for an operation.

Roncalli wrote, "On the evening of August 11, they told him he must leave the next morning. He received the news with an expressive yet fearless look and said, "Oh, ho! I understand." Then raising his arms he quoted in Latin: *And another will gird you, and lead you, you know not whither.*"

Don Angelo rode beside his Bishop in an open automobile over the hills to Bergamo. He recorded that as the car began the long descent to the Valle de Serio, "The blazing sun of August shooting its rays over the crests and peaks of Alban in a glory of gaiety and color and all the mountains around us, like a magnificent stage setting, appeared to be giving the final salute to their pastor . . ."

An exploratory operation in Bergamo showed that nothing could be done for the Bishop. The cancer had spread through his whole system. It was only a matter of days. The doctors came to Radini-Tedeschi soon after the operation and said, "We can do no more; you are now in the hands of God."

He said, "Very well, I understand. Thank you for your care of me, and now I bless the Lord and turn to him alone."

But when the doctors had gone, his dark hour came as it comes to all men. Alone with Don Angelo he sobbed like a child. The young priest tried to comfort him saying, "Take heart, Monseigneur, are we not all in the hands of God who gives strength and life?"

"Oh, my son, it is the thought of my responsibilities that

troubles me. I am a bishop, and God will judge me by the power I had for good, and how I exercised it. I have not done enough . . ."

But soon the black mood passed. The Bishop recovered his courage never to lose it again. "Death," he said to Don Angelo, "you know I am not brave in the face of death. It scares me. However, I am not a coward either. If God really wants to send me death now for His glory, I don't only say to Him that I resign myself to accept it, but I say, 'I wish it.' "

They had many talks in those final days of August, 1914. They were terrible days for Don Angelo and his pain-wracked Bishop in the quiet chamber of death in the Episcopal Palace, terrible for the whole world which seemed to have become a great chamber of death.

That was the time when the first great battles of World War I were fought, and the horrible potential of modern weapons was first demonstrated in mass slaughter as history had never known. News of it coming to that quiet room in Bergamo troubled the dying bishop as it did all humane men the world over.

But one death touched him more closely than all those others. In the evening of August 20, word came of the death of Pope Pius X, worn out by his efforts to stem the tide of war. When he heard the news, the Bishop said to Don Angelo, "May the love of the Pope be always in your heart. You know it was one of the most beautiful ideals of my life . . . I am strengthened by a knowledge that my love for him never lessened. That I am able to show it to our Lord as whole, pure and delicate as the day He lit it in my heart, as it was on the day I was made a bishop."

Then Radini-Tedeschi smiled and added, "Do you know what the Pope whispered to me that day? He said, 'When you die I shall come for you and we will be together forever in Paradise.' Our Holy Father is in Paradise now. I sense his voice. He is calling me and calling me. I will go to see him soon."

Two days later, death was very near. Roncalli recited the last prayers for the consolation of the dying, and his Bishop feebly responded to them. Then he became silent and the young priest thinking him unconscious was silent, too. The Bishop opened his eyes and said, "Courage, courage, my dear Don Angelo. It goes well. Continue, I understand every word you say."

And after a few moments Radini said, "Ah my Jesus, crucified, I voluntarily offer you the sacrifice of my life, in the hope you will forgive my sins and those of my people . . . And I offer it for the Church . . . and the new Pope, whoever he may be, and for my priests and seminarians, for all my friends near and far, for my country . . ."

He paused and a far vision seemed to light his eyes. In a clear strong voice he said, "And for the peace, for the peace. . . ."

Church of Velo d'Astico after Austrian Shelling

CHAPTER FIVE

"THE BLOODY FIELDS..."

The sergeant wore a fine, full mustache with a touch of wax at the tips. His military great cape swirled around his shoulders and his kepi had a slightly rakish tilt. It was difficult to recognize Don Angelo in Sergeant Roncalli, but his inner life was unchanged.

After the death of his Bishop, Don Angelo had remained at his post under his successor, Bishop Marelli, only a short time. It was evident that the new bishop had very different ideas from his predecessor. A close and inspiring association had come to an end.

He packed up his dearest treasures which his Bishop had bequeathed to him, the purple robe in which Radini-Tadeschi had been consecrated and his favorite zucchetto, and moved to the familiar Seminary where he continued to teach. It was a brief and poignant interval in his busy life, for, despite his confidence that the Bishop was indeed with his beloved Pope in Paradise, Don Angelo missed him dreadfully. He occupied his greater leisure with work on St. Charles of Borromeo and a new project, a life of Bishop Radini-Tedeschi.

In May, 1915, Italy entered the war on the side of the Allies. Like millions of other young Italians Roncalli was called to the colors. Dressed in lay clothing, he reported to the great Military Hospital in Milan, and was assigned to a medical unit; its base was at Bergamo.

Whatever Roncalli did, he did with all his heart, which explains his rather swash-buckling appearance in uniform. In his work he was both nurse and priest, consoling the wounded, while tenderly caring for their hurts, and preparing their souls for death while striving to keep life in their bodies. In every situation he asked himself how Radini-Tedeschi would have met it, and tried to act accordingly.

A certain anti-clericalism still persisted among his superior officers. In fact, the Lieutenant Colonel who was in command did not like having a soldier-priest in his outfit and rode Roncalli rather hard. However, the young priest's good-natured acceptance of every humiliation finally wrung from the Colonel an odd little apology. With a small, tight smile he said, "Don't be offended by me, Sergeant. You see, I am at bottom a poor man, glad to be able to add one more gold leaf to the visor of my kepi. You, on the other hand, are on your way to the top—monsignor, bishop, cardinal . . ." They laughed together and were friends.

In March, 1916, all the priests in the Italian Army were made chaplains and promoted to the rank of lieutenant, Don Angelo among them. He was still stationed at Bergamo, and in addition to his military duties, continued to teach at the Seminary, though his classes steadily diminished as Italy called ever younger boys into service to replenish the wastage of war.

One of his pupils pictured him coming into class. He was dressed as a priest except that there were two gold bars on the sleeves of his cassock and two gold cords around the flat crown of his clerical hat. As he came into his first class he made the sign of the Cross, and smiling, quoted from the Epistles of St. Peter, "Let none of you suffer as a murderer or a thief, or a slanderer, or as one coveting that which belongs to others. But if he suffers as a Christian let him not be ashamed; let him glorify God under this name."

The war was a time of intense suffering for Don Angelo, a time of testing and of learning through sorrow. The military hospitals in which he worked were extremely primitive at best. There were no sulfa drugs to cleanse the wounds, and the long wards were foul with the smell of putrid flesh and loud with shrieks and groans of men crazed by fever or, less mercifully, fully conscious of their condition.

With the great defeat and slaughter at Caporetto, a few hundred miles from Bergamo, the torrent of wounded over-flowed the hospitals and were laid on pallets in all the lovely churches of the city. Then four hours' sleep was far too much indulgence, and Don Angelo worked all day and all night giving the last rites to the dying boys who lay in the familiar naves and chapels.

He also served on the terrible battlefields. Pope John still speaks of that time as the most moving experience of his long life. In the rain and mud of the dreadful spring of 1917, his cassock stained with blood, he moved among the troops "on the plateau of Asiago and the blood-soaked fields along the Piave," bringing help and comfort to the wounded, and, as he says, "to the dying the last consolations of friendship and the reconciliation of final absolution . . ."

Speaking of the philosophy which guided his efforts, Pope John said, "The chaplain's is a deeply human and brotherly ministry where in the midst of fighting men the priest becomes the witness to the highest moral and religious ideals for which those valiant men have not hesitated to give their lives." Despite the horror, the physical hardships and the spiritual pain he endured, Roncalli said long afterward, "I thank God that I was a sergeant and a military chaplain in World War I. How much I learned of the human heart at that time; how much experience I gained; how great the grace I received. . . ."

The war ended in November, 1918, and soon after that Roncalli was discharged from the Army. Since he had received no pay during his service, he went to Doctor Giuseppe Fuma-

galli, paymaster of the Bergamo District, for a final reckoning.
The doctor immersed himself in complex calculations putting
spidery figures in great ledgers, and finally came up with the
sum of a few hundred dollars due Lieutenant-Chaplain Roncalli for nearly four years' service. Doctor Fumagalli handed it
over with an apology for its meagerness.

Don Angelo laughing said, "Look, it's not much. But I
can use it. I have a plan to open a students' clubhouse in
Bergamo."

The idea was a badly needed innovation in 1919. Post-
war Italy was in a chaotic condition. Her radicals, beguiled
by Marx and Lenin, were adopting the emblem of the ham-
mer and sickle and trying to make her a Communist state.
The arch-conservatives were listening to the voice of a former
socialist named Benito Mussolini and organizing under the
sign of the rods and the ax, the fasces, symbol of the power of
ancient Rome.

Both groups of extremists were recruiting Italy's youths
into armed bands who roamed through the streets of her cities
shooting and looting their political opponents, and indulging
in bloody "rumbles" with each other. The democratic government was helpless. It was time somebody got the young men
off the streets and reminded them of another sign—the Sign of
the Cross.

For his Student House, the first of many in Italy, Don
Angelo secured the lovely old Palazzo Asperti. He arranged it
with a pretty little chapel, study and recreation rooms, and
sleeping quarters for the young men on the second floor. The
walls of the rooms were hung with ancient tapestries and some
fine old pictures. Don Angelo hung a full-length mirror on the
final landing of the grand stairway where everyone going up
saw himself. Above it he put a Latin inscription: "Know
thyself."

With such a jolly priest running the club it became a place
of youthful gaiety and idealistic thinking. A short distance off

was "Sant' Alessandio," the headquarters of the student branch of Catholic Action where the young people of Bergamo and students from other cities met in a truly religious spirit to dedicate themselves to Christian activities throughout their distraught country. Don Angelo lived in his *Casa dello Studente* and spent every moment he could with his young people. They loved him for his simple friendliness, his goodness, and his wit; they trusted him because they knew that he was saintly rather than sanctimonious. They brought him their problems, as they might never have to their own parents, and he gave them good, sensible advice. He was always ready to help them with their studies, or alleviate their loneliness by his warm friendship, or get them out of youthful jams or advance a small loan. Above all, he inspired their devotion by his transparently simple faith.

Of course, Don Angelo took on a multiplicity of other jobs. He was Spiritual Adviser of the Union of Catholic Women and the Union of Catholic Youth. In 1919, Bishop Marelli made him Spiritual Director of the Seminary as well. At night, when all his young people were asleep he worked on his book about St. Charles Borromeo.

All this not being enough—he had twenty hours a day— he was one of the principal organizers of the first International Eucharistic Congress to be held after the war. The Pope had chosen Bergamo, his "most Catholic city," as its site. Cardinals, bishops, priests, and laymen flocked to Bergamo from all over the world. Don Angelo was everywhere at once, with his immense energy and beaming face, attending to a thousand details but never too rushed to extend a warm greeting to every new arrival.

He knew how proud his Bishop would have been that Bergamo had been chosen for this honor; for his own address to the Congress Don Angelo chose Radini-Tedeschi's favorite theme, "The Eucharist and Our Lady." He was inspired by the thoughts of his dear friend and spiritual leader. Those who heard him speak were impressed by the simplicity of his holiness.

With all the jobs he had taken on, Roncalli might have been considered an indispensable man in Bergamo. He was too humble and too busy to think that of himself. And yet, in November, 1920, when the letter came from Cardinal van Rossum in Rome he was stunned and uncertain.

The Cardinal was known as the "Red Pope," because he was the Prefect of the Congregation of the Propagation of the Faith. His letter said that Pope Benedict XV, the successor of Pope Pius X, had directed him to write to Roncalli asking him to come to Rome as the Director of the Society for the Propagation of the Faith in Italy. Don Angelo knew that this was a great honor. It would bring him under the eyes of the Holy See and put him in the direct line of promotion. He was heartbroken.

He already had more honors than he wished or felt he deserved, having been nominated as an honorary Canon of Bergamo. He had no ambition to become one of the hierarchy of the Church, confined to Rome, immersed in bureaucracy, and deprived of a pastorate. Nor could he bear to think of leaving the work so well begun in Bergamo: his beloved young people and his *Casa dello Studente* (in fact it gradually desiccated after he left). To leave Bergamo seemed almost to be betraying his beloved Bishop.

In his distress Don Angelo wrote to ask the advice of old Cardinal Ferrari, the Metropolitan of Milan. The Cardinal, who was so terribly ill that he could hardly speak, nevertheless quickly replied in a gay little letter: "Dear Professor: This business has a quantity of good wishes. It is the wish of the red Pope and the wish of the white Pope; therefore it is the wish of God. Leave everything and go. You will be followed by a great benediction of the Lord."

Obediently Don Angelo went.

Twin Churches—Piazza del Popolo

CHAPTER SIX

THE ARCHBISHOP OF
AREOPOLIS

Pope Benedict XV, who had succeeded Pius X in 1914, was an Italian aristocrat who had been Cardinal Giacomo Della Chiesa, Archbishop of Bologna. His last name meant "of the Church." He was a small, lean man with bright, heavy-lidded eyes and a big Roman nose with rimless spectacles perched on it. He was a great intellectual with a mathematician's love of order. Bishop Radini-Tedeschi had been one of his dearest friends, and in the comparatively serene years before the war he had, of course, known young Roncalli.

There has been quite a bit of speculation about how the Pope happened to choose a little-known priest from the provinces for such an important position in Rome. Some historians say it was due to Benedict's friendship for Radini-Tedeschi; others hold that Roncalli's brilliant speech at the Eucharistic Congress brought him to the attention of the Holy See. The most likely reason is the expert way in which Don Angelo handled the arrangements for the Eucharistic Congress.

Since the virtues and temperament of many to whom vocations to the priesthood have been given do not necessarily produce good executives, the Vatican is usually desperately in need of administrators for its multitudinous departments. Roncalli was not only a dedicated priest, but a man of great vigor and a proven organizer. Furthermore, as the Rector of the Seminario Romano had said to Radini-Tedeschi, everybody got along with him. The Holy See needed such a man.

When he reached Rome in January, 1921, Roncalli went to work immediately in the offices of the Propagation of the Faith, which were then housed in a splendid, square Renaissance palace on the Piazza di Spagna. In the confused state of Italy and indeed of the whole world, the work of the Italian Society for the Propagation of the Faith was both difficult and delicate. Pope Benedict summoned Roncalli to the Vatican to tell him personally what he wanted done.

It was the first time Don Angelo had ever been in the Papal Apartment with its tall windows looking down on St. Peter's Square and over the tumbling roofs and domed churches of the old city to the green Campagna with its rim of gentle hills. He knelt in awe and kissed the Fisherman's Ring. Then the Pope raised him and made him sit beside the desk, and gave him his instructions and a warning.

"The ways of the Society are too old-fashioned to meet the dangerous conditions of modern times," he said. "We want you to reorganize it and bring it up to date. Impart to it some of your youthful vigor. But you must be tactful. You will meet opposition from the older men in the organization who have performed great services for the Church, but are now suffering the rigidity of age and are wedded to the old ways. You must make the innovations without hurting them. It will take much charity and patience."

The Pope indicated that it was the ultimate intention to bring all the national societies for the Propagation of the Faith to Rome and elevate them to the dignity of a papal institution. "We want you to visit all the important centers of the movement in Italy and in Europe to see what needs to be done," he said. The smiling Pontiff added, "You will be God's traveler," and gave Roncalli his blessing.

In March, 1921, Roncalli was officially named Director of the Italian Society for the Propagation of the Faith. Later he was given the titles of Domestic Prelate to His Holiness and Monsignor. As Pope Pius XII once observed, it was a title which meant nothing except that one had to work a little harder to justify it. Roncalli took this obligation very seriously.

Though he was now thirty-nine years old and rather portly with only a small peninsula of hair left on his balding forehead, he still retained his youthful enthusiasm; in fact, he does today. Soon he permitted himself the boyish pleasure of a quick trip to Sotto il Monte to see his family and neighbors.

There once again the whole village gathered in San Giovanni and waited outside to greet Monsignor Roncalli after the Mass. As he walked among them, talking gaily and joking with his former playmates in his fine new cassock with a purple cape and broad purple ribbon belted over it, one awe-stricken villager said to the Monsignor's proud mother, "Why is Don Angelo dressed up like a bishop?"

"I'm not quite sure," Maria Anna answered. "You know priests arrange these things among themselves."

Pope Benedict XV died in January, 1922. Once again, Roncalli saw the solemn pageantry of a papal funeral, but this time he was part of it, both outwardly as a member of the Curia and in his inward grief for the Pope who had also been his friend. The ensuing Conclave quickly elected Achille Cardinal Ratti, who took the name of Pius XI. Roncalli was in the Sistine Chapel the day that all the cardinals gathered there for the ceremony of the third adoration, watching as they prostrated themselves before the man who had been his kindly mentor in the Ambrosiana Library.

As the Holy Father left the Chapel, Cardinal van Rossum, walking beside him indicated Monsignor Roncalli who knelt while the new Pope recalled their old friendship. Then the Cardinal said, "As soon as we heard of the election of a Pope, this Monsignor said to me, '*Signor Cardinali,* I hope that the business of the societies for the Propagation of the Faith will not be delayed.' "

The Holy Father smiled at the younger man's zeal, and blessing him moved on. But only a week later Pope Pius issued the decree elevating the societies to a pontifical institution and concentrating all their headquarters in Rome. Monsignor Roncalli helped him to write the decree.

However, it was not done as easily as that. The Society for the Propagation had been founded in France in 1822, and had always had its headquarters in Lyons. Working in the same field were the Society of the Holy Childhood, whose headquarters were in France, and the Society of St. Peter the Apostle, which specialized in the Japanese missionary field, and was based in Switzerland. Consolidating them under one head in Rome meant a lot of toes would be stepped on, feelings hurt, and national pride outraged. The Pope gave Roncalli the mission of placating them and making them like it.

The man who set out on this diplomatic mission was no longer the naive country boy who had graduated from the Seminario Romano. True, he was still bluff, genial and kindly; his pure simple faith was untouched, and he still talked with the harsh intonation of northern Italy. Ten years of close association with Bishop Radini-Tedeschi had given him, however, some of the best qualities of an aristocrat without altering his honest nature. He had acquired poise, courtly manners, tact, and a certain subtlety in dealing with people in high places.

He journeyed first through Italy reorganizing the work of the Society there. Then he went to Brussels, Aachen, Vienna, Munich, several Swiss cities, Paris, and Lyons. His mission in France was the most delicate of all because the two Societies for the Propagation there had been founded by the French, and their members had a proud nationalism.

But Roncalli was becoming quite familiar with that lovely land and its people, and was fluent in French, though to this day he speaks it with a guttural accent which makes him sound like a well-educated German. He was able to talk to the French heads of the societies with understanding and sympathy, and convince them that far from being a set-back the transfer of the headquarters of the societies to Rome was a recognition of their importance and an assurance for their future. It was not accomplished without some nimble egg-treading, but it was done, and done without any open breaks and a minimum of injured feelings.

In 1924, Roncalli returned to Bergamo when the body of his Bishop was transferred from the city cemetery to its final resting place in the crypt of the cathedral among the Bishops of Bergamo, the renovation of whose tombs had been the first act of his episcopate. At the solemn memorial service on April 29, Roncalli delivered the principal address which was his final tribute to the man who had been his teacher and spiritual father:

"As this sad occasion draws to a close," he said, "the heart yet experiences the gentle solace that comes from a task completed and well done. Courage, therefore my brothers, and let us go forward, all together, along the path of peace. Let us be guided by the words which that truly great servant of God and the Church whom we have just honored addressed to us in his last testament: 'I commend justice, truth and charity to all.' "

Perhaps, Roncalli was thinking of that last sad night in the Bishop's room with the soft summer air bringing unbearable sweetness through the open windows, and the faint voice speaking with a terrible effort. His own voice was choked with tears as he said, "May the invocation that came from his dying lips, the last words he spoke be also ours, 'Peace! For the Peace. . . .' "

Pope Pius XI declared 1925 a Holy Year. He expressed the hope that it would have two results: to bring Rome closer to the souls of his people and their souls closer to Rome in the true missionary spirit of the Church. As Roncalli called it at the time, "Holy Year, missionary year."

But while inspiring souls, bodies had to be cared for. This meant that enormous preparation must be made to receive hundreds of thousands of pilgrims in Rome. Arrangements for lodgings were of prime importance. Many, of course, could afford the hotels and boarding houses of the city, but there were many more who would use their last lire for transportation and thousands who would come on foot. So that none of these might suffer for their piety, free lodgings and food had to be provided, tent cities raised in the fields outside the walls, and religious houses prepared as hostels.

Arrangements for transportation from all parts of the world must be coordinated; steamship companies and railroads must be encouraged to offer special low-fare excursions. Above all, a corps of priests and brothers had to be organized to provide for the spiritual welfare and inspiration of the pilgrims.

Pope Pius relied heavily on Roncalli for this tremendous job of organization. In fact, their association became so intimate that Roncalli with humble pleasure once said that he believed that the Holy Father had "transferred to me the friendship he felt for the late Bishop. . . ."

In the midst of these multitudinous activities Roncalli might easily have been cut off from the pastoral duties which he held to be his first function as a priest. But the twenty-hour day he maintained allowed him time even for these. He heard confessions, held spiritual exercises for laymen, and, most enjoyable of all to him, taught religion to the children. What a delightful Sunday school teacher he was with his clear simplicity of thought, his humor and his God-given love that embraced his little pupils and made their Sunday morning sessions not a duty but a joy.

Early in 1925, when the Holy Year arrangements were running smoothly, Roncalli was called on to teach on a considerably higher intellectual plane. Cardinal-Vicar Basilio Pompili asked if he would be willing to add to his other activities the task of Professor of Patristics (Lives of the Church Fathers) at his old Alma Mater, the Seminario Romano, now moved to fine new quarters near St. John in the Lateran and called the Pontifical Lateran Athenaeum. Of course he agreed.

We have Pope John's own word for it that the course of lectures he delivered, ranging from the Apostolic Fathers to St. Cyprian, were good. With the endearing naiveté that enables him to be pleasantly astonished at any success he achieves, Pope John said on a visit to the Seminario in 1959, "Those fifteen lectures . . . were of such lively interest to us that even now, at a distance of thirty-three years, we find them a cause for humble but real exaltation. We do not know the reason for our success, but we remember very well the attention and applause with which our beloved students followed and punctuated every lecture. . . ."

Of course, the Holy Father never realized the reason for his success, but it was certainly due to the lively and moving way the lectures were written, and, especially, to the enthusiasm with which they were delivered.

It was evident to Pope Pius XI that a man of Roncalli's diverse abilities should not be wasted on routine jobs. He was only waiting for some really challenging task to come up. It came when Monsignor Eugene Tisserant, who had been on a mission to Bulgaria, proposed that an Apostolic Visitor be appointed to that country. The Pope thought Roncalli was the right man for this delicate mission. In order to give him the necessary authority for the work, the Holy Father decided to make Roncalli titular Archbishop of Areopolis, an ancient diocese in Palestine long since lost to its Arab conquerors.

Roncalli heard the news without elation but with a deep sense of obligation. As he said, "In reality, to be named a bishop or to remain a simple priest is no different to those who seek only the glory of the Lord and not the evanescent glitter of earthly satisfaction."

Suddenly relieved of his many duties, Roncalli went to the country for a few days to prepare for his Consecration by meditation and prayer. From there he wrote to a friend: "I find

myself in an ancient Roman villa, alone and secluded, to prepare my spirit for my Episcopal Consecration on the Feast Day
of St. Joseph . . . Thank you for your love and paternal words
on the occasion of my nomination . . . In this thing I see an
honor to our Congregation (The Sacred Heart) and submit
quietly to the Lord. For the rest, there remains neither embar-
rassment nor confusion. My spirit is therefore tranquil and
my heart at peace. I shall make obedience conquer my strong
repugnance to this undetermined adventure, and dismiss all
uneasiness. Yes, *Obedientia et Pax:* There is my episcopal
motto. Thus it shall ever be. . . ."

St. Joseph's Day, March 19, 1925, had been chosen for the
Consecration. That morning Angelo Roncalli dressed himself
in the cassock in which his beloved Bishop had been consecrated and which he always wore thereafter on occasions of
great spiritual significance until he became Pope. Then he was
driven to the church of San Carlo al Corso named after his
favorite St. Charles Borromeo.

The little marble church was filled with his friends, high
prelates, young seminarians, and many laymen. Among them
was a delegation from Bergamo headed by Bishop Marelli.
Roncalli's father and mother were there, and all his brothers
and sisters. However humble and fearful were the feelings of
their son as he approached this moment, Giovanni and Maria
Anna Roncalli were filled with pride and joy that few parents
can ever know.

Pope Pius had asked Giovanni Cardinal Tacci, Secretary
of the Congregation of Oriental Affairs, to consecrate Roncalli.
The co-consecrators were Bishop Francesco Marchetti Selvag-
giani and Bishop Gustavo Palica. The consecration of a Bishop
is one of the most solemn and awe-inspiring rites of the Church,
conferring the ultimate completion of priesthood. According to
the Scriptures, bishops "rule the Church." They rule by Divine
Will; it is a fearful responsibility.

As he went through the long, beautifully symbolic ceremony Roncalli was swept by torrents of strong emotion—awe, fear of unworthiness, high resolve, and total submission to the Will of God. At last it was ended. He stood there wearing the miter, which is the old Mosaic symbol of leadership and holding the crozier signifying the Shepherd. On his finger was the episcopal ring to symbolize his marriage to his flock; around his neck hung the jeweled pectoral cross, emblem of his faith in Christ and his readiness to die for this faith. He stood there and trembled. . . .

The morning after his Consecration Angelo Roncalli, accompanied by his father and mother, went to St. Peter's to celebrate his first Mass as an Archbishop at the altar over the tomb of St. Peter, where the young priest had gone after his ordination. Then, Giovanni and Maria Anna Roncalli went with the Archbishop to the Pope's apartment in the Vatican where the Holy Father blessed them. But more important to them than his blessing was the affection he showed for their dear son.

The Cathedral—Sophia, Bulgaria

CHAPTER SEVEN

"A CANDLE IN MY WINDOW"

Before going to Bulgaria, Archbishop Roncalli went to Sotto il Monte for a few days to be with his family. He stayed at Colombara Farm, enjoying its sweet simplicity and renewing his strength by contact with the burgeoning earth and the people he loved. Spring comes early to Italy. The evenings were already soft and a delicate green veil lay across the fields.

Though Roncalli had assumed the episcopate with such solemnity and gravity, he was no more a sad bishop than a sad priest. In a picture of him taken at that time in his robes and lacy vestments he looks very young and very handsome. It is a picture of a happy man.

In the evenings he sat with his family and the old friends who dropped in to greet him on the gallery of Colombara Farm. Later they proudly painted the episcopal coat of arms he had chosen on the wall of the gallery. It was the round crenelated tower from the arms of the first Maytino de Roncalli on a field of red crossed by a white band and underneath the motto which Angelo Roncalli had borrowed from Cesare Cardinal Baronio, *Obedientia et Pax.* But on this visit there was so much good talk and simple merriment that they almost forgot he was an archbishop.

77

In order to insure his return to Sotto il Monte during his vacations and to keep his roots there, Roncalli rented for a small sum the ancient villa that his ancestor Maytino had built on a hillside near Colombara. He kept it until he was elected Pope. He also arranged for two of his sisters, Ancilla and Maria, to come to Bulgaria as soon as he was settled there to keep house for him. He thus assured himself of those strong family ties which were part of his strength and joy of living.

Then he started for Bulgaria.

Sophia, the distracted capital of a country in turmoil, could not have been more of a change from the serenity of Sotto il Monte. Roncalli, accompanied by his Benedictine secretary, Father Constantino Bosschaerts, arrived in Sophia on April 25, 1925. Only nine days before his arrival Macedonian terrorists had expressed their disapproval of the Government of King Boris III by exploding an "infernal machine" in the great-domed Orthodox Cathedral of Svate Nedelia during the funeral services for Prime Minister General Kimon Gheorgiev, whom they had previously assassinated. The high cupola crashed down on the worshipers. The king escaped, but one hundred and fifty men and women were killed, and over three hundred were wounded. The Archbishop's first sad duty was to make the rounds of the hospitals to comfort the survivors.

As a result of this murderous act, the Bulgarian Government cracked down with the violence of frightened rulers—curfews, nightly police searches of sleeping houses, mass arrests, and executions. It was a reign of terror.

The religious situation in Bulgaria was almost as confused, though not as explosive, as her politics. The great mass of the people belonged to the Bulgarian Orthodox Church which, like the Greek and Russian Orthodox churches, was schismatic in that it did not submit to the authority of the Pope. However, unlike the case of the Protestant churches, the validity of its sacraments is recognized. The Holy See has never ceased to hope for its eventual reconciliation. Though some

Orthodox Bulgarians shared this hope, most of them, including Exarchate Stefan of Bulgaria, were definitely anti-Rome.

There were about fifty thousand Catholics in Bulgaria of whom forty-five thousand were of the Latin rite. The others were Catholics of the Byzantine or Eastern rite which, while acknowledging the Pope as their supreme Pontiff, used the Byzantine liturgy, almost exactly like the Orthodox, and had a Code of Canon Law differing from that of the Latin Church. In addition to the Bulgarian Catholics there were about three hundred thousand refugees from Macedonia, which had been reconquered by Turkey, living in temporary camps of whom twenty thousand were Catholics who had their own bishop. It was Roncalli's job to reconcile all these divergent elements, and to bring to all the spiritual benefits of which they had been deprived by their isolation and poverty.

When he first arrived in Sophia, Roncalli stayed in a small white house in the court of the Svate Bogoroditza Church as a guest of Monsignor Kurteff, a priest of the Byzantine rite. This diplomatic move was intended to honor this minority group and make them feel wanted in the Mother Church. He held a press conference there. The reporter for *La Bulgarie* described his astonishment at the number of books the Archbishop had brought with him which filled the shelves of the small library he used as an office. Among them were many works of the Church Fathers, as well as the Italian poets, Dante and Petrarch, and his favorite novelist, Manzoni. The reporter went on to say, "The Apostolic Visitor is still young and his physiognomy strikes me by its energy, sincerity and sweetness. . . ."

In the first sermon Roncalli delivered in Sophia the day after his arrival, he made clear the course the Catholics of Bulgaria should adopt toward the Orthodox majority in the country. "It is not enough to have the kindest feelings toward our separated Christian brothers," he said. "If you really love them, give them a good example, and translate your love into action." In his dealings with the Orthodox Churches, he himself has always followed this precept.

The sermon was delivered in Italian, but in it he promised to learn Bulgarian. Wasting no time he engaged Father Methodius Ushtikoff, a Bulgarian priest, as his second secretary, and began to study with him immediately.

Although, unlike a papal nuncio, Archbishop Roncalli had no official diplomatic standing, he was received by King Boris only four days after his arrival in Sophia. As his car drove through the high, wrought iron gates and along the long, classical façade of the royal palace, the peasant of Bergamo was no more concerned, and less excited, than if he had been arriving at Colombara. Worldly splendor never impressed Roncalli; in a palace or a hut he was exactly the same person.

King Boris and his visitor became friends immediately. Roncalli has recorded his impression of the King's wide knowledge, common sense and goodwill; Boris made his feelings about the Archbishop clear in many ways during Roncalli's nine years in Sophia. Their friendship was especially important because of a harsh exchange between the King's father, Czar Ferdinand I of Bulgaria, and Pope Leo XIII.

The Czar, who was born a Catholic, had made his son join the Orthodox Church to secure his throne. Pope Leo became very angry about this; to placate him, the Czar came in person with his high officials to the Vatican. Unfortunately, their discussion developed into a hot argument which ended when the diminutive Pope in splendid anger pointed at the door and said to his royal visitor, "Get out!"

"I was treated like a dog," Ferdinand said.

Naturally, relations between the Holy See and the Bulgarian royal family were decidedly chilly until Roncalli's arrival in Sophia.

No sooner had the Archbishop settled in Sophia than he started to visit his widely scattered flock. It was a voyage roughly comparable to crossing America in a covered wagon. The moment his car left the vicinity of the capital it plunged into dirt roads that were hardly more than goat tracks. He went first to the port cities of Bargas and Yamboli, then swung through the little villages of the rich farming countryside.

Roncalli's next trip took him to Svilengrad and on to Adrianople which the Turks had recaptured from Bulgaria. Here he found a distressing situation. Abandoned by fleeing worshipers, the churches, standing forlornly among the beautiful flowers of June, were half ruined and violated, with broken icons and ceremonial vestments scattered about. A visit to the magnificent mosque of Sultan-Selim at the hour of vespers further deepened the melancholy of his spirit at this loss to Christianity.

Returning to Svilengrad, Roncalli started for Pokrovan. His car followed a road that was no more than two ruts in the ground over the rugged mountains rising one behind another in desolate beauty. After about fifty kilometers he came to a place where a flood of the Arda River had washed out the road. Roncalli secured a small, leaky scow, and was rowed across the muddy torrent with the water rising around his ankles. On the other side he borrowed a work horse and rode on to Pokrovan.

The town had a beautiful onion-domed church but the parish house was a little old Turkish granary. Its wall were made of rose-colored stones piled on top of each other with no plaster either inside or out, and the dusty gloom of its interior was unlighted by a single window. In one corner were two beds of straw in which the Archbishop and his secretary slept.

After a dubious night's rest, Roncalli rode on, bouncing about in the saddle of his borrowed work horse, to the village of Ateren. From there, in a torrent of rain, he rode through a dense forest to reach Armuth, a Catholic village whose inhabitants lived in miserable huts. Its poor chapel, hardly larger than the rickety dwellings, had been sacked and the tabernacle profaned. Soaked to the skin, but radiating the warmth of his love for these unhappy but devout people, Roncalli ate supper with the priest before a smoky fire and bedded down, on straw

again, in his cabin. As in every other village he visited, the
ragged people surrounded Roncalli amazed that such a great
dignitary of the Church had time to visit them. And before he
left them they forgot their awe in the joyful assurance of having
found a friend and protector.

Several days more of riding through unrelenting rain
brought him in a wide circle back to Pokrovan. Since his automobile was still held up by the floods, Roncalli rode back
toward the Bulgarian border. Here he was intercepted by the
frontier guard and taken to a command post where he enjoyed
the luxury of a camp cot while poor Father Ushtikoff, who did
not know what becoming the secretary of such a rugged archbishop entailed, slept on the ground beside him.

In the morning came further luxury. The saddle-sore
Archbishop was able to exchange his horse for an "Arabia," a
local springless carriage drawn by two mountain ponies, which
the officer of the guard had summoned by telephone. As Roncalli parted from his military host, the lieutenant, a kindly
fellow of the Orthodox Church, said, "Perhaps it would be
wise for you to leave your pectoral cross and your ring with
me, or at least hide them under your hat so as not to attract the
attention of the bandits."

"Bandits?" asked Roncalli.

"The mountains are full of them," the officer assured him.

Roncalli thanked him gravely and took his advice. On the
lonely trip through the barren mountains the Lord protected
the Archbishop, however, because on that particular day the
bandits were busy holding up the mail wagon, and his carriage
passed unnoticed.

Starting out from Svilengrad again in the carriage, Roncalli visited the Thracian refugee camps where conditions were
even worse, if possible, than among the villages. At Mostratli
he stayed in a monastery which two hardy priests had built
with their own hands. He came then to Soudzak, one of the
loveliest villages in Bulgaria, where at last he rested.

Archbishop Roncalli encountered many such situations on

his apostolic visits in Bulgaria. Since he was "God's traveler," he continued them until he had seen every village in the land that contained a Catholic church or chapel. Everywhere he went his genial manner, his simple faith, and his genuine love for the unfortunates of his flock brought new courage to these people who had kept the faith even while imagining themselves forgotten by their Pope. Roncalli was the first ranking representative of the Holy Father to visit Bulgaria in six hundred years.

Archbishop Roncalli was not the man to give unhappy Christians a kind word and his blessing and then to forget them. He was determined to do something concrete. Neither good will nor money was enough; this matter required the utmost diplomacy.

The Orthodox Church was the official Church of Bulgaria and was jealous of its power and its independence of Rome. Although many Orthodox Bulgarians would have liked to rejoin their Mother Church, a majority of them, and almost all the higher clergy, were violently against it. They suspected the Holy See of devious machinations to produce this result and watched every move the Archbishop made with hostile eyes. They were right about his desire to arrange a reconciliation someday—it remains in truth the great ambition of his life and was one of his reasons for calling an Ecumenical Council—but they were totally wrong about his methods. This man could not conspire, nor would he attempt to bring them back to the fold against their wills. He realized, however, that he had to prove it to them before he could accomplish anything in Bulgaria.

And he did. Before two years had elapsed, he was on friendly terms with the Exarchate of the Orthodox Church and many of its clergy. When an earthquake struck in 1928, bringing death and suffering to thousands of Bulgarians, Roncalli rushed down to the devastated towns and villages as unsparing of himself as he had been on the battlefields of the Piave. He brought material assistance as well with gifts of supplies and money, some of which he raised among his friends in Rome, and a large share of which came from the Holy See. Roncalli saw to it that his help was distributed to all of those in need.

Pope Pius XI was eventually able to make Archbishop Roncalli permanent Apostolic Delegate to Bulgaria. King Boris alone could not have permitted this advancement of the Catholic position in Bulgaria if he had not had the consent of the Exarchate.

Yet this same King Boris brought Roncalli his greatest diplomatic defeat and great spiritual sorrow. In 1930 a royal marriage was being discussed between King Boris and Princess Giovanna, the daughter of King Victor Emanuel III of Italy. Politically this alliance had many advantages for both countries, but there was one almost fatal difficulty: King Boris belonged to the Orthodox Church and the princess was a Catholic.

In 1929, the Holy See and the Italian Government of Benito Mussolini had at last reached a conciliation of their long quarrel. Taking advantage of this new—and temporary— friendship, Mussolini pressed hard for the Pope's consent to the marriage. "If we could arbitrate the great difficulties between us," he said to Papal Secretary of State, Cardinal Gasparri, "surely we can settle this little Bulgarian business."

"It is not that easy," said Gasparri. "The marriage must conform to the canons of the Church or we cannot sanction it."

Roncalli was entrusted with the delicate mission of convincing King Boris that he should accept the Pope's conditions which were that the marriage must be solemnized in the Catholic Church *only*, and that the children must be raised as Catholics. The King was apparently willing enough, but the Bulgarian constitution specifically stated that only an Orthodox prince could reign in Bulgaria.

Roncalli had long conferences with the King almost every day in the hot summer of 1930. The two men genuinely liked and respected each other, and the discussions were very friendly.

Gradually Roncalli's firm persuasiveness seemingly convinced the King. He finally accepted the Vatican's conditions and solemnly promised to fulfill them. It was a great diplomatic triumph for Roncalli. Nevertheless, he was too wise in the ways of men, and kings, to exult prematurely. On the day before the marriage he wrote, "This has gone fairly well; but it is only natural that the devil will use all his arts to upset it."

The devil got busy even more quickly than he feared. The royal couple were married at Assisi in Italy on October 25, 1930. As soon as Boris got his bride back to Bulgaria he forced her to marry him again at a magnificent ceremony in the Orthodox Cathedral of St. Alexander Nevsky in Sophia.

Archbishop Roncalli was profoundly shaken. That the King, whom he really liked, should forswear himself so quickly proved that he had never meant to keep his word. Sadly the Archbishop wrote, "My life has passed through a stormy time. The affair of the marriage in the Orthodox Church has distressed me deeply. My consolation and my hope is that from this great evil a greater good may come . . . to lift this heavy weight from my conscience."

One good did come of it: it enabled the Holy See to bring enough pressure to bear on the King to force him officially to recognize the Apostolic Delegate—a diplomatic nuance that was more important than it sounds. To mark the occasion Roncalli moved to a much larger house, where in the great red salon graced by a beautiful Italian painting of Christ the Savior, he received the prelates of the Church and the *Corps Diplomatique*.

But diplomatic triumphs were, as he well knew, illusory. The next blow was heavier. On January 13, 1933, Queen Giovanna gave birth to a daughter. Boris, faithless again, though doubtless under tremendous political pressure, had her baptized by Exarchate Stefan with great pomp in the Orthodox Church.

Archbishop Roncalli lodged an energetic protest with the Prime Minister, and called at the Royal Palace. The King refused to receive him—probably he was too embarrassed—so Roncalli deposited another stiff protest. He knew it would do no good. In colloquial Italian he said unhappily to a friend, "I've been had."

Nevertheless, he did not altogether blame King Boris. He knew that the Government had brought all its democratic power to bear on the monarch and that Boris had yielded for what he believed to be the welfare of his people, who after all were 85 per cent Orthodox.

However, Roncalli had a heated interview with the Italian Minister to Bulgaria, Signor Piacenti, who had helped to arrange the marriage. With typical Roman cynicism Piacenti is reported to have said, "Don't be so upset, Your Excellency. After all King Boris is Orthodox and it's a matter for his conscience. As to Queen Giovanna, she'll just have to go to confession."

This frivolous attitude fired a rage in Roncalli such as he had seldom known. He tongue-lashed Piacenti for ten minutes until the Minister rang for a footman and angrily ordered him to show the Archbishop out.

Poor Queen Giovanna, in fact, had been completely helpless. The King had walked into her room, taken the baby in his arms and carried her off to the Cathedral, even though the Queen Mother of Italy was actually on her way to Bulgaria to be godmother for the child's Catholic baptism.

Despite the coolness of the King, Roncalli spent many hours at the Royal Palace that winter consoling Queen Giovanna. He was able to assure her that the Holy Father, in love and understanding, absolved her from all blame.

With the exception of the royal marriage, Roncalli's nine-year mission to Bulgaria was a record of solid accomplishment. He induced the Government to recognize diplomas granted by Catholic schools against the vehement protests of Orthodox fundamentalists. At his suggestion the Byzantine rite Catholics were brought under an Apostolic Administrator and he accompanied the appointee, Monsignor Kurteff, to Rome for his Consecration in the ancient church of San Clemente which was associated with the Bulgarian Saints Cyril and Methodius.

Roncalli also brought the two dioceses of the Latin rite together. He encouraged an embryonic Catholic Action organization; he secured permission to found the first Catholic seminary in Bulgaria for both Latin rite and Byzantine rite instructions. In addition, Roncalli energetically encouraged the building of new schools, churches and religious institutions, and worked to ameliorate the unhappy condition of many Bulgarian Catholics.

By 1934, things were in excellent shape. Roncalli could look forward to seeing the results of his labors come to fruition. But he had no such good fortune. On November 24, 1934, he received word that he had been appointed Vicar Apostolic and Apostolic Delegate to Turkey as well as Apostolic Delegate to Greece. The news of his promotion—this dual post was far more important in the eyes of the Holy See—came as a blow both to Roncalli and his Bulgarian friends, Catholic and Orthodox alike.

The whole Bulgarian Orthodox press expressed their regret and eulogized the departing Archbishop. The Catholics of all classes mourned the loss of a great spiritual leader and protector. One bearded priest of the Byzantine rite expressed their sentiments in the words, "Monsignor, you have shown to us the gentleness of David and the wisdom of Solomon."

Roncalli's many Orthodox friends spoke of how they would miss the warmth and wit which had endeared him to them at the many social functions which he had attended as a duty, but also enjoyed. Roncalli's own feelings at leaving his Bulgarians were expressed eloquently in his farewell address (in Bulgarian) on Christmas Day, 1934, in the Church of the Capuchin Fathers in Sophia which was broadcasted throughout the country:

. . . "Leaving for the new post to which I have been assigned I carry with me a precious remembrance of Bulgaria. I have asked the Holy Father to change my titular archbishopric to that of a marvelous place, which is truly a jewel of Bulgaria. From now on I shall no longer bear the title of Archbishop of Areopolis but shall be known as the Archbishop of Mesembria. Thus each day I shall be reminded of Bulgaria, a remembrance that will echo in my heart each time I raise my hand solemnly to bless the people and every time I sign a document.

"And you, my beloved brothers, do not forget me . . . who will always remain, beyond wind and sea, the fervent friend of Bulgaria. There is a tradition in Catholic Ireland that on Christmas Day each family puts a lighted candle in the window of their home, so that if Saint Joseph and the Virgin Mary should be passing by they may know that within, beside a fire and a table blessed by the Grace of God, the family awaits them.

"Wherever I may be throughout the world, if a Bulgarian, who might be in distress, should pass my house, he will find the candle of welcome burning in the window. Let him knock on my door and it will be opened to him, whether he is Catholic or Orthodox. My Bulgarian brothers, you have only to enter to find in my house the warmest and most affectionate hospitality. . . ."

It is said that even now he sometimes weeps for those good friends who disappeared behind the Iron Curtain and can no longer enter his house.

Roncalli left Sophia on January 4, 1935. Almost ten years before he had arrived alone with his secretary. Now the station plaza was jammed with people and the whole *Corps Diplomatique* was on the platform, as well as the representative sent by King Boris, and, more touching still, a delegation of bearded Orthodox priests representing his good friend the Exarchate Stefan.

The Third Hagia Sophia—Istanbul
(Built by Justinian)

CHAPTER EIGHT

BOTH BANKS OF
THE HELLESPONT

In Turkey, Roncalli started all over again from scratch—from behind the mark, in fact—because of the anti-religious attitude of Kemal Ataturk's government. A single priest met him at the station in Istanbul to avoid attracting governmental attention, and they drove in a cab to the Apostolic Residence in the Pera district.

Despite its imposing title, the Apostolic Residence was a rather dingy old house with a moderate salon on the first floor and a warren of rooms upstairs. Roncalli and his sisters, Ancilla and Maria, lived there for the next ten years. The staff was limited to one in the beginning; later, two secretaries and one or two servants were added. No automobile was provided; therefore, the Vicar Apostolic traveled on foot, in trolleys or buses or, on special occasions, in cabs. Roncalli preferred this because it gave him closer contact with the Turkish people, and he was able to know them much better.

Roncalli's mission was complicated by a variety of adverse factors. Kemal's young Turks were not only opposed to Catholics, but they were also against all religions, including the Mohammedan and Orthodox. One of Roncalli's tactful triumphs was to persuade the authorities not to turn the famous

Cathedral of St. Sophia, which had been a Mohammedan mosque for five hundred years, into a secular museum. He so thoroughly convinced them of its historic and artistic importance that they began restoring it. As the paint and plaster with which the Ottomans had erased its Christian character were removed, the beautiful Byzantine mosaics of the Holy Family emerged from the obscurity of half a millennium.

Further difficulty was caused by the open hostility of the Patriarch of Constantinople, whose "Primacy of Honor" theoretically made him the senior prelate to all the Orthodox churches. He was, therefore, intensely jealous of the position of the Pope whom he called the Bishop of Rome. In addition, the five different Catholic rites of Roncalli's vicarate—Latin, Byzantine, Coptic Catholic, Armenian, and Syrian—had their own private feuds.

Unlike the position Roncalli held in Bulgaria where the King had accorded him unofficial recognition, Roncalli was barely tolerated in Turkey. The Turkish Government, carrying the ideal of separation of Church and State to absurd lengths, acted as if there were no such things as churches, or worse, as if they were hostile organs of propaganda. Kemal Ataturk once expressed the opinion that a man who prays is a coward or, in any event, a useless person.

A few months after Roncalli's arrival in June, 1935, the government passed a law which forbade the wearing of religious habits in public. Although they grudgingly made an exception of the heads of churches, Roncalli felt it was more tactful to conform to the letter of the law. He humorously remarked that he had spent ten years in mufti. Trotting through the colorful streets in his black business suit and derby hat, with only a clerical collar to mark his priesthood, the Archbishop might have been mistaken for a jolly Dutch burgher who had strayed a long way from home. But he was not to feel a stranger long. Because of the strict limitations on diplomatic or missionary activities, his principal service during those first years was as a pastor, the service which he loved best. To him, this was always the highest duty of his vocation—fulfilling it gave him a true sense of spiritual contentment. Intellectually he realized that his various other missions for the Church were perhaps more important religious duties, but none of these gave him the same sense of direct communion with God. His flock mainly consisted of the Catholics of the Latin rite in Istanbul, of whom there were only about ten thousand, but he also visited all the churches of his vicarate as he had done in Bulgaria. In some parts of Turkey there was only one Catholic in every hundred square miles, so this meant a great deal of travel to see very few Catholics, but Roncalli was not a shepherd who stayed in the sheepfold.

The Catholic schools were his next greatest concern. At that time, they were among the best educational institutions in the country, but a vast improvement in secular schools has since been made. Ironic as it may seem, Kemal himself was educated partly in a French Catholic school. Roncalli was particularly devoted to the school conducted by the French Capuchins. During Lent he indulged in the pleasure of teaching the children their catechism as he had in Rome and Bergamo.

Although he was cut off from all contact with the heads of the government, Roncalli made many trips to Ankara, the capital, where he was on friendly terms with many of the *Corps Diplomatique*. He did not meet Kemal Ataturk, but, in spite of the Kemal's antireligious attitude, Roncalli respected his integrity and his desire to improve the condition of his people. In return, Kemal managed to convey to the Vicar Apostolic his admiration for the tact and prudence with which Roncalli conducted his difficult mission, especially because he had ordered that certain prayers and sermons in Catholic churches be said in Turkish.

Roncalli made a good friend in the lower echelons of the Government—the Under Secretary of the Foreign Office, Naman Rifat Menemengioglu. Their first conversation is recorded by Leone Algisi in his biography of Pope John. Roncalli had received word that Menemengioglu would unofficially receive him to discuss the new Turkish laws which applied to foreigners. Roncalli went to Ankara, whose bare, broad streets and ugly, but comparatively efficient, modern buildings seemed to typify the hustle of the new Turkey. The meeting which followed was a delightful minuet of diplomatic courtesy and polite verbal fencing.

"I have come to Ankara to compliment the minister and to offer my homage to the representatives of Turkey," Roncalli began.

"I am happy to know you personally," replied Menemengioglu, "and to tell you of the great respect the Turkish government has for the illustrious tradition you represent."

"For that I thank you. I hope that the Turkish authorities have noted the regard Catholics have displayed for the laws of the country, even though they do not like them sometimes. That is proved by the clothes I am wearing."

"That is a fact," said the Minister smiling. "On the other hand, I want to assure you of our concern for the liberty of your ministry as long as it does not violate the law of the land. And also, of course, as long as it does not imply any rapport on our part with a religious power."

"Understood," said Roncalli mischievously. "But that does not impede this 'religious power' from taking pleasure in the rise of Turkey and also in finding in your new constitution some of the fundamental principles of Christianity, although we naturally disagree with its antireligious spirit."

Menemengioglu said, a little pompously, "The secularity of the State is our fundamental principle and the guarantee of our liberty."

"The Church will be careful not to infringe your liberty," said Roncalli. Then with an infectious grin he added, "But I am most optimistic. In every case I aim for that which unites rather than that which separates. So we are in accord. Your natural principles can take us down the same street. For the best thing is mutual confidence. Of course, on our part we

only want one step more: for the Turks to enter the Church."
Laughing, they shook hands and parted.

Despite all the difficulties, Roncalli was serenely happy
during his first years in Istanbul. The exercise of his priestly
vocation, teaching, and a sense of slow, but real, accomplishment in promoting good relations between Catholics of different rites assured this. His personal life, with one sad exception,
was also happy. At last he found leisure hours to devote to
prayer and meditation, and to read and learn Turkish. He was
particularly interested in the history of the Oriental Church,
and he became one of the world's greatest scholars on this subject. Roncalli's interest was further stimulated by visits to many
of the historic shrines of early Christianity in his vicarate and
to other countries of the Middle East.

One of his rare secular indulgences was an occasional
walk down to the crowded, aromatic, colorful bazaars of Istanbul where, poking among the open stalls of the merchants, he
sometimes unearthed an ancient Byzantine object of art, or
an ancient book or manuscript which he purchased. His natural
good taste and his wide knowledge of the period afforded him
some gratifying bargains. Roncalli's favorite bookshop was run
by an old Italian named De Gregori, whose innocent ignorance
of his wares gave the Archbishop many a kindly chuckle. De
Gregori would pull out some huge tome and say: "Look, Monsignor, here is a great bargain. It weighs at least ten pounds."
Nevertheless, Roncalli was careful not to take undue advantage of this friendly old literary grocer who sold books by the
pound.

Roncalli was fortunate in the assignment of secretaries to
the delegation. The first was an ardent young Italian, Father
Angelo Dell'Acqua, who is now one of the most valuable members of the Curia. He was replaced by Father Thomas Ryan,
who became one of Roncalli's closest friends, and who is now
a member of Pope John's personal staff. Father Ryan, a big,
full-blooded man with blue eyes and a high color, was the

clerical equivalent of a fighting Irishman. His fulminations against non-Catholics and bureaucratic infidels, which he considered the Turks to be, once led Roncalli to say with a gentle smile, "You Irish are impossible. The moment you come into the world, even before you are baptized, you begin damning everybody who doesn't belong to the Church, especially Protestants!"

Father Ryan, like Roncalli, was a happy priest with a great sense of humor. His faith was strong and his devotion to God profound, and he was the most loyal of friends and subordinates. All these things made him a wonderful companion for the Archbishop who was sometimes a little lonely in that far-off foreign land.

This was especially true in the summer of 1935, when a cable arrived telling Roncalli of the death of his father. The deep love he felt for the simple, good man who had been so naively proud of his son's position made a torment of Roncalli's grief. Although Giovanni Roncalli was eighty-one years old and had lived a full and happy life, his son was heartbroken not to have been able to be with him—to hold his hand once more and to give him the consolation of the sacraments. As soon as possible Roncalli returned to Sotto il Monte to comfort his mother, and found the sweet, sad consolation of praying at his father's grave.

We must not forget that Roncalli was also Apostolic Delegate to Greece, for he certainly did not. In the first year, he made three journeys to the second object of his double mission. In Athens, his position was only slightly less difficult than that in Istanbul. Although the Greek government was less hostile officially, Metropolitan Damaskinos of the Greek Orthodox Church was perhaps even more antipapal than the Patriarch of Constantinople. He viewed the arrival of the new Apostolic Delegate with anything but a welcoming glance. And once more, as Roncalli went about the business of the Lord, he had to walk very softly.

As a child, Angelo Roncalli lived in a simple farmhouse *(above)* in Sotto-il-Monte *(below),* a village typical of farming towns in the Italian Alps. Most of its residents are farmers, who still live as they did when young Angelo lived there. They have but two TV sets, seven autos, and one church, where Pope John XXIII was baptized.

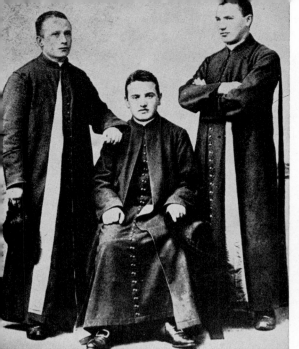

To attend grammar school Angelo walked six miles daily, in bare feet. Understandably, his grades were poor, but at the seminary in Rome *(left, in center)* his work excelled, partly as the result of the warmth and understanding of one of his instructors—Eugenio Pacelli, soon to be Pope Pius XII.

In 1904, Angelo was ordained and, by chance, met the Pope, who encouraged him and gave him his special blessing. At the time of his first Mass Angelo posed for this portrait *(right)*.

"I cannot remember a day when I did not want to serve God as a priest," the Pope once said. But he had his own parish only briefly —in 1913, after "his Bishop" died and before World War I. Then he could be Father Roncalli *(left)*.

Early in World War I Angelo became a medical service sergeant in the Italian army and grew a fine mustache (*below*). As Pope he said it was "a weak moment on my part."

Wide World

United Press International

When Angelo became a chaplain his mustache was gone. *Above:* He poses with two of his brothers, Zaverio (*in center*) and Giuseppe.

In 1921, as Director of the Italian Society for the Propagation of the Faith, a busy Father Roncalli (*above*) briefly visited at home. Four years later he was consecrated Titular Archbishop of Areopolis and departed from Rome for Sophia as Apostolic Visitor to Bulgaria.

Archbishop Roncalli hoped to remain in Bulgaria to continue his work with its Church, government, and people; but in 1934 he was promoted to Vicar Apostolic and Apostolic Delegate to Turkey and Apostolic Delegate to Greece. This picture was made at that time.

Wearing a bishop's biretta, Archbishop Roncalli *(front row center)* posed with his new associates in Istanbul.

On October 29, 1953, Angelo Cardinal Roncalli *(left, above)*, who had just arrived from Paris, where he served as Nuncio, waited at Castel Gondolfo for Pope Pius XII to bestow upon him the *galero,* the cardinal's red hat. With him are Cardinal Ciriaci and Cardinal de Arriba y Castro *(right)*, both of whom received the red hat at that time. Cardinal Roncalli was also appointed Patriarch of Venice. At *left* he is shown in his formal portrait as Cardinal and Patriarch, taken after his arrival in Venice, his last See before he was chosen the Supreme Pontiff.

The years in Venice were the happiest before Roncalli became Pope, for he fulfilled a lifelong desire to serve mainly as a shepherd of souls. *Above:* The Patriarch is a central figure in Venice's annual historical regatta.

Giordani

Giordani

In Venice Cardinal Roncalli endeared himself to the many clergy-men who visited at his palace, as did Cardinal Spellman *(above)*.

The Patriarch enjoyed talking and joking with the Venetians, who loved him for it. *Below:* He jokes with an athlete at the regatta.

Giordani

Cardinal Roncalli was unusually active as Patriarch. His salon was regularly open to the public, with whom he loved to talk, confer, or just gossip. He was the first patriarch of Venice ever to attend the International Biennial Art Exhibit. *Above:* He speaks before the Conference on Childhood, and votes in the general elections.

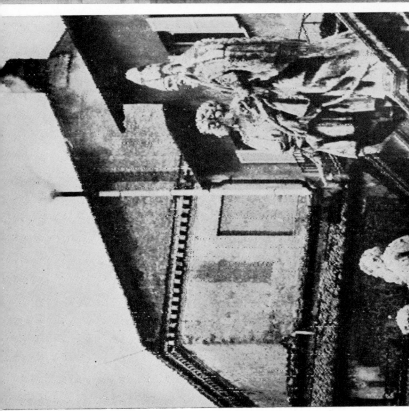

Pope Pius XII died on October 9, 1958, and the saddened Cardinal Roncalli left for Rome. *Right:* October 16—he leaves the Vatican after a meeting of cardinals. *Left:* Twelve days later white smoke rising from the chimney beside the Sistine Chapel marks the election of the new pope—Angelo Cardinal Roncalli, Pope John XXIII.

The coronation of Pope John XXIII was celebrated on November 4, in St. Peter's Basilica. *Above:* During the Communion of the Mass John drinks from the jeweled chalice, held by Cardinal Tisserant.

After his coronation as the two hundred and sixty-second pontiff of the Roman Catholic Church, Pope John imparts his first papal blessing, to hundreds of thousands of people gathered below in St. Peter's Square.

Many members of Pope John's family arrived for the coronation. *Above:* His sister Assunta and a brother, Alfredo, are leaving their train at Rome. Two other brothers and eighteen nieces and nephews also arrived. *Below:* In middle row, from left to right, Assunta, Zaverio (a brother), Alfredo, an unidentified man, and Sister Anna Roncalli, a niece who arrived from Ethiopia, witness the ceremonies.

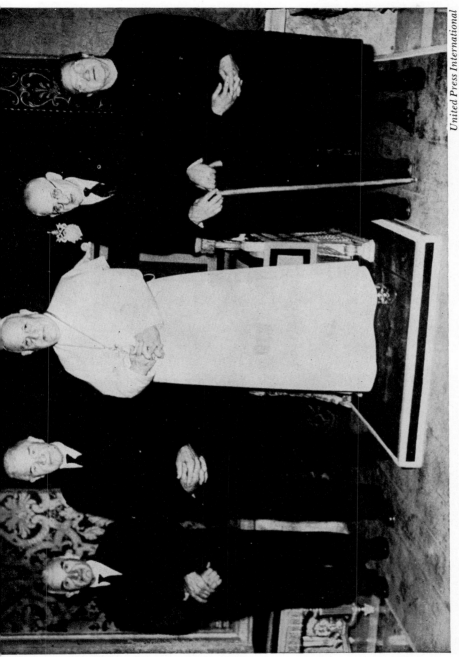

The Pope poses with his brothers and sister. From left to right, they are Giuseppe, Zaverio, Alfredo, Assunta.

Wide World

Wide World

Wide World

After the coronation farm life returns to normal. Zaverio *(top left)* and Alfredo *(below)* harvest corn. Giuseppe picks apples, while within the farmhouse Marie, Zaverio's wife, and Assunta knit and gossip.

Wide World

There were fifty thousand Catholics in Greece—Latin and Byzantine—scattered over the mainland and the lovely islands of the Aegean Sea. Extreme poverty was the normal condition of these people, and their priests suffered along with them. Roncalli went vigorously to work to help them in every possible way, especially in the islands, where the small isolated communities of Catholics could feast their eyes on beauty but had very little to put in their stomachs.

As Roncalli traveled throughout Greece to see and be seen by his parishioners, he also visited as many of the classic ruins of the country as possible. Although these lovely marble temples had been erected to false gods, they were symbolic of the highest aspirations of mankind in the beauty of their outward form which was the legacy of ancient Greece to mankind.

As usual in Roncalli's unstable spheres of activity, the Apostolic Delegate was faced with political unrest. In 1936, the government of Greece, which had degenerated into the chaos of political strife, was overthrown in a coup d'etat by General John Metaxas who established a right wing dictatorship with the full support of King George II. One might suppose that this would have resulted in a less anti-Catholic attitude than that of the radical, socialist-leaning politicians who had been ousted. Not at all! The new Government passed some extremely rigorous anti-Catholic laws which, in the name of limiting proselytizing, made it very difficult to publish or import Catholic books in Greece, and absolutely impossible to carry on any missionary work.

Roncalli promptly got to work to induce the Government to relax these laws. Using all his gentle charm he succeeded in making a friend of King George, as he had of King Boris, and also won a considerable degree of confidence from General Metaxas, while taking the utmost care to do nothing that would irritate the Metropolitan.

His efforts were surprisingly successful. Not only did he manage to have the laws modified, but he secured permission to build a Byzantine cathedral in Athens on the foundations of the ancient cathedral which had been built in the days before the Orthodox Church broke away. In this effort, the Apostolic Delegate got fine assistance from the Holy Father, who pleased the Greeks by announcing that the new edifice would be the Cathedral Church of the Byzantine Bishop of Athens who would have jurisdiction over all Greek Catholics including those in Turkey, because "Athens, the capital of Greece, is also the capital of all the Hellenes."

As usual a diplomatic triumph was followed by a diplomatic defeat, or what seemed like one. The extreme anti-Catholic faction of the Greek Orthodox Church gleefully announced an agreement with the Church of England by which each recognized the validity of the other's Holy Orders. But Roncalli was genuinely pleased. To the Greeks who slyly asked him what he thought of the arrangement, he said sincerely, "I have nothing but praise for our separated brothers for their zeal in taking a step toward the union of all Christians."

Nineteen Thirty-Nine was a year of despair for all people. To Roncalli it brought private as well as public grief. In February, 1939, his friend Pope Pius XI died. As he conducted the Memorial Mass in the Cathedral in Athens where he happened to be, Roncalli kept thinking not of the Pope lying in State in St. Peter's in his white and gold vestments, but of the round-faced librarian of the Ambrosiana who had been so helpful to an eager young scholar.

On March 2, 1939, word came of the election of a new Pope, Eugenio Cardinal Pacelli, who took the name of Pius XII. Pacelli had been Papal Secretary of State ever since the retirement of Cardinal Gasparri in 1930. Naturally, in his semi-diplomatic position Roncalli knew him well. He remembered the thin, ascetic lecturer of the Seminario so long ago, and he had had many conferences with the Cardinal-Secretary of State, who mingled an astute knowledge of the wiles of professional diplomats with the other-worldly serenity of a man whose inner being moved on a higher spiritual plane. If any mortal could confront the darkening future and pilot St. Peter's Bark through the coming storms with technical skill and unshaken faith, this was the man.

In August, 1939, Roncalli received another of those sad cables from Sotto il Monte telling him of the death of his mother. By this time the world situation was so dangerous that he dared not leave his post even for a brief visit to her grave.

On September 1, the thing that good Christians dreaded most exploded in the world. Hitler sent his armored legions smashing across the Polish Border and on across the level Polish plains in his long-planned blitzkreig. The nations of Europe, one after another, tumbled into war. In a special service in the Cathedral at Istanbul Roncalli prayed that the city might be spared the horrors of war and characteristically added: "This we ask of Thee equally in behalf of all those who live under this same sky whatever their race may be, for we are equally brothers no matter what our religion, our ethical customs, our traditions or social position."

Inevitably, neutral Turkey, the link between Europe and Asia-Minor astride the ancient crossroads of the Dardanelles, became a hornets' nest of spies. Their cloak-and-dagger activities, which would provide ample material for thrillers for years to come, were boiling in Ankara and Istanbul. Agents of all nations and every ideology were spying on each other, corrupting each other, and even murdering each other. Sometimes it seemed to Roncalli that all of them, British Intelligence, French *Deuxieme Bureau*, Russian N.K.V.D. and Nazi Gestapo, were watching him. "I learned to recognize them all," he said.

The Apostolic Delegate was also gathering information in a highly efficient manner from a far-flung network of clergy, monks, and laymen, and passing it on to the Vatican. But the object of his activities was not lethal but philanthropic. Because of his unique position at the nerve center of information, Roncalli's delegation became one of the most important clearing houses for tens of thousands of queries from anxious men and women of all the warring nations and of all religions—and none—about their loved ones who had disappeared in the war. This, of course, was one of the humanitarian services, which the Holy See had rendered during World War I and reactivated in the second global conflagration.

Pope Pius XII was a great diplomat, but he took sides firmly against the inhumanities of the Nazis whatever the consequences. He dared to denounce in caustic invective Hitler's ruthless barbarities. Roncalli, whose greatest goal was peace, was equally indignant at the Nazis. One of the hardest things he had to do was to mask his feelings in genial suavity in order to retain the confidence of the German diplomats which was necessary to his work of gathering information about the Allied prisoners who had disappeared behind the German lines.

On one occasion, though, he let himself go. When Germany declared war on Russia, Roncalli's colleague, German Ambassador Franz von Papen, came to him with the suggestion that now that Germany was fighting the atheistic Communists perhaps he could influence the Pope to give them his moral support. Roncalli's face got red and his blue eyes flashed in a rare burst of splendid anger as he said, "And what shall I say about the millions of Jews your countrymen are murdering in Poland and in Germany?"

Von Papen, an old style German diplomat and a Catholic, later secretly helped Roncalli save thousands of Jews from countries overrun by the Nazis and sent them to safety in Palestine. In turn, Roncalli tried to help von Papen when he was tried at Nuremburg after the war. Fifteen years later in January, 1959, Pope John XXIII received him in private audience at the Vatican.

The Turkish Government's confidence in Roncalli enabled him to perform a great humanitarian service. A shipload of Jewish children who had escaped from Germany arrived in Constantinople. Kemal Ataturk in order to preserve his precious neutrality ordered them shipped back to Germany.

To a man who loved children as much as Roncalli, the thought of these innocents going back to the horror of Nazi

Germany was not to be borne. He immediately went to work on their behalf, and was so insistent that Ataturk decided that neutrality would be better served by shipping them to another neutral country. Hundreds of Jewish children were saved by the Vicar Apostolic from the Holy See.

Though Roncalli's work in Turkey was difficult it did not involve the heartbreak of his work in Greece. Neutral Turkey escaped the direct impact of war, but in 1941, Greece was conquered and enslaved by a ruthless enemy with all the bloodshed and misery that implies.

During the war, Roncalli made many trips to Greece by whatever means of travel he could find. On one of these, shortly after the Nazi-Italian conquest, he went by train to Sophia, where all his friends, including Queen Giovanna and even Exarchate Stefan, received their friend. Then he motored through the familiar countryside, over the Macedonian Mountains and down through the deep, war-wasted valleys of Greece to Athens, where on August 25, 1941 he found a desperate situation.

A whole brave nation was literally starving to death with tens of thousands of its young men and women confined in the huge stockades, and a frightened peasantry desperately trying to wring bare subsistence from the infertile earth. Trade and industry were at a standstill leaving the population of the cities without work.

The natural bitterness of the remaining Grecian officials against the invaders made any arrangements with them difficult, and the hatred they saw in the eyes of the people did not incline the Italian occupation authorities to mercy. In such stringent conditions Roncalli could not hope to accomplish much. He said philosophically, "The best thing is simply to try your best."

His first move was to make friends with both sides. Roncalli's good will was never more valuable to him or to his people. Greeks, Germans, or Italians had only to meet him to realize that he was a man they could trust because he loved all men. At one point he asked to visit the 4th Italian Division on the Greek-Albanian border. The troops were on dress parade, because Italian regulations required that an archbishop be accorded the honors due a lieutenant general. As they stood in ordered ranks, grumbling at the annoyance caused by visiting brass, a small black car bumped over the field, and out of it jumped a round little man with a jolly round face all dressed in black. Before anybody found out who he was, the Archbishop was walking through the lines of troops who were still "at ease," laughing and joking with them and getting to know them.

After celebrating a field Mass he went in to talk with the general and his staff. When he came out, the whole division surrounded him, cheering and calling affectionate God-speeds. A corporal came forward timidly in spite of the frowns of the officers.

"What do you want, dear boy," Roncalli asked.

The soldier dropped on his knees to kiss the Archbishop's ring. "May I embrace your Excellency for all of us?" he asked.

In his efforts to alleviate misery, Roncalli found an unexpected ally in the Metropolitan Damaskinos. The grand old man of the Greek Orthodox Church, who had been an adviser to Kings and Prime Ministers, was desperately trying to perform his last and greatest service to his country. He was aware that if the people of Greece were not to die of starvation they had to have three hundred and seventy thousand tons of wheat from the Allies. He succeeded in obtaining permission to bring it into the country from the Italian and German authorities because, after all, it was to their advantage to be relieved of the burden of a starving people. But persuading the hard-pressed Allies to provide the food and to allow it through the blockade was another problem.

Meanwhile, Roncalli was working along the same lines. Their efforts converged when the security-conscious German

Commander in Chief asked Damaskinos, "Who is going to be your contact with the enemy?"

"I shall work with a Christian church with whom my own church was once united," the Metropolitan replied.

Hearing of this, Roncalli took the initiative. He sent a message to Damaskinos asking if he would be willing to meet with him at a time and place of Damaskinos' choosing. This delicate deference to his position touched Damaskinos. He accepted eagerly.

The youthful-looking Catholic Archbishop and the white-bearded Orthodox Metropolitan met for the first time in a conference room of the Paleophaleron Palace. After their formal greetings, stiffened by a thousand years of mutual suspicion, the two men relaxed. The Metropolitan told Roncalli what he had done so far, and said in desperation, "A thousand Greeks are dying every day of starvation. We must do something."

"We will," Roncalli answered warmly.

At another more intimate meeting, Metropolitan Damaskinos performed what was probably the most difficult act of his life. He told Roncalli that the Church of Greece officially requested the good offices of the Holy See in negotiating with the Allies for food for Greece. He then handed the Apostolic Delegate a letter to Pope Pius XII from the highest laymen of the Orthodox Church asking for help.

With all the warmth of his nature Roncalli accepted the mission and somehow contrived to make the proud old man feel that it was the Metropolitan who was doing the Holy See a favor. It is a matter of history that the joint efforts of the two churches were successful in saving thousands, perhaps hundreds of thousands, of Greek lives.

The representative of Rome and the Metropolitan had a number of other meetings before Roncalli started back to Istanbul on October 7. When they parted for the last time the Metropolitan leaned forward almost shyly. With a sudden flash of joy, Roncalli understood his intention. They parted with the "kiss of peace" used in the Catholic liturgy and Orthodox liturgy as a sign of forgiveness, of charity, and of love.

The study office in Istanbul was rather dreary on that day in mid-December, 1944. Of course, Archbishop Roncalli realized that there was much for which to be grateful. The people of Greece had been spared. The anti-human forces of Nazism had recoiled everywhere before the Allied armies. Italy had been freed of her own errors and the iron grip of Nazi domination. France was liberated—or almost.

But Roncalli's high hopes for a quick peace had been ground down by the gradual stiffening of German resistance, the new fierce battles that postponed the hoped-for end of killing. In Turkey the stringencies imposed by the war were reducing the people he loved to further privations. And the devil's dance of spies and counterspies was reaching a peak of frenzy.

Even to a man as hopeful as Roncalli the prospect seemed gray. The weary round of death and intrigue continued into an indefinite future. As he worked at his routine tasks, he prayed that all people everywhere be released from the trap of man-made havoc, and that there soon be a great renaissance of faith.

The Turkish houseboy knocked on the door and brought him a telegram from Rome. He knew it was urgent because it was in the special code. Father Ryan was away from Istanbul on business of the diocese so Roncalli got the code book out of the old-fashioned iron safe and began laboriously to transcribe the message. As the words slowly took shape, he thought he must be doing it wrong. He checked and rechecked, but the evidence imposed itself upon his disbelief. The coded message made sense and yet no sense. Aloud he said, "I think they must have lost their minds."

A few days later Roncalli was in Rome in the magnificent but chilly office of Monsignor Domenico Tardini, Acting Secretary of the Office of Extraordinary Affairs of the Holy See. He knew Tardini well, a compact, bullet-headed man with tremendous energy, ability, and a warm heart. His conversation was salted by a gay but caustic sense of humor.

When they had greeted each other Roncalli said, "Look here, old friend, are you sure that cable I received is not a mistake. Surely the Holy Father did not intend to appoint me Nuncio to France."

Tardini chuckled. "It's no mistake," he said. "His Holiness makes his own decisions. But you can be sure of one thing: none of us thought he would do this."

The Gargoyles—Notre Dame, Paris

CHAPTER NINE

THE CHURCH AND
LIBERATED FRANCE

The small reception room on the ground floor of the Elysée Palace, residence of the Presidents of France, was cold and shabby. Its brocaded walls were dingy with dust which fogged the luster of the beautiful crystal chandelier. The furniture was dilapidated, and the long windows facing the park-like garden were crusted with dirt. In fact, the whole beautiful edifice showed the neglect of nearly six years of war and four years of enemy occupation; it was a reflection of France herself.

De Gaulle's Chief of Protocol, M. Losé, met the Papal Nuncio on the portico of the Palace and escorted him through the marble hall to the reception room. As he waited, Roncalli noted its condition, and smiled gently at someone's attempt to brighten it up with a vase of beautiful red roses. Then the double doors were flung back, and General de Gaulle, President of the Provisional Government of France, entered, followed by Foreign Minister Georges Bidault. There was nothing shabby about the General. His uniform was immaculate, and the brigadier general's stars glittered. He wore one clean white glove and carried the other in his left hand. On his breast was a single decoration, the double-barred Cross of Lorraine.

Roncalli advanced to meet his host, smiling in his friendly way, but the General was as cold as the cheerless room. Towering over the little prelate, he bowed stiffly and murmured a formal phrase of welcome. Roncalli could do nothing but begin his prepared speech: "In presenting Your Excellency with the letters which accredit me as Nuncio to the President of the Provisional Government of the French Republic . . . my thoughts go back to the distant days of my young priesthood . . . during which I learned to know and love your country.

"Your Excellency can therefore appreciate the feelings with which I begin the mission that the Holy Father has entrusted to me. . . . Even more than expressing these feelings it is my duty to present to Your Excellency the pledge of esteem and affection with which the Holy Father has charged me, with the assurance of his particular benevolence for your country.

"To this pledge of my August Sovereign permit me to add my own which I make to you in the ardent hope that I, with the help of God and the precious cooperation of your Government, will be allowed to draw even closer the existing relations between the Holy See and the noble French Nation."

The odd thing about this flowery speech was that Roncalli meant every word of it. He presented his credentials which General de Gaulle accepted with a few stately phrases.

Then there was an awkward pause while Roncalli sought a way to melt the ice. Looking at the vase of roses with a tentative smile he said, "How lovely those are. I love flowers and all the beautiful, gay things God has created."

He had struck exactly the right note. De Gaulle had a passion for red roses. A glimmer of warmth appeared in the General's ice-blue eyes as he said, "So do I."

At first glance it might appear that Roncalli's appointment to France would be a pleasant vacation after the stress of his two previous missions. As Nuncio he would be officially received by the government of a predominantly Catholic nation instead of being an alien with no diplomatic status whose presence was tolerated by a hostile government. Roncalli knew the situation in France too well to be lulled into false security. He was more than ever the Pope's trouble-shooter.

After the Fall of France in 1940, Papal Nuncio Valerio Valeri had been ordered to accompany the Pétain Government to Vichy. The Archbishop of Paris, Cardinal Suhard, and almost all the other archbishops and bishops of France had felt it their duty to remain in their dioceses and to carry on under the occupation. This necessarily meant having official relations with the Germans and even receiving those who were Catholics in their churches. In doing this they were following a basic policy of the Church in all the wars and confusions of nations throughout its history.

However, the men of the French Resistance, who had fought for their country's freedom in little bands in her wild forests or alone and secretly in her cities under the very noses of the invaders, and who had witnessed the massacres of the innocents by which the Nazis had taken revenge on the French people for their activities, had no use for anyone who had "collaborated" with the enemy. When France was liberated, the men of the Resistance came into power under de Gaulle. Many of them were Communists or free-thinking socialists, and even the Catholics among them, though not irreligious, were not inclined to forgive this of the clergy.

General de Gaulle, a devout Catholic, understood the conscience of the clergy, and sympathized with them. But, to a considerable extent, he was the prisoner of his own legend and of the men who had brought him to power. He felt obliged to ask the Holy See to recall Valeri, and to request the removal of no less than thirty-three bishops. He did not want, however, to sever diplomatic relations with the Vatican or play the Communists' game. Thus, he urgently requested the appointment of another Nuncio.

If Roncalli had had any illusions about the prickly situation he was getting into they were extinguished during the brief audience he had with Pope Pius XII before going to Paris.

After confirming Tardini's words about Roncalli's appointment
—"It was I, Monsignor, who thought of you myself, and I made
the decision—no one else"—the Pontiff realistically outlined the
unhappy position of the Church in France, and the necessity
for restoring it. He made it plain that he was relying on Roncalli's tact, judgment, and devotion to accomplish this, but he
did not expect him to work miracles. "In your position," the
Pope said with a twinkle, "you can only do, as they say in
France, *aussi bien que possible.*"

Roncalli was told that he must get to Paris as fast as possible. On New Year's Day by custom the *Corps Diplomatique*
in Paris called *en masse* on the President. Their address was
read by the dean of the Corps—the Papal Nuncio if there was
one, or the ambassador who had been there longest. At this time
the Soviet Ambassador qualified. Nobody wanted this to happen. On December 29, the French Government was so concerned that they sent a military airplane to bring the new
Nuncio to Paris.

On December 30, Roncalli flew to Paris in an uncomfortable bucket seat, and presented his credentials on December 31.
As he wrote to the Bishop of Bergamo, "I seemed to be seized
by surprise, like Habakuk, and transported suddenly from Istanbul to Paris by a sort of incantation. Also my interior discipline
was turned topsy-turvy . . . the more so since it seemed absolutely incredible to me and certainly I had neither the courage nor the imagination nor the desire for it. I was stupe-
fied . . ."

On the morning of January 1, 1945, the Papal Nuncio
dressed in the colorful robes of his episcopate took the salute
of the brass-helmeted Garde Republicaine in the Elysée courtyard, and appeared in the Salle d'Armes of the palace at the
head of the *Corps Diplomatique* to read the address. He lavished
compliments and flattery on de Gaulle. Such phrases as "Thanks
to your far-seeing statesmanship and your energy, this beloved
country has found its freedom and its faith in its own destinies"
. . . and "With her lucid spirit, her love of work, her love of

freedom, and her spiritual splendor . . . (France) will know how to point out the way to a unity of hearts and a spirit of justice that may lead our society toward an era of tranquillity and peace . . ." rang through the room.

The gratification of the French staff officers was evident, and though de Gaulle's face remained impassive his eyes showed that his patriotic spirit was touched. As Roncalli wrote to a friend, "I think it went off very well."

M. Jacques Domaine, former Chief of Protocol of the French Foreign Office, has described how Roncalli expressed his conception of his mission at their first meeting. As he came into Domaine's office the Nuncio clapped his hand to his head to straighten his zucchetto, which was always slipping askew, and said simply, "My role in France is like that of St. Joseph: to be a guardian over our Lord and to protect him with discretion."

The Nuncio knew that oratory was not enough. The situation could only be eased by action and by gaining the intimate friendship of French leaders. As he was seeking a concrete expression of the good will of the Holy Father toward the new French Government, an Italian political leader, Giuseppe Saragat, who happened to be in Paris, gave him a valuable tip. "Why not make Saliège a cardinal?" he said.

Jules Saliège, Archbishop of Toulouse, was one prelate whom the Resistance leaders loved. Though he had been paralyzed from the neck down for years, his spirit was indomitable. At the height of the Nazis' vengeance and repression, he had himself carried to his Cathedral on a stretcher and laid in the pulpit, where he launched a denunciation of them and their barbarous methods that equaled many of the words of the classic masters of invective from Cataline to Edmund Burke.

Roncalli could take a hint and the Pope trusted his advice. At the first post-war consistory in February, 1946, Saliège was elevated to the rank of Cardinal. Roncalli, beaming with pleasure, went to Toulouse to present the red biretta to the frail but fiery Archbishop.

Roncalli was able to dispose of the matter of the thirty-three allegedly collaborationist bishops in a typically diplomatic manner. Instead of haughtily refusing the government's request, he asked for formal charges. After examining them he called on General de Gaulle and said, "What I have here is mostly newspaper clippings and gossip. These are not evidence in any system of justice. If you can't supply something more concrete, I am afraid that any action against these men would be discreditable both to me and the justice of France."

De Gaulle admitted the point, and, in the end, only three bishops were removed.

Meanwhile Roncalli was preparing to make friends and influence the rulers of France. The first step was to refurbish the nunciature, a lovely, classic house at 10 Avenue Woodrow Wilson, which he bought from the Prince of Monaco. Like all the other buildings in Paris, it had been neglected during the war. Workmen came, and painters swarmed through the graceful rooms, banging, hammering, painting and polishing until that house became a place of beauty and comfort again.

But there was very little comfort for the Nuncio while the work was going on. He was driven from room to room, and it took all his powers of concentration to go on with his work or to find peace for his daytime devotions and meditations. He remained unruffled—except for one occasion. They tell the tale which seems well authenticated, that Roncalli was working at his desk one day when a workman in the next room dropped a plank on his foot. The man's howls of pain were mixed with blasphemous appeals to every member of the Trinity.

The Archbishop bounced out of his chair and into the room and without the slightest hesitation said to the astonished painter, "*Alors, qu'est-ce que c'est ca? Vous ne pouvez pas dire merde comme tout le monde?*"

When the house was finished it was a rare combination of elegance and intimacy. The large drawing room was decorated in a surprisingly harmonious combination of deep red, ivory and gold. The dining room was hung with tapestries, which

Roncalli picked up in Paris at post-war bargain prices for the Vatican. Although the dining room could seat fifty people at dinner—and often did—its lightness and graceful decor encouraged good conversation.

After embellishment came entertainment. Roncalli was acutely aware that, whether the adage holds good for the rest of the world or not, the way to a Frenchman's heart is through his stomach. He hired the best chef he could find in Paris, Roger, who is now the proprietor—and soul—of the famous restaurant *La Grenouille*. He did not stop, of course, with offering his guests French delicacies with which they were familiar. Because the French are imaginative eaters who like to adventure in new fields, Roncalli thought that they might appreciate some of his favorite dishes from Bergamo. He conferred with Roger, and between them they managed to concoct such gastronomic surprises as ravioline polenta with small birds, hare or chamois in salmi, deviled chicken, and tripe Bergamasque. The wines and cigars were carefully chosen.

These Lucullan menus infer perhaps that Roncalli himself was a gargantuan eater. We have the word of Roger, "He is as fat as a curate although he eats like a bird. It is the books he devours that make him fat." Although this is true, "the bird" was no ostrich. For though Roncalli was a moderate eater he had a very discriminating palate. A true gourmet, he enjoyed good food just as he enjoyed all the other "beautiful, gay things which God has created."

His luncheons and dinners soon became famous in Paris, not only for the fare, but for the conversation. With the Nuncio leading the talk with his deep knowledge of politics, art, and literature, and, above all, his spiritual inspiration, combined as it too rarely is with wit, the world gathered to feast its ears as well as its mouths. Regulars at Roncalli's table included many of the men who were shaping the destiny of France. Among them were Bidault, of course, and such other cabinet ministers—past, present and future—as René Mayer, Edgar Faure, Robert Schuman, René Pléven, Antoine Pinay, men representing almost the whole kaleidoscope of French politics, as well as such great men of letters as François Mauriac. Perhaps Roncalli's greatest friend was the grand old socialist and anti-clerical, Eduard Herriot. The Archbishop's greatest spiritual triumph, because heaven so rejoices in the return of lost lambs, was when, on his deathbed, this upright defender of secular philosophies asked for and received the sacraments of the Catholic Church.

Roncalli's favorite "infidel" was Naman Menemengioglu, who had been made Turkish Ambassador to France.

In Paris, as on his other missions, Roncalli walked the diplomatic tight-rope, skillfully avoiding commitment to any political party. On one occasion Pierre de Gaulle, the General's brother, tried to trap him by saying in a speech celebrating the two thousandth aniversary of the City of Paris, "The presence of the Nuncio with us here today is proof that the Church considers the Gaullist Party as being *the* Catholic party."

There was nothing Roncalli could do then, but the next time he saw Pierre de Gaulle he gave him a book by the sixteenth-century humanist Gasparino Barsizza, saying crisply, "This book was written by a man of Bergamo like me. It concerns good manners. I suggest you read it."

Although it was a considerable drain on his energies, Roncalli also accepted as many as possible of the hundreds of invitations that poured in on him. He knew that this was the best way to widen the circle of his influence so that from these contacts it would spread through all the echelons of the French government. The jovial presence of the Nuncio became an assurance of the success of a party. Of course, the people realized that he had a purpose in charming them, an episcopal ax to grind, but they did not mind. They also knew that his friendship was not deceitful, and that he enjoyed them, even loved them, as they loved him.

Robert Schuman best expressed the remarkable effect that the Archbishop had on these gatherings of sophisticates when he said, "He is the only man in Paris about whom you feel that he is the physical embodiment of peace."

If Roncalli's friendships with French laymen have been emphasized it is because it was in this way that he did so much to restore the Church to her former position in France. However, he was also on intimate terms with many French prelates, though he tactfully avoided interfering with their diocesan authority unless they asked him for advice.

And one of the greatest French cardinals—Eugene Cardinal Tisserant—became his devoted friend. Cardinal Tisserant, who was head of the Congregation of the Oriental Church (and appropriately wore a patriarchal beard), of course, lived in Rome, but he made many visits to Paris during Roncalli's stay there. Whenever he came, these two conversed for long hours. Tisserant shared Roncalli's great and abiding ambition to pave the way for eventual unification of the Orthodox churches with Rome.

Nor did Roncalli neglect the people themselves. Although the nunciature was provided with a chauffeur-driven limousine, he preferred to walk to his destinations when possible. Ambling along with a single companion he became a familiar figure in the streets near the Avenue Woodrow Wilson, stopping to talk to the passersby and the tradesmen who soon felt he was an old friend. Often he managed to stray off his direct route to visit the bookstalls along the Seine, where when he had time he spent an hour or two browsing among the old books looking for bargains—and finding them. In this way, as in Turkey, he made intimate contacts quite literally with "the man in the street."

Another way of becoming acquainted with the people was by traveling to all parts of the country. He even went to French North Africa, not only to the coastal cities, but over the rugged bandit-infested mountains to small villages. In thirty-eight days he drove ten thousand kilometers from Tunisia through all of Algeria and on through Morocco to the Pillars of Hercules and the Spanish border. His French friends said that like the Roman Scipio he should have the title *Africanus*.

In France he visited all but two of its eighty-odd dioceses and many of its shrines. His favorite shrine was Lourdes which had so moved a young priest long ago. He made a pilgrimage there every year while he was in France. He expressed the emotion Lourdes aroused in him on the occasion of his last visit there when, as Patriarch of Venice, he consecrated the vast underground basilica of St. Pius X.

First he praised the Marian devotion of France which, "rising from the crypt of Chartres to the sublime heights of La Salette now returns to find expression underground in Lourdes in the largest church in the world except for St. Peter's."

Then in a voice exalted by his love of the Virgin, he said, "Mary is always here . . . always in the act of fulfilling her pious mission. She is here as she is in the grotto, the crypt, the upper and lower basilicas. She is always here, the Mother of Jesus. Always she is here, ever in the act of carrying out her maternal mission, the mission proclaimed by her Son Jesus. She listens, enlightens, consoles, heals and encourages all those who appeal to her . . ."

In addition to ameliorating the diplomatic relations between France and the Holy See, Roncalli faced a difficult problem within the Church. This was the matter of the worker priests. Realizing that more and more French workers were straying from the Church a group of priests originating in the *Mission de France* had decided to try to regain these workers by living and working alongside of them. Cardinal Suhard supported the plan.

It was a splendid idea and fruitful for a time. However, some of these priests became so emotionally involved with the problems of their friends, the workers, that there was danger that instead of the workers being converted, the priests might be converted to some of the practices, though not the atheistic dogmas, of Communism. The good things and the bad in the movement became a mixed matter.

The Nuncio, of course, had no authority over the French bishops, but he inevitably became involved in the problem be-

cause they came to him for advice. Roncalli, no authoritarian
bureaucrat but a rather spontaneous humanitarian, was intensely sympathetic to the worker priests. Their flaming missionary spirit appealed to his ardent heart. At the same time,
he was too good a theologian and too obedient to the dogmas
and canons of the Church not to recognize the dangers of the
situation.

While he was Nuncio he tried by wise advice, prudent
encouragement, and patience to hold a delicate balance, saving
what was good and mitigating the evils. By the time he became
Pope, the situation had gotten out of hand and he reluctantly
issued a decree altering this idealistic experiment by substitut-
ing missionary trained laymen for the worker priests.

Another duty that was entrusted to Roncalli during his
final years as Nuncio placed him on the world stage of diplomacy. He was appointed Observer for the Holy See to the
United Nations cultural agency, UNESCO.

Soon his rotund figure in its swinging, tent-like cape became as familiar in the chilly halls and conference rooms on
the Avenue Klèber as it was in bookstalls on the quays or the
salons of the Rue du Faubourge St. Honoré. His ability to
speak languages such as Bulgarian, Turkish, modern Greek and
even a little Russian endeared him to the delegates from those
countries. Indeed, there is a photograph of him in amiable
conversation with his great opponent, Soviet Ambassador Bogo-
molov, showing that even there he sought "what unites rather
than what divides."

From the first, Roncalli recognized the danger that
UNESCO would tend to propagate a mass materialistic culture
rather than encourage the precious individual spiritual and
artistic values of its many nations. His most eloquent address
to the general conference in July, 1951, was a masterpiece of
the diplomat's subtle art; instead of viewing the danger with
alarm he contrived to point it out by lavishly praising UNESCO
for doing the very things it was in fact neglecting.

"UNESCO," he said, "is no longer what one feared it might become, a big museum dedicated to diluting culture for the benefit of a curious throng. Instead it is a great, blazing fire whose sparks fly forth to arouse enthusiasm and cooperation on behalf of justice, freedom and peace for all peoples without destruction of race, language or religion . . .

"If I underline this clear purpose of UNESCO, contained in its constitution, it is not because the racial, literary or religious values of different peoples are being ignored or neglected, but to insure that these values may always continue to be upheld by it. UNESCO . . . must never become either blind or deaf to the basic psychology of each of its peoples, that is to their national ideals and their religious spirit . . . Regard for these will insure the trust and cooperation of the vast majority of mankind in this great international organization . . ."

Roncalli would have been less than human if he had not sometimes wondered if his long service in the Church would be crowned by its penultimate accolade—the Red Hat. On a visit he paid to Sotto il Monte in the summer of 1952, his family and old friends brought up the question in their long talks with him as they watched the shadows reach across the valley from the gallery of Colombara Farm. Pope Pius XII had not created any new cardinals since 1946. However, the Sacred College was dwindling because of the deaths of several cardinals, and he might be expected to do so before long.

Answering the eager questions, Roncalli said, "The Nuncio to France is usually made a cardinal at the end of his tour of duty. However, if I stay there for ten years, as I hope to, I then will be seventy-four, which is rather late in life to have need of a scarlet biretta."

Roncalli took the long way back to Paris staying two days in Milan and visiting many of the small Italian towns he loved. He also took the opportunity of stopping in the little cities in the Alps Maritime part of France, like Grasse, Cannes, Frejus and Avignon, to see for himself how things were going there.

Back in Paris in November he received two disparate pieces of news in the same day. The first was a letter from Monsignor Giovanni Montini, the Pope's Acting Secretary of State for Ordinary Affairs, saying that the Holy Father had included his name in the list of new cardinals who would be created at a consistory to be held January 12, 1953. Hardly had he savored the happiness that this mark of the Pope's confidence brought him when a telegram arrived from Sotto il Monte that plunged him in sorrow. It told him that his sister Ancilla, whom he loved deeply, had contracted a mortal illness and could be expected to live only a few months. It seemed a Biblical reminder of the vanity of earthly glory.

However, if Roncalli's joy was extinguished, there was no damper on the enthusiasm of the friends he had won in France. Congratulations, flowers, and presents poured into the nunciature. Prime Minister Antoine Pinay rushed over alone to extend his congratulations and those of his cabinet. So great was the outpouring of felicitations that Roncalli dryly reminded himself of an epigram coined long ago by wise and witty Father Jolpa, when he was secretary to St. Filippo: "Are they saying bad things about you? They are speaking truly. Are they paying you compliments? They are fooling you."

He wrote to a friend saying that his promotion was neither a sacrament nor sacramental, but more like a winning post that he had passed. And he added, "Perhaps Providence is preparing me for the responsibilities which are, after all, a heavy reckoning to pay."

He had no idea how heavy . . .

Just before Christmas Roncalli paid a flying visit to Sotto il Monte to see Ancilla and comfort her. She was not suffering and was cheerful in her faith in God's love. In the bright sunshine and crisp snow-smelling air from the mountain so appropriate to that gay season, it seemed incredible that he would never see her again. Then he hurried back to Paris for the New Year's Day ceremony at the Elysée. There he learned that his good friend, Patriarch Carlo Agostino of Venice, had died. The Patriarch was to have been made a cardinal at the same consistory as Roncalli. The harsh irony was surely food for reflection on submission to the will of God.

A few days later the Nuncio received another letter from Montini telling him that Pope Pius had appointed him to replace his friend as Patriarch of Venice. It was a splendid see, and had Archbishop Roncalli been given his choice, he could not have asked more. Nevertheless, he was far from elated; he felt that, as in his missions to Bulgaria and Turkey, he was being taken away from France before his work was done. However, after long meditation he wrote, "I end up by becoming convinced that this is a grace for which I must thank God, and which will gain for me some other (grace)."

After his decision was made, he exclaimed in characteristic exuberance, "I think I will address myself first to the wonderful spirit of the people, the spirit of joy that is so easy to find along the canals of Venice."

A deputation of prelates and citizens from Venice soon came to greet and congratulate him. He liked them all, but there was one young priest whom he particularly liked. Father Loris Capovilla was a tall, thin, eager man with a brilliant mind and plenty of energy. With his searching brown eyes and his horn-rimmed glasses he might have been a young intellectual from a university or an aspiring writer. Even in that first brief meeting Roncalli felt that he was a kindred soul and his intuition was right. He and Capovilla were to establish the same loving, filial relationship as he had known with his dear Bishop of Bergamo.

It is truly said that when Roncalli departed from Paris he left behind him a host of friends and not a single enemy. This was because his sense of humor, combined with his genuine affection for the French, endeared him to a people who enjoy wit. On one occasion a politician of the French Catholic MRP tried to trap the Nuncio into supporting his party in the elections. *"Cher Monsieur,"* Roncalli said, "you know that at the end of Lent all the holy images in our churches are covered with a violet veil; please allow the Nuncio to cover himself with a veil during an election campaign."

The President of France, Vincent Auriol, had become very fond of the Nuncio and always looked forward to his New Year's Day address because Roncalli invariably produced some apt French quotation as his text. The last one Roncalli delivered was on January 1, 1953. The Nuncio began with the lines from La Fontaine:

> *Troublez l'eau, vous y voyez vous?*
> *Laissez-la reposer*
> *Vous verrez votre image.**

Then he went on to say that this knowledge of self is pleasing to God, and that the President had this knowledge in great measure which enabled him to serve the common good of the French people. When the ceremony was over, President Auriol said teasingly, "I enjoy your French quotations, especially now that I am used to your accent."

Twinkling Roncalli replied, "It took me quite a while to get used to yours."

A few days later Auriol was able to give convincing proof of his affection for the Nuncio. The question had arisen as to how Roncalli should receive the cardinal's red biretta. He could, of course, go to Rome and receive it from the Holy Father. However, the tradition was that in countries which had diplomatic relations with the Holy See when the nuncio was elevated to cardinal, the biretta was placed on his head by the Chief of State. This, of course, presupposed that the ruler was a Catholic. Since the separation of Church and State in France the President of the Republic had seldom performed this ceremony. Furthermore, Vincent Auriol was a Socialist and an agnostic. Despite these difficulties, Auriol was so fond of his Nuncio that he wanted the pleasure of presenting the Hat. Roncalli wanted him to do it; it was soon arranged.

> * Trouble the waters; do you see yourself there?
>   Let them be calm.
>   You will see your image.

At first, out of delicacy, the President proposed a very private ceremony, but it grew. The Canadian Ambassador begged for an invitation. Then Turkish Ambassador Menemengioglu called on the President and asked to be allowed to see his old friend receive the crowning symbol—as he thought— of his long career of service in the Church. Finally the CardinalElect told Madame Auriol that he would like the Bishop of Bergamo, the parish priests of Sotto il Monte, and his three brothers, Alfredo, Giuseppe and Zaverio Roncalli, to witness the ceremony.

The Roncalli brothers arrived at 10 Avenue Woodrow Wilson two days before the ceremony, very excited by their first trip outside of Italy. Early the next morning they came into their brother's study properly dressed for the big city except for neckties. "We don't know how to tie them," they confessed sheepishly. "Will you help us?"

Smiling affectionately Roncalli said, "But you were wearing them when you arrived last night."

"Assunta tied them for us before we left," Giuseppe explained.

"Don't bother with them," Roncalli advised. "We peasants shouldn't put on airs."

However, on the great day in the Salle d' Armes of the Elysée they were in full evening dress with snap-on white ties thoughtfully purchased by their brother who knew they would want to do him honor.

The scene was splendid if extraordinary. The purple-clad Papal Ablegate, Monsignor Giacomo Testa, who was Apostolic Delegate to Turkey and who brought the biretta from Rome, was escorted by a detachment of the Noble Guard in their brilliant uniforms and silver helmets. The *Garde Republicaine* almost outshone them in the full panoply of gilt cuirasses and classic Roman headgear. The French officials were in black and white evening dress which was relieved by the flash of color of their decorations. Across President Auriol's breast was the tri-color sash of his office. Of course, the central figure was

Angelo Cardinal Roncalli in the lace vestments and brilliant scarlet robes of his new rank.

There was a moment of dramatic irony as the Prince of the Church knelt before the President of the Republic. But Roncalli felt no hesitancy in making obeisance. By virtue of his charge, the benevolent but agnostic Frenchman became the personal representative of the Holy Father, and it was to him Roncalli knelt. Having solemnly placed the biretta on Roncalli's humbly bent white head, Vincent Auriol by a diplomatic incantation became again the President of the Republic addressing the Papal Nuncio—and also a warm-hearted man speaking to a dear friend.

"The French Government has been deeply sensible of your constant cordiality and the concern which you have shown for all the generous undertakings and for works of peace in accordance with the noble and paternal teachings of the Supreme Head of the Church.

"And I, myself, *Monsieur le Cardinal,* recall our conversations on the first of January with a very special emotion. Your messages will remain for all of us as examples of wisdom, good taste, and friendship. The regret that the imminent departure of your Eminence occasions us and your distinguished colleagues of the *Corps Diplomatique* is tempered by the joy we feel in seeing a Prince of the Church, who is a great connoisseur of the good things of France, number us, as you have often said, among your sincere and certain friends."

Then the President took from its purple velvet box the glittering Grand Cross of the Legion of Honor, and hanging its broad red ribbon around the Cardinal's neck embraced him on each cheek with a little bear-hug that imparted personal warmth to formal protocol.

As the President of France finished there were tears in his eyes. Cardinal Roncalli was also close to tears as in a husky voice he replied, "It will be enough if every Frenchman who recalls my humble name and my stay among you is able to say, 'He was a loyal and peaceful priest.' "

Cathedral of San Marco—Venice

CHAPTER TEN

"A BRIDGE BETWEEN
WEST AND EAST"

Before he left Paris, Cardinal Roncalli gave a farewell dinner for his friends. The guests included politicians of the Right, the Left, and the Center united on this one occasion in their affection for their genial host. There were also a number of French writers and academicians. As a compliment to his French guests, Roncalli wore the Grand Cross of the Legion of Honor which dangled from the broad red ribbon just above the jeweled cross of his episcopacy.

Robert, the chef, outdid himself. The wines were the finest vintages of France, which is to say of the world, and the conversation sparkled more brilliantly than the champagne. It was such a delightful occasion that, paradoxically, it made them all sad at the thought of losing their favorite Nuncio.

Roncalli left Paris on February 23 for Rome, where Senator Luigi Einaudi, who later became President of Italy, administered the oath of loyalty which the Government requires all bishops of Italian Sees to take. Roncalli was also to have received the *galero*, the ceremonial Red Hat which cardinals never wear but which is placed on their coffins when they die, from the hands of the Supreme Pontiff. However, Pope Pius

141

was suffering one of the severe attacks of hiccups which cul-
minated the following year in the critical illness from which
he only recovered, as he firmly believed, by miraculous inter-
vention. The ceremony was postponed until October when it
finally took place at Castel Gandolfo. The titular church assigned to Roncalli in Rome was Santa Prisca on the Aventine
Hill, one of the oldest in that ancient city.

From Rome, Roncalli went to Bergamo and Sotto il Monte
for a few days. The welcome he received led him to remark
rather sadly, "It is true that among us princes are esteemed
more than people." Thence he went on to the Abbey of Praglia
where he made a three-day retreat to commune with God and
meditate on the new responsibilities that faced him.

The arrival of the new Patriarch in Venice on March 15,
1953, was the gayest, most colorful occasion in which Roncalli
ever played a part. For although his coronation as the Supreme
Pontiff was more magnificent it was neither as picturesque nor
uninhibitedly joyful as the welcome the Venetians gave him.

It was a brilliant, sunny day with the bite of winter still
in the air. Every gondola, launch, and barge in Venice had
been chartered by the faithful to escort the launch provided
by the city government from the railroad station to the Piazza
San Marco. All the buildings, palaces, and bridges along the
Grand Canal were decorated with banners of the ancient Republic of Venice with its winged Lion of St. Mark; beautiful
ancient brocades and tapestries hung from balconies and windows. Spring flowers were banked everywhere on buildings,
boats, and docks.

The floating procession was headed by the official gondolas
of the mayor and city councilmen and the private gondolas of
the nobility with the gondoliers in their colorful livery. Other
boats with golden lanterns and religious standards at their
prows carried priests and deputations from hundreds of parishes
of the diocese. In addition to the vast floating crowd in the
slowly moving mass of aquatic vehicles, every spot dry enough

to stand on was jammed by happy Venetians shouting, waving, and laughing in their joy, while church bells led by deep-voiced Marangona filled the air with metallic clangor.

Patriarch Roncalli, in the brilliant scarlet robes of his rank with a short little ermine cape for warmth, was the jolliest person of all. He gave his smiling blessing left and right so vigorously that his round, broad-brimmed hat kept slipping to one side. If he had not caught it in the nick of time, it would have fallen into the canal.

The launch drew up to the Piazza San Marco where Venice opens her arms to the sea, and the Patriarch stepped out and kissed the crucifix. Then he stood for a moment looking in awe at the incredibly lovely, glittering golden domes and intricately embellished romanesque arches of the great Basilica.

After exchanging his hat for the red biretta and greeting the waiting mitered bishops, he walked in procession, still smiling broadly, down the lane made by the carabinieri, between the shouting people across the Square, and onto the portico of San Marco, where he turned again to give his blessing. After the Te Deum was sung inside San Marco, the Cardinal-Patriarch made his first address to the Venetians. Its simplicity, contrasting sharply with the Byzantine splendor of gold, rare carved marbles, and superb mosaics of the interior of the famous Basilica, set the tone of his pastorate.

"Behold the man! Behold the priest! Behold the pastor!" he said . . . "I am like every other man who lives down here (on earth). I have the grace of good physical health, and a little good sense to see things quickly and clearly, and a disposition to love mankind . . ."

Then he went on to tell them that although he was known best as a politician and a diplomat, they must think of him only as their priest and their shepherd which he had always wanted to be. He spoke of how Providence had led him "to travel the roads of the world in the East and in the West," and, he added, "At the end of my long experience I return to Venice, the land and the sea familiar to my great grandparents throughout four centuries, and to me through my studies and personal sympathy. No; I have not the courage to call myself a friend of Venice like Francesco Petrarch, nor do I have tales to tell you like Marco Polo. But certainly strong bonds bind me to Venice . . .

"The position confided to me in Venice is very great and far surpasses my merit. But I commend to your benevolence the man who wishes simply to be your brother, amiable, approachable, understandable . . . a man who wishes above all else to be your loving brother. Such is the man, such is the new citizen which Venice has been kind enough to welcome so festively today . . .

"May the protecting Saints of this illustrious See assist me! . . ."

Cardinal Roncalli soon settled into the routine of his new position. Routine is really the wrong word because he made so many pastoral visits in his See and so many pilgrimages beyond it. He is said to have made "more than one visit" to every parish of his Venetian diocese and to have celebrated Mass in each. In his first year he personally officiated at all the confirmations in his diocese. Even at home in Venice, the religious ceremonies and duties of the Patriarch were so numerous and varied that he certainly had little leisure.

A "normal" day, then, was the exception rather than the rule. It began at 5 A.M. or earlier when Roncalli rose, in what most people regard as the dead of night, to pray and read his Breviary. Often he went up to the terrace he had built on the roof of the Patriarchal Palace to meditate as he watched the sun rise over the exquisite city, tinting its domes, marble palaces, and the still, blue mirror-surfaces of canals and lagoons with delicate pastel shades. He reveled in this beauty as much as any aesthetic. In his creed, the lovely things of life were created by God for man's inspiration and enjoyment, and it would be sinful not to appreciate them.

At seven the Cardinal said Holy Mass, and at eight he breakfasted on coffee, hot milk, a roll, and some fruit. Then he began to work, answering his far-reaching correspondence, reading the newspapers, and attending to the administration of his extensive See, which included the metropolitanate of the Province of Veneto and nine dioceses, among which were Padua, Verona, Vicenza, and Vittorio Veneto. In addition, the Patriarch was ex-officio President of the Tri-Venetian Episcopal Conference whose members, besides the nine bishops of the dioceses, included the Archbishops of Udine and Trento and the Bishops of Bresanone, Gorizia, Gradisca, and Trieste-Capodistria.

From ten until one almost any Venetian who wished to see his Patriarch could call on Roncalli. He received them in the great marble salon called *La Sala dei Banchetti*—The Hall of the Banquets—where the Doges of Venice had given audience to its citizens. When his secretary protested against his open-door policy he said, "Let them come! They might want to confess." Luncheon was at one, followed by a prayer in the lovely chapel and thirty or forty minutes of rest; after his rest, Roncalli went back to work, finishing up the morning's business, receiving official visitors, attending diocesan meetings, or visiting the sick in the city's numerous hospitals. At quarter of eight in the evening he joined the members of his household in the chapel where he said the first two decades of the Rosary, and they all recited the third decade in unison.

Dinner was at eight o'clock and after a brief time for reading in his library or, perhaps, to work on the final volume of "St. Charles Borromeo," Roncalli went to bed about ten. That was a rather strenuous day for a man well over seventy years old, but it was unusually quiet. According to members of his household, when Roncalli had a speech or pastoral letter to write he often worked in his study from dinner time until four o'clock in the morning and slept only from then until seven-thirty. Occasionally he went to bed before nine in the evening, but on those nights he often got up at one, and spent the rest of the night in prayer and study.

His enormous physical vitality sustained this schedule without apparent effort. His official Venetian doctor, Paola Venchierutti, says, "I never remember being called in to care for His Holiness in all the years he was in my charge."

In fact, one day when Roncalli noticed that Venchierutti was looking overtired, he said, "Doctor, I keep telling you to take better care of yourself. You're not looking at all well today. You'd better take some of that medicine you're always trying to give me!"

Roncalli's predecessor, Patriarch Carlo Agostino, had also done an immense amount of work. But he had driven himself by sheer will power—indeed, he drove himself to death. As a result he was nervous and occasionally irritable, giving an impression of arrogance and certainly lack of patience. Roncalli, by the grace of his powerful peasant constitution, never seemed hurried and was always serenely patient and sympathetic. As he once said, "There's nothing wrong with my liver and nothing wrong with my nerves so I enjoy meeting people." The more they saw of him the more the Venetians loved him because they knew he loved them. They jokingly called him "the calm after the storm."

They saw a great deal of him. Despite the magnificence in which he was now lodged—the great, ornate halls and salons of his palace in marble and gilt and brocade, the exquisite chapel with its *cinquecento* embellishments, his own study with silk-hung walls, heavy carved furniture, and over four hundred books ranging from religious works and history to the plays of Moliere and the poems of Rimbaud—which he loved to show visitors, engaging them in historical discussions—in spite of the panoply of his surroundings, he maintained the simplicity in living that he always liked. For example, he had no private launch or gondola but either took the *Vaporetto,* the public launch-bus, or hired a taxi launch or gondola when he had need of it. He always made friends with the gondolier. As often as his busy days allowed, he still took the long walks he had enjoyed in Istanbul and Paris, and he often managed to get out among the people, strolling in the Piazza San Marco or shopping casually in the arcades.

The Ai Leoncini coffee shop was next to the Patriarchal Palace on the Piazza. When the high spring floods flowed over the great Square, turning it into a reflecting pool in which the domes and cornices of the surrounding buildings were repeated in shimmering distortion more lovely than reality, the Patriarch would take a short cut from the back door of the Palace through the back door of the coffee shop to keep from getting his feet wet. The patrons were used to seeing him in the simple black cassock he always wore on informal occasions and the familiar round broad-brimmed black hat, bustling between the tables, stopping at every other one to exchange a merry greeting with friends or with people who simply wanted to be friendly.

While making new friends Roncalli did not forget his old ones. Many of those he had made in Paris came to stay with him. Among them the French authors François Mauriac and Wladamir D'Ormesson. After Vincent Auriol retired as President of France, he, too, came to stay with his old friend. As he entered the great hall of the Palace, he saw the Patriarch standing before a group of kneeling Venetians. Auriol confessed later that he did not quite know whether to drop on his knees or not, but his dilemma was solved as Roncalli trotted over and enfolded him in a great hug.

Later he took Auriol to see the small, austere room which St. Pius X had occupied when he was Patriarch. It had been kept just as it was the day the Saint had left for Rome. One of Roncalli's first actions had been to have it cleaned and restored. He never entered it without thinking of the day a newly-ordained priest had knelt before the great Pope in the corridor of the Vatican. The same emotion swept him as he said to Auriol, "This is where Pius X lived."

With French flattery Auriol remarked, "Perhaps the successor to Pius XII will also have lived in this palace."

Roncalli only grinned affectionately at his old friend, thinking that his remark was too foolish to require an answer.

Of course, far more prelates than laymen came to stay with the Patriarch. Among those whose names were known through-

out the world were Cardinals Lercaro, Constantini, the bearded
Armenian Agagianian, and Cardinal Feltin of France. One day
when the latter was staying with Roncalli, they strolled out to
hear a band concert in the Piazza San Marco. On a sudden impulse the Patriarch left his guest and trotted over to have a
word with the conductor of the band. An instant later Cardinal Feltin was touched to hear the martial strains of the Mar-
seillaise reverberating through the Square, while the Venetians
cheered. Another guest who came to stay with Roncalli soon
after his arrival in Venice was Cardinal Spellman of New York.

One impulsive gesture of Roncalli's hospitality should be
noted because it is so typical. His friend, Eugenio Bacchion,
President of the Venetian Catholic Action, lost his wife at
almost the same time that Roncalli's beloved sister, Ancilla,
died. On Christmas Eve that year Roncalli telephoned to Bacchion saying, "Tomorrow will be your first Christmas with an
empty place at the table. Will you and your children come and
have Christmas dinner with me?"

If their Patriarch's simple, friendly ways led the Venetians
to suppose that he was altogether easy-going they soon realized
their error. As his secretary, Monsignor Gino Spavento, said,
"No one should be deceived by the Patriarch's simplicity into
thinking him a simpleton. His simple manner is the result of
his holiness, but he is a very complex and profound personality, keen, alert and anything but stupid."

In matters of principle and religious doctrine Roncalli
was like an immovable human rock. When the young liberals
of Catholic Action sought to associate their wing of the Christian Democratic Party with the Communist-oriented Socialist
Party in a so-called "opening to the left," the Patriarch sternly
called it "a very grave doctrinal error and a flagrant violation
of Catholic discipline." He added, "The error lies in participating . . . and sharing the ideology of Marxism which is the
negation of Christianity and cannot be reconciled with the pre-
suppositions of the Gospel of Christ."

But though Roncalli abhorred Socialist doctrine he loved Socialists as his fellow men, and only six months later he wrote a message to his flock in which he said, "The Congress of the Italian Socialist Party is about to meet in Venice with representation from all parts of the peninsula . . . As a good Venetian, who holds hospitality in great honor and also in accordance with the Pauline precept which teaches that a bishop should appear *"hospitalis et benignus,"* I am saying a respectful word about it . . . It is always very painful for a pastor of souls to have to recognize the fact that many honest, intelligent, and noble men . . . ignore or pretend to forget the basic principles of that divine message . . . which was the heartbeat of twenty centuries of history . . . and who (believe) in another ideology which is not inspired by the Gospels of Christ.

"But having said that . . . the wish remains in our heart that the people of Venice, welcoming and amiable as is their custom, will help to make this meeting of so many of our brothers from all the regions of Italy a contribution toward the ideals of truth, goodness, justice, and peace."

Sometimes the Patriarch had to maintain discipline among his clergy in spite of his own feelings. When Auxiliary Bishop Augusto Gianfranceschi was sent to the Diocese of Casena, there was great dissatisfaction among the clergy there because of Gianfranceschi's reputation as an officious and difficult person. With typical Italian humor they circulated cards edged with black mourning bands announcing the appointment. The Patriarch wrote a stern pastoral letter reprimanding them for this discourtesy. But he remarked to Monsignor Spavento, "If that fellow, Gianfranceschi, had been present at the Creation, he would have wanted to help God make the world."

Another matter on which the Patriarch had strong views was womanly modesty. Every July and August, Lido Beach, just across the lagoon, looked like a Garden of Eden inhabited by thousands of Eves who had lost their innocence—certainly their modesty. Because he was careful never to go there in the season, Roncalli knew it only by report, but when the feminine

tourists invaded the Piazza San Marco in very brief shorts he
publicly objected. With the humor that often lightened even
his urgent protests he said, "I do not say that people need
come to Italy in furs and woolens. They can come dressed in
that modern American silk, fresh and soft, which is a veritable
refrigerator at low cost. On the other hand Italy is not on the
equator, and even there lions wear their fur coats, and croco-
diles are protected by their expensive skins."

He forbade scantily dressed women to enter his Basilica,
and Paul Christopher Perrotta, author of "Pope John XXIII:
His Life and Character," records approvingly that his own
niece was refused admittance because she was wearing a sleeve-
less dress.

Another cause of anxiety to the Patriarch was the annual
Film Festival held in Venice because of the salacious nature of
some of the films shown and the amoral attitude of many of
the participants. In 1953, his first year as Patriarch, he personally celebrated the traditional "Movie Mass" in San Marco.
Then, speaking in French, the language likely to be most generally understood by that international assemblage, he reminded
the sophisticates of their great responsibility in influencing the
customs of people all over the world, and added, "Messieurs, my
brothers! As artists you must have considered the question
whether beauty can exist independently of goodness. It is an
undoubted fact that goodness and truth enhance the splendor
of beauty; the spirit governs even entertainment. The world
of today is shrouded in a suffocating atmosphere. Purify it! Let
the fresh air into it! And you will make a contribution both to
the cinema and to society as a whole.

"You will say that it is difficult to do this. Without doubt!
But you can put your trust in the power of prayer. Let us
pray; I for you, you with me."

A similar anxiety was caused Roncalli by the International
Biennial Art Exhibit. The first held during his Patriarchate, in
1954, had a few pictures that ranged from the obscene to the
blasphemous. Roncalli did not see them, but he heard about

them. Although he was always reluctant to interfere in matters outside his sphere, the Patriarch spoke strongly to the city officials in charge of the exhibition. As a result the Exhibit of 1956 was more carefully chosen. As a token of his appreciation—and also because he loved beauty in whatever form—Roncalli attended the exhibit; he was the first Patriarch ever to do so. Afterward, he gave a reception for the officials and artists in the *Sala Maggiore,* the Grand Salon of the Patriarchal Palace. At that time he officially removed the ban former patriarchs had imposed against the clergy attending the exhibit. As usual the extreme conservatives were shocked, but Roncalli's intention was to acclaim modern art as "a noble human activity," even as his predecessors of the Renaissance had done in their time.

Perhaps the happiest time of Roncalli's life was the period he lived in Venice, because those years were the only ones during which he was able to realize his wish to be above all a priest and a shepherd of souls. The administrative details of his See and the mundane problems in which he was involved were secondary to that sacred charge into which he flung himself with all the energy and ardor of his nature. He was, in fact, joyfully fulfilling a spiritual need of his own.

His numerous parochial visits, mentioned before, brought him into close contact with the country people as well as those in Venice itself. He loved to celebrate Mass in the ancient, but often impoverished, churches of the small country towns and villages and to preach afterward to the congregations of peasants, who were similar to his own people. According to the biography of Pope John by Ugo Groppi, he once preached ten sermons in a single day at San Lorenzo in Mestre. His closeness to the people and the spiritual inspiration he felt they drew from him was a source of great satisfaction to him.

Though he loved the beautiful Basilica of San Marco, which he once described as being a place where in the words of Dante "heaven and earth joined hands," he was troubled by the fact that the greater part of its congregation was excluded from the high altar by the iconastasis which screened the sanctuary from the main body of the Church.

In itself, the iconastasis was an exquisite work of art. Columns of oriental and African marble supporting the archetrave were connected by six large marble panels decorated in intricate designs of Venetian-Gothic style. Statues of the twelve Apostles and of the Virgin of San Marco by Jacabello and Peter Paul della Masegni embellished it, and from its top the silver crucifix of Jacope Bennato dominated the nave of the Basilica. This lovely relic of the days when San Marco was a ducal chapel shut from the view of most of the worshippers not only the golden altar pieces and the brilliant mosaics in the cupola of the apse, but deprived them of the precious privilege of seeing and hearing the celebration of the Mass.

Roncalli felt very strongly that this was not right. Beauty and tradition must not impair the basic principle that a church should serve all the faithful. In 1954, he suggested that the marble partitions be removed so that the congregation could see between the columns; the traditional character of the structure would not be destroyed. In fact, he thought it would improve it because the heavy marble panels spoiled the airy transept which della Masegni had designed.

Naturally, conservative opinion was opposed to change as it always is. Civic and religious groups fought it on the grounds that it would "compromise the nobility and beauty of the architecture." They also expressed the fear that the sanctuary would suffer a certain profanation by "the curiosity of tourists —Orthodox, Protestants, Mohammedans, Taoists, and even by Catholics with cameras."

Roncalli thought this latter objection was nonsense. The high Altar of St. Peter's, standing openly in glory for all to see, had not been profaned by the millions who had gazed upon it. It was his firm conviction that the Lord was capable of making use even of tourists for the greater glory of His Name. However, the Patriarch said, "I am not making this a matter of war even though I wish everyone could be convinced of the value of my proposal. If you were to tell me that to gain my objective I would have to kill an ant, I would not kill it."

There the matter remained throughout Roncalli's Patriarchate despite his gentle prodding. After he became Pope his opponents had a change of heart. It was finally decided that pivoting the marble panels on rods so they could be swung down would allow the faithful a view of the sacred mysteries.

In his handling of this problem Roncalli abided by his principle of avoiding both authoritarianism and paternalism. He said that, "Authoritarianism truly suffocates truth by . . . rigid exterior discipline . . . It arrests lawful initiative; is incapable of listening and confuses inflexibility with firmness.

"Paternalism is a counterfeit paternity. It takes its objects into custody in order to preserve its power of authority. It makes its liberality felt by everyone, but fails to respect the rights of its subordinates. It speaks in a tone of protection and refuses to accept collaboration."

Like his "Pole Star," Bishop Radini, Roncalli undertook as extensive a program of building and renovation as the budget of his See allowed. During his five years in Venice he established thirty new parishes, built a new minor seminary, and established a new center for the Patriarchal archives. The Seminary had been housed in the beautiful Villa Fietta at Paderno del Grappa which former patriarchs had also used as a country residence. Before building the new seminary, Roncalli sold the Villa to the Maestre Pie Filippini. A gentleman of Paderno tried to change the Patriarch's mind by describing the quiet, lovely days and restful nights he would be denying himself if he gave up the Villa.

"I realize how lovely it is," Roncalli said. "But, as a matter of fact, I sleep perfectly well in Venice. The seminary and the needs of the diocese are much more important. What counts is the salvation of souls."

Roncalli also refurbished the Sanctuary of the Immaculate Heart of Mary in Mestre and entrusted its care to the Order of the Sons of St. Jerome Emiliani. He acquired and renovated the historic San Giorgio in Alga and reorganized the houses of the canons around the Patriarchate.

Roncalli also improved the Basilica of San Marco and increased its splendor. The tomb of St. Mark was raised from its hidden crypt to a place beneath the main altar where the faithful could see and venerate it; the superb Byzantine mosaics were cleaned until they sparkled; the remains of many of his forty-three predecessors were brought from the burial Isle of Cypresses and placed in the renovated crypt near the relics of St. Mark. There the Patriarch planned to lie himself when his work was done.

Roncalli's invitation to Stravinsky to conduct his oratorio, "Sacred Canticle in Honor of St. Mark the Evangelist" in the great Basilica was a startling innovation. The Patriarch attended the first performance on September 13, 1956.

During his Patriarchate Roncalli took every occasion to celebrate not only the great liturgical ceremonies of the Church, but also anniversaries peculiar to Venice, with solemn splendor calculated to impress the faithful with their profound significance. On these occasions the Venetians found their friendly, jolly Patriarch transfigured into an imposing symbol of the dignity, glory, and tradition of the Church, worthy to be the forty-fourth Patriarch and one hundred and thirty-ninth bishop of his historic see.

A particularly impressive ceremony marked the five hundredth anniversary of the death of the fifteenth century Patriarch, St. Laurence Giustiniani. Roncalli was amazed at the neglect of the most illustrious—and most Venetian—of all the patriarchs. He decided to recall his memory to the Venetians in a dramatic way. A solemn pilgrimage was organized in which St. Laurence's body was carried through the seventy-seven parishes on the mainland, the littoral and the remote islands of the diocese. At the end of the pilgrimage in the splendid solemnity of the service in San Marco, Roncalli spoke movingly of the apostolate and of the contemplation which nourished the spirit of the saint with whom he felt himself in mystic harmony.

The last great ceremony that Roncalli conducted as Patriarch was the celebration of the centenary of St. Pius X on September 13, 1958. Roncalli had expressed his feeling for that other peasant lad who had been Patriarch of Venice on the occasion of the fiftieth anniversary of his own ordination in 1954 when he said, "Oh Holy Father Pius X! On the day of my first Mass you stretched your hands above the head of the new priest as you passed by in the Vatican. I have always kept in my heart the memory of that gesture and the sweet words of benediction that accompanied it . . . You . . . have been lifted to the glories of the saints and all Christian people invoke you. The humble Levite of long ago has been placed on the Chair of St. Mark, where you sat with so much splendor of doctrine, virtue and example.

"Oh Holy Father Pius X! I trust in you . . . Help me with your powerful arm that I may, during what is left of my life, direct all my actions to the edification, benediction and joy of these most dear sons of Venice with whom it is most sweet to live . . ."

Knowing instinctively how St. Pius X would desire it, Patriarch Roncalli held the centenary celebration, not amid the golden glories of San Marco, but in the simple church at Castelfranco in Veneto in which St. Pius X had been ordained.

During his time in Venice Roncalli's journeys were not confined to his own See. In fact, he was probably Venice's most-traveled Patriarch. In Italy he attended seven Eucharistic Congresses in different parts of the peninsula. In 1954, he organized a pilgrimage of all the Tri-Venetian bishops to Lourdes. When he left Lourdes, Roncalli took off his scarlet robes, and in an unadorned black cassock went on a humble pilgrimage to the shrine of Santiago di Compostela in Spain.

He returned to Lourdes again in 1958 as Papal Legate to dedicate the great underground Basilica of St. Pius X on the hundredth anniversary of the Virgin Mary's appearance to Bernadette Soubirous. Always eager to adapt modern inventions to God's use, he flew there in a jet plane and made the prescribed three circles of the ritual blessing of the huge basilica, second in size only to St. Peter's, in an open convertible. As he boarded his jet for the return to Venice, reporters asked him for one last message to the French people. In reply Roncalli quoted the Blessed Virgin's words to the peasant girl of Lourdes: "Penance, penance, penance!"

Of all the cities of western Europe Venice is the most closely bound to the Near East and the Orient. For centuries her merchant galleys crisscrossed the Mediterranean to all the ports of the Levant, and her caravans treked eastward over the vast plains and deserts of Asia. It was no accident that Marco Polo was the first European trader to reach Cathay. In San Marco itself hang the standards of Lepanto where the Venetian fleet under Don Juan of Austria broke the naval power of the Sultans and kept the sea lanes of *Mare Nostrum* in Christian hands.

This affiliation with the East was another cause of Roncalli's happiness in Venice, which he thought of as a bridge between West and East—even his title of Patriarch was an echo of the Orient. He had never given up the hope of reuniting the Orthodox churches with Rome—and eventually all Christian sects. Wherever he went, to the Pro-Orient Week in Palermo in 1957, or even on visits to places less sympathetic to this cause, he never ceased to work for it. He once mentioned to ex-Mayor Gurgio La Pira of Florence that he prayed for it daily.

Early in his Patriarchate, in September, 1954, Roncalli was delighted to be chosen by Pope Pius XII as Papal Legate to the National Marian Congress at Beirut in Lebanon where he presided over the touching ceremony of crowning Our Lady of Lebanon; while he was there he renewed his ties with many prelates of the Near East. One with whom he had long earnest discussions on the subject nearest to his heart was Cardinal Agagianian of Armenia. Full-bearded in accordance with the tradition of the Oriental Rite, tall, and strong-featured, Agagianian was deeply in accord with Roncalli's views, and it is probable that their conversations laid the groundwork for great events in an unforeseeable future.

That same year Patriarch Roncalli held a series of conferences on this subject in the Hall of St. Basso in Venice. In these conferences he emphasized, as always, "that which unites rather than that which divides." In fact, his liberal views shocked his audience. "The road to unity of the various Christian Confessions is charity, so little observed on either side," he told them; he went on to urge strongly the necessity of studying true Christian thought, seeking the many points of contact between the different sects. He ended by quoting Joseph's exultant shout to his brothers who had betrayed him, "I am Joseph, your brother!" and added, "My heart is big enough to enfold all the people of the world in my desire for unity."

It is said that those gathered in the great ornate hall were astonished. They were not yet prepared for so Christian a doctrine.

All through his Patriarchate, Roncalli persisted in his efforts to prepare men's minds for its acceptance, never pushing too hard, but working softly, persuasively, and diplomatically. Although he made progress he was unhappily aware of how little one man could do even though he was Patriarch and a Prince of the Church. If ever ambition stirred in him, if ever he thought of the improbable possibility of steering the Bark of Peter, it was for the leverage it would give him to lift the world a little nearer his great dream.

Roncalli's last six days in Venice were full of agony and sorrow—a sorrow shared by all the Catholics on earth and by millions of Protestants, infidels, and atheists. Pope Pius XII, known throughout the world for his quiet holiness, was dying, and by the electronic communications which he had been foremost in using to spread God's truth, all the world seemed to be watching by his death bed in a small room of Castel Gandolfo.

On Monday, October 5, 1958, as he was receiving visitors, Roncalli heard that the Pope had suffered a stroke. He im-

mediately retired to his private chapel to pray for the Holy
Father. He spent most of the next three days on his knees,
praying in public and in private. During that time he must
have thought often of the slender, vibrant man who had delivered such fascinating lectures to the young seminarians at the
Apollinare, and of the gaunt, white-robed figure who had said
to him in the Vatican, "It was I, Monsignor, who thought of you
myself . . ."

Like many priests of the Church, wherever they were in
the world, Roncalli did not go to bed the night of October 8;
he spent the night praying and listening to the radio. Just before
four o'clock in the morning of October 9, the dreaded news
came. The Pope was dead.

After celebrating a High Requiem Mass for the dead Pontiff in San Marco on October 11, Patriarch Roncalli packed his
clothes to go to Rome. Among the very few things he took with
him was his Cappa Magna, the great scarlet ceremonial cape in
which according to tradition he would pay homage to the new
Pope. He had never had occasion to wear it; he never did.

On Sunday morning, October 12, Cardinal Patriarch Ron-
calli went to his beautiful golden Basilica and knelt before the
Altar of St. Mark for the last time to say the *Itinerarium Cleri-
corem* which is the prayer for priests about to go on a journey.
Particularly appropriate was its plea *"Procedamus in pace"*—
Let us proceed in peace.

Then Roncalli sailed in a launch back along the same
route he had come on that brilliant March morning nearly six
years before. This time there was no formal procession, but
boats full of well-wishers followed him to the station, and the
banks of the Grand Canal were crowded with Venetians shouting their good wishes for an easy journey and a quick return.
In the minds of nearly everyone, however, was the thought of
that other Patriarch, Giuseppe Sarto, who had left Venice to
become Pope Pius X.

A vast crowd at the station cheered Roncalli respectfully,
and lined the platform as the station master escorted him to his

compartment. Roncalli lowered the compartment window for a few last words with his friends. Someone in the crowd, voicing the thought in the back of everyone's mind, said significantly, "I wish you luck."

Roncalli answered smiling, "The best luck that could happen to me would be to return here in two weeks."

Then the train began to move, and the crowd raced after it to catch a last glimpse of the round little man in his black cassock and big round hat waving and smiling so sadly at them.

White Smoke Signifying the Election of a Pope

CHAPTER ELEVEN

THE PENTECOSTAL
CONCLAVE

Between moss-green stone walls and lush green fields where the Via Aurelia curves up the Aventine Hill stands the Domus Mariae (The House of Mary), the headquarters of Women's Catholic Action in Rome. Before the conclave, Cardinal Roncalli stayed in this large, modern, brick structure. Its high wall commands an inspiring view of the many-domed city which, even from that height, is dominated by the greatest dome in the world.

Roncalli arrived Monday morning, October 13. Much to his surprise many of his friends from the Curia and exiles from Bergamo and Venice were waiting at the station.

"Do this many people greet all the cardinals?" he asked.

"Oh no," was the answer. "You're both a cardinal and a patriarch so you drew twice as many."

Roncalli laughed at the little joke and blessed everybody in sight.

He went from the station to the Domus Mariae which he had deliberately chosen because it was isolated from the excitement of the city, and yet it was within ten minutes' drive of the Vatican.

Roncalli's first sad duty was to attend the burial of Pope Pius XII in the Crypt of St. Peter's, near that other Pius over whose canonization he had presided. It was the third day of the *Novendiali,* the nine days of prayer and mourning for the Pope which would culminate in the final High Requiem Mass on the ninth day. During the *Novendiali,* Roncalli and all the other cardinals put away their scarlet vestments and wore purple cassocks and birettas.

The days that followed were full of activity and of such great emotional stress that it is wonderful that men in their seventies and eighties, as most of the cardinals were, could survive them—in fact, not all of them did. The Patriarch rose very early and had several hours for prayer and meditation before the affairs of the Church engulfed him. He celebrated Mass every morning in the chapel of Domus Mariae, dedicated to the Sacred Heart, and attended a second Mass said by his secretary, Monsignor Loris Capovilla. At half-past ten every day, Roncalli met with all the cardinals who were in Rome in the General Congregations held in the great Hall of the Consistory under the presidency of his old friend, Cardinal Tisserant, Dean of the Sacred College.

Each day, more Princes of the Church arrived from all parts of the world. Cardinal Wyszynski of Poland was the only cardinal from behind the Iron Curtain who was able to come to Rome. Cardinal Stepinac of Yugoslavia, who was under house arrest in his native village of Carso, was ill. He was afraid to leave because Tito's Communist Government might then refuse him permission to return to his dangerous archdiocese; Cardinal Mindszenty of Hungary, who had taken sanctuary in the American Embassy in Budapest, was refused permission to attend by Dictator Kadar in spite of the diplomatic appeals of the United States Government.

In the superb Hall of the Consistory, with its elaborate decorations and its high, painted ceiling, the cardinals in purple mourning vestments sat on throne-like chairs conducting the necessary preliminaries to the conclave. They also received deputations bringing condolences from nations and organiza-

tions throughout the world. These congregations lasted until
noon when Roncalli returned to the Domus Mariae for lunch
and prayer in the chapel.

In the afternoon, after a brief rest, Roncalli sometimes
revisited the places in Rome that were dear to him. Chief among
them was the Church of Santa Maria in Monte Santo on the
Piazza di Popolo where he had been ordained fifty-four years
before. He lingered a long time at the altar in St. Peter's where
he had said his first Mass, and visited the Church of San Carlo
al Corso where he had been consecrated a bishop. As always
when he was in Rome he went to the Chiesa Nuova to venerate
the body of St. Philip Neri, who had so greatly inspired his
youthful days. He also visited the grave of Cesare Cardinal
Baronius whose motto, *Obedentia et Pax*, he had made his own.

Roncalli had many earnest talks with his fellow cardinals
about their fears and hopes for the future of the world. During
these conversations the Patriarch constantly stressed his hopes
for the ecumenical movement, the gathering of all Christians
under one Shepherd. He had several especially interesting conversations with frail, silvery Celso Cardinal Constantini, who
was head of the Sacred Congregation for the Propagation of
the Faith. Constantine was a liberal who had done all in his
power to make it easy for Chinese and other Orientals to accept
the liturgical practices of the Church. He and Roncalli agreed
on the vast importance of the Catholic missions in the Orient
and in awakening Africa.

It was a heavy blow to Roncalli, when Cardinal Constantini
died suddenly about a week before the conclave opened.

On the ninth day of the *Novendiali*, Sunday, October 19,
a High Requiem Mass was said for Pope Pius XII in St. Peter's.
Cardinal Tisserant, looking like a Biblical patriarch with his
long gray beard and lean ascetic face under a tall miter, was
the celebrant of the Mass, which was attended by twenty-five
thousand people within the great Basilica and thousands more
standing in the Square. To Roncalli, as to all those present, it
was an elevating ceremony. This man, this Pope, had lived so
holy a life and served God and His Church so well that there

was little doubt in the minds of the faithful that he, like St. Pius X, would someday be "lifted to the glories of the saints."

The faithful, though sorrowed by the death of the Pope, were actively engaged in speculation as to his successor. Both Canon Law and traditional propriety forbade the cardinals to discuss the coming election even with each other, but they would have been less than human, if they had not thought about it constantly, and tried to learn as much as possible about the ideals and characters of the different candidates.

The cardinals who were considered likely possibilities, called *papabili* in Italy, were discussed in the Press of all the world. As in mundane politics there were three schools of thought among the cardinals: the conservatives who held strictly to the old ways; the liberals who were in favor of making any changes necessary for modern society, and the middle-of-the-roaders. In addition, there was the question whether it would be best if a "pastoral" pope, who would be mainly concerned with the religious aspects of the Papacy were elected, or a "political" pope, who, having experience in worldly affairs, would be more capable of steering the Bark of Peter through the stormy times everyone could foresee. There was also much talk of an "interim" pope, an older man who would bring the College of Cardinals up to its full strength of seventy—from fifty-four—and serve as a brief bridge between one strong Pope—Pius XII —and another who would also have to be forceful.

In the speculations of the Press the leading conservative *papabili* were the Italian Cardinals Ottaviani, Masella and Ruffini. The liberal leaders were the Italian Cardinals Lercaro, Siri and Archbishop Giovanni Battista Montini of Milan, who had been offered the Red Hat in 1953 and refused it because he felt he could serve his beloved Pope Pius better in the position he then held of Pro-Secretary of State.[1] For the first time

---

[1] The Pope-Elect need not be a cardinal or even a priest. He can be any duly baptized member of the Catholic Church who has reached the age of reason, i.e. seven years old.

in four centuries several non-Italians were considered to have a very good chance of election. Cardinal Agagianian, a liberal, was the strongest of these despite the fact—or perhaps because of it—that he belonged to the Oriental Rite. Another was Cardinal Tisserant whose wisdom and long experience as a world traveler and his position as head of the Sacred Congregation for Oriental Rites made him an eligible candidate. The American newspapers publicized the chances of Francis Cardinal Spellman, a conservative who had a brilliant record as Archbishop of New York.

The man considered both middle-of-the-road and a possible interim pope was Cardinal Roncalli. As the day set for the opening of the Conclave approached, he was mentioned more frequently as an eligible candidate.

Although Roncalli meticulously adhered to the oath he had taken on arriving in Rome before the Chamberlain, Aloisi Cardinal Masella, to obey the canon governing the election, which included not discussing it, he would have been blind and deaf had he not known that he was considered a strong contender. He laughingly turned aside those who mentioned this to him by quoting the old proverb: "He who enters the conclave a Pope comes out a Cardinal."

But his serious thoughts about the conclave and how he should exercise "the most delicate and terrible power" of the cardinalate are apparent in three letters he wrote from the Domus Mariae in the stressful days before the conclave opened. In the first letter, to the Rector of the Seminary in Venice, he said in part: "As for the Pope who died and ascended to glory. . . . Long live the Pope! And pray that his successor, whoever he may be, will not represent a break in continuity; rather may he progress in following the eternal youth of Holy Church, whose mission is always that of being a leader of souls to the divine heights of evangelical realization and sanctifications of human life with a view to life eternal. . . .

"Now I am about to enter the conclave and bear with me the face of the Madonna della Salute and the image of my dear seminarians with whom I intend to work even more closely and devotedly as soon as I return to Venice. . . . I should not fail to mention that I count greatly on the prayers of my seminarians whom, together with their worthy superiors, here from the tomb of St. Peter, who called Mark his son . . . I embrace and bless."

To his friend Giovanni Montini, the slender, dark and fiery Archbishop of Milan, he wrote, "I have great need of the saints. Therefore I apply to you, who are very near to the saints of my special devotion . . . (who were buried in Milan) Recommend my soul to St. Ambrose and St. Charles Borromeo . . ."

Finally, on the day before the conclave, he wrote to Bishop Giuseppe Piazzi of Bergamo saying, ". . . One point about my entrance into the conclave: It is like an invocation . . . to everything dearest to my heart as a good man of Bergamo. In thinking of all the venerated and beloved images of Mary spread throughout the diocese and with the memory of our patron saints, the bishops and illustrious and saintly priests as well as both men and women of outstanding virtue in religious orders —as I remember these my soul is comforted with confidence in the new Pentecost which will enable us to give a new vigor to the victory of truth, to what is good, and to peace through the renewal of the Head of Holy Church . . .

"It matters little whether the new pope be from Bergamo or not. Our common prayers should be to obtain as pope a man who will be a wise and gentle governor, a saint and a sanctifier. Your Excellency understands what I mean . . ."

In that final enigmatic paragraph lies, perhaps, a premonition of what was to come. More important is the reference to the "new Pentecost" which affirms Roncalli's belief that, even as He descended among the Apostles at the first Pentecost, the Holy Spirit would inform and guide the cardinals in conclave, and that whatever their decision might be, it would reflect the Will of God to which he would be resigned.

The conclave began on Saturday, October 25. That morning the fifty-two cardinals who were in Rome, once again clad in their scarlet robes, assisted at a Votive Mass of the Holy Spirit in St. Peter's and listened to an exhortation given in Latin by Monsignor Antonio Bacci who spoke to them of these perilous times when in many nations "religion is either forgotten . . . or what is worse persecuted."

"For this reason," he said, "we have need of a pontiff with great strength of mind and ardent charity; a pontiff who knows how to tell the truth even to those who do not wish to hear it; who knows how to defend the rights of Christian and human civilization, but at the same time to open the arms of pardon to all, even to those who make bloody the heart of our common Father . . . He must be a teacher . . . and a pastor . . . but also a father. . . .

"May the new Vicar of Christ be like a bridge between heaven and earth . . . may he be like a bridge between social classes . . . Finally may he be like a bridge between nations, even among those who reject, repel, and persecute the Christian religion. . . . Above all, Eminent Fathers, there is need of a *holy* pope because a holy pope may obtain from God things which natural gifts cannot provide. . . . Give the Holy Roman and Universal Church (such a) shepherd in the briefest possible time, and with the greatest zeal, forsaking any earthly considerations and keeping your eyes on God."

After the Mass the cardinals returned to their quarters and packed their things so that they would be ready for their confinement in the conclave. For weeks the whole working force of the Vatican had been preparing apartments for them in that part of the Apostolic Palace surrounding the Sistine Chapel. This area was sealed off by a temporary brick wall with a single door that could be locked from both inside and out and six revolving sections into which food and necessary supplies could be placed and swung inside without unlocking the door. The windows facing the outside were whitewashed; the telephones were disconnected, and radios were removed so that no signal could be transmitted from without or within the area of the Conclave.

Each cardinal was allowed to bring with him one or two "conclavists"—one of whom could be a layman—to help him as needed, to carry messages, or to do secretarial work. Roncalli brought his secretary, Monsignor Loris Capovilla. Each cardinal was assigned an apartment consisting of three or four austere little rooms, or cells, furnished only with a cot-like iron bed, a prie-dieu, a crucifix, desk, lamp, and writing materials. Although some of the apartments were real rooms which were normally used as offices, others were formed simply by putting up partitions in the large public rooms. Some of the apartments did not have running water, and their occupants had to use a communal lavatory.

Two temporary kitchens were set up, and several sisters of Santa Marta were assigned as cooks. Because of the culinary reputation of this Order, cynics predicted a very short conclave. In addition, there were two doctors, a surgeon, a chemist, various officials and their staffs, electricians, elevator operators, workmen, etc. In all, over two hundred people were immured within the Vatican.

Cardinal Roncalli left the Domus Mariae about three o'clock and arrived at the Vatican at ten minutes after three just as the other cardinals in flowing scarlet vestments were pouring through St. Peter's Arco delle Campane. Cardinal Tien-Ken-Sin of China, who had been in an automobile accident in Germany and was encased in plaster casts, was carried into the conclave on a stretcher.

A terrible shock awaited the cardinals. It was the news that Edward Cardinal Mooney of Detroit, who had been at Mass that morning, had died of a heart attack in the North American College where the American cardinals were staying. Now there were only fifty-one cardinals.

An official of the conclave escorted Cardinal Roncalli to his quarters which had been the office of the commander of the Noble Guard. As they reached it, the official pointed significantly to the sign still on the door which read: *IL COMMANDANTE.*

Roncalli said, "Do you believe in signs, Signor? I don't."

With his conclavist, Roncalli joined the other cardinals in the Sala dei Paramenti, from which the cardinals and conclavists

went in procession, each escorted by two Swiss Guards, to the
Pauline Chapel, where the papal choir sang *Veni Creator*. With
the papal cross carried before them, the cardinals and conclavists
then proceeded to the Sistine Chapel. In the pale light from
the whitewashed windows Michelangelo's superb ceiling was
starkly shadowless. The terrible beauty of his "Last Judgment"
above the altar was partly covered by a tapestry symbolically
depicting the descent of the Holy Spirit. Around the walls of
the chapel, under the pictures in which the great artists of the
Renaissance had told the story of the Bible, stood the chairs
and writing desks for the cardinals. Above each was a purple
canopy, or baldachin, signifying their joint sovereignty until a
pope was elected. The black iron stove in which the ballots
would be burned stood in one corner, with its long stovepipe
snaking up to a high window.

When the doors of the chapel were closed, Cardinal Tisserant began the Collect, *"Deus qui corda fidelium. . . ."* Then
the new Apostolic Constitution, promulgated by Pope Pius XII,
which was the law of the conclave, was read to them, and again
they took the long oath prescribed for its members. "Standing
in the presence of this man of God, touching with my hand the
Holy Gospels, I swear that I will observe a rigorous and inviolable secrecy on each and all of these things which in any
way come to my knowledge concerning the election of the new
pontiff. I will keep secret all matters dealt with and defined in
the Congregation of Cardinals in the conclave . . . all matters
concerning the voting . . . I promise I will carry no radio,
telegraph, microphone or other instrument for the transmission
or reception of messages, and no photographic or cinematic
equipment. I will observe this pledge under penalty of excommunication which can find absolution only by special ruling of
the future Pontiff." After the Cardinals were finished, their
conclavists and the other officials took an oath of secrecy.

The cardinals then retired to their quarters. Meanwhile
the traditional cry, *"Extra Omnes!"* rang through the reserved
area, meaning that all unauthorized people must leave. When

it was certain this had been done, Prince Chigi, hereditary
Marshal of the conclave, locked the door from the outside,
and Monsignor Alberto di Jorio, who had been appointed Secretary to the conclave, locked it from within. At 6:08 the big bell,
thrilling the still air and vibrating through the ancient stones,
signalled that the conclave was sealed.

The secrets of the conclave have been well kept, perhaps
due to the stern insistence of Pope John XXIII. All that is
definitely known are the unimportant details, which in the
jargon of generals are "unclassified." After the conclave was
sealed, Roncalli dined with his fellow cardinals in the refectory
set up in the great salon of the Borgia Apartments. How he
spent the night is not known, but one may imagine that through
much of it he was on his knees invoking the Holy Spirit.

On Sunday morning, March 26, all the cardinals, except
Cardinal Tien-Ken-Sin who was confined to his bed, assisted at
Mass in the Pauline Chapel. When they took their places in the
Sistine Chapel, Roncalli's stall was to the right of the main door
between Cardinals Valeri and Cicognani. An empty seat next
to Cardinal Agagianian was a sad reminder of Cardinal Mooney.
Cardinal Tien-Ken-Sin's seat was also vacant. When the voting
began, a committee of three cardinals went to his quarters to
get his vote.

The first ballots were cast promptly at ten o'clock. Each
cardinal, disguising his writing to keep the ballot secret, wrote
the name of his choice on a form printed in Latin with the words
"I elect as Supreme Pontiff the most reverend Lord Cardinal ——," and carefully sealed it with wax. When Roncalli's
turn came, in order of seniority, he walked to the altar and
knelt in fervent prayer. Then he rose and stood before the table
covered with green baize on which was an ancient silver chalice,
saying the traditional Latin words, "The Lord Christ, who shall
be my judge, is witness that I choose the one whom I believe
should be chosen according to God."

When all the cardinals had voted, the *scrutators* (cardinals
chosen as tellers of the election) counted the ballots and then

opened them, reading each name aloud, and marking their tally sheets. When this was done, they read this list and the number of votes each candidate had received. Then the ballots were mixed with straw and burned in the iron stove. Out in St. Peter's Square and in all the streets leading to it a vast crowd, numbering perhaps half a million people, stood watching the stove pipe, waiting for a sign—white smoke if the Pope had been elected; black smoke if he had not. The smoke was black.

For two days, as the cardinals voted twice each morning and twice each afternoon, the smoke was black. Some unofficial accounts of what happened during those tense days make it sound like a political convention with all the heat and even "bitterness" of contested partisan politics. There is no doubt that this was true of the conclaves held in earlier days when the pressures of national interests or personal ambition did indeed produce a tumultuous atmosphere. But, in all frankness, it was not true of this conclave. In fact, it was so untrue that Pope John XXIII in one of his two recorded comments on what went on, once said, "I was very amused by the newspaper accounts of the conclave."

On ballot after ballot some candidates gained votes and seemed to be winning and then halted short of the necessary two-thirds plus one vote. But if so honest a man as Cardinal Tisserant is to be believed—as he surely is—there was neither heat nor bitterness. Solemn dedication existed and the prayers of men seeking guidance of the Holy Spirit in an anguished desire to ascertain and follow the Will of God.

The political aspects and the ferment were all beyond the walls of the Apostolic Palace where, as the black smoke proclaimed one indecisive ballot after another, speculation mounted to feverish intensity. All sorts of rumors ran through the world on the cables and airways. In Rome itself, gamblers were even making book on the outcome, setting up slates with the names and odds chalked on them like the bookies at Epsom Downs.

Strangely enough the varying odds did reflect in some measure the varying fortunes of the *papabili*. This was not due

to leakage from within; it was due in part to intelligent ap-
praisal that the delay meant that none of the "strong" candidates
was quite strong enough. Although one bookmaker's slate gave
Roncalli 7-1 odds, 5-1 odds, and finally 2-1 odds, no one would
claim that these figures represent what was actually happening.
For example, according to such meager leakage as there has
been, Montini, who at one time had 5-1 odds, was never a real
contender, and may not have received any votes at all. On the
other hand, the rapid drop of the odds against Roncalli does
seem rather prescient.

On the third morning of the conclave, Tuesday, October
28, the tension was at a peak when the weary cardinals gathered
in the Sistine Chapel. Most of them had spent the night in
prayer asking the Holy Spirit for guidance. Now they seemed
to be waiting for enlightenment.

We get a hint of what must have happened from a sentence
spoken by Pope John long afterward. "I knew by certain signs,"
he said, "that I would be chosen." Perhaps, that meant that on
the second morning ballot the scrutators had read his name on at
least a majority—though not two-thirds—of the ballots.

From that morning, the tension dissipated rapidly. It was
as though the cardinals had indeed received the enlightenment
they had sought. All but one felt a sense of relief, but that one
was fearfully oppressed. The terrible responsibility that weighed
upon Cardinal Roncalli made him inexpressably sad and fearful. Only the absolute conviction that it was God's Will that he
bear the burden of the Papacy upheld him.

There is not a shadow of doubt that Roncalli did not want
to be elected. He had spoken truly on the station platform in
Venice when he said that the best thing that could happen to
him would be a speedy return to the city he loved so well, the
city where he had passed the happiest days of his life. Characteristically, he allowed his thoughts to dwell only a few minutes
on the joyful past. During the lunch hour and after his fervent
prayers before the prie-dieu in his room, Roncalli's thoughts

were busy forming the words he would say when the dreaded moment came. He gave thought also to the name he would choose, and how he would explain it to the cardinals and the world.

The first ballot on the afternoon of Tuesday, October 28, was the eleventh and last of the conclave. Again and again the scrutators called the name "Roncalli," far more often than two-thirds of the time. When the last vote had been recorded and the final tally read, Cardinals Tisserant, Van Roey and Canali rose and walked solemnly to the place where Roncalli, white-faced but gravely serene, sat. In the Latin words prescribed by tradition, Cardinal-Dean Tisserant asked, "Do you accept your election, made canonically, as Supreme Pontiff?"

There was a long, seemingly endless pause. Then in a low voice Cardinal Roncalli replied in scriptural phrase, "Hearing your voice, 'I tremble and am afraid.' The consciousness of my own poverty and insignificance should explain my confusion. But seeing in the votes of my brothers, the eminent cardinals of our Holy Roman Church, the sign of God's Will, I accept the election made by them, and I bow my head to the chalice of bitterness and the yoke of the Cross. On the feast of Christ the King we have all sung: 'The Lord is our Judge; the Lord is our Lawgiver, the Lord is our King. He will save us!' "

At the moment Cardinal Roncalli finished speaking, all the other cardinals pulled the strings that lowered the canopies above their heads. Only the one above Roncalli's chair remained, signifying that from that moment he was the Supreme Pontiff of the Holy Roman and Universal Church.

Pope John in the Sistine Chapel after his Election

CHAPTER TWELVE

"FATHER OF PRINCES
AND OF KINGS"

Within one moment of the time he became Pope, former Cardinal Roncalli broke his first precedent. Cardinal Tisserant, still standing before him asked the second prescribed question in Latin, "How do you wish to be called?" The new Pope replied, "Vocabor Joannes" (I would be called John). A sweet name, a gentle name, a solemn name.

A whispering sound of surprise ran around the circle of cardinals. For five hundred and fifty years no Pope had chosen to be called John, because the last of that name had been the anti-Pope John XXIII whose election had been held invalid. Since that time, no Pope had wanted to be called "John XXIII." The new Pope was prepared for the cardinals' reaction and explained his choice. "This name is sweet to us," he said, "because it is the name of our father. It is sweet to us because it is the name of the humble parish church in which we were baptized; it is the name of innumerable cathedrals . . . and first of all the sacred Lateran Basilica, our cathedral (as Bishop of Rome).

"It is the name which has been borne by the most popes in the long list of Roman pontiffs; in fact, there are twenty-two supreme pontiffs of undoubted legitimacy with the name of John. Virtually all of them had short pontificates. We have preferred to cover the smallness of our name behind the magnificent succession of Roman Pontiffs."

The new Pope then went on to mention that St. Mark also bore the name John, and he spoke of John the Baptist and John the Disciple and Evangelist, "beloved of Christ and his Mother . . ." "May John the Evangelist . . . (and) Mary the Mother of Christ," he said, "support together this exhortation which is meant for the life and joy of the Catholic and Apostolic Church and also the peace and prosperity of all nations. 'My little children love one another'; love one another because this is the great commandment of our Lord.

"May God graciously grant, Venerable Brothers, that we . . . by the aid of divine grace have the same holiness of life and strength of soul that we may, if God wills, even be prepared to shed our blood."

When Pope John XXIII finished speaking, the Secretary of the Conclave, Monsignor Alberto di Jorio, came forward and kneeling in front of the new Pope offered him the white zucchetto, or skullcap. As Pope John took off his own scarlet zucchetto, he placed it on the head of Monsignor di Jorio as a sign that he would be made a cardinal. Then the Pope went to the main altar and knelt for a long time in silent prayer while the others sat in silence, perhaps praying inwardly for him.

Returning to his chair which had become his throne, Pope John signed the Act of Acceptance, which Monsignor di Jorio witnessed. After that, he retired to the sacristy of the Sistine Chapel, which is known as "the room of tears" because new popes are always robed there, to put on the white papal vestments with the help of his ecstatic conclavist, Monsignor Capovilla, who had been summoned into the Sistine Chapel. The Vatican tailor had made three sets of white vestments of different sizes, but he had not figured on Roncalli. The white cassock was terribly tight. "I felt all tied up," the Pope said later.

When he was robed, Pope John went back into the main part of the Chapel and gave his first blessing to the kneeling cardinals. Then he mounted a throne which had meanwhile been placed on the platform in front of the main altar, and promptly broke another precedent. Cardinal-Dean Tisserant was the first cardinal to approach the throne to make the submission. Kneeling, he kissed the Pope's hand, and started to kiss his foot in the traditional ceremony. Pope John refused to allow it; instead he immediately embraced him with the kiss of peace, a gesture which he continued with the other forty-nine cardinals. When all had paid him homage, Cardinal Tisserant slipped the Fisherman's Ring on Pope John's finger.

Meanwhile, the ballots had been burned without straw so that the smoke was white, and the great crowd in St. Peter's Square was wild with joyful excitement, shouting, "We have a Pope. Long live the Pope!" More and more people tried to jam into the Square as radio and television told of the white smoke; the noise was deafening.

Excitement reached an apex as lights went on and windows opened in the Hall of Benedictions, behind the central balcony beneath St. Peter's dome, which glistened in the floodlights. By now it was early evening. An official appeared and hung a huge white and scarlet banner embroidered in gold with the Arms of the Holy See over the balustrade; the crowd, in a mood for cheering anything, shouted loudly. A long wait followed, while through the Square ran the continuous questions, "Who? Who? Who?"

At exactly six o'clock the carabinieri band began the triumphant Pontifical March; on the balcony appeared the glittering three-barred Papal Cross. Officials in red medieval robes followed it, and then the tiny, scarlet-clad figure of Nicola Cardinal Canali, Dean of the Cardinal Deacons, appeared. Very solemnly he stepped to the microphone. As the crowd was suddenly stilled he announced, "I bring you joyful news. We have a Pope! He is the eminent Lord Cardinal Roncalli who has taken the name of Pope John XXIII."

The roar of cheers seemed to rattle Bernini's colonnade and make the great dome shiver while all the bells of the Basilica boomed their joy. It appeared impossible that more sound could be compressed on the shaken air, but as the rotund figure of the Holy Father in his white vestments and scarlet cape appeared on the balcony, the roaring doubled to an incredible pitch. Pope John stood there in the storm of sound under the white glare of flood lights, serene and smiling.

Whatever his inward feelings had been, however much he had, in fact, trembled at the burden put on him, that feeling was past. Now he was completely in God's Hands, confident in Divine Love and like a father to the tens and hundreds of thousands of people below him and the millions more listening by radio and watching by television. He radiated benevolence and love for all of them so strongly that many of those most remote from him seemed to feel the force of that powerful, mysterious current.

When at last the people quieted down a little and began to call, "Bless us! Bless us!" the Pope prepared to speak. An official whispered in his ear something about the traditional procedure and the sensitive microphones caught Pope John's reply, "I know, I know."

Then he raised his hand, and a stillness, as incredible as the sound had been, fell on that vast throng. In a strong voice to which still clung something of the harsh accent of a peasant from the northern hills, Pope John gave in Latin his first blessing *Urbi et Orbi,* to the city and to the world: "Blessed be the name of the Lord! Now and also forever! Our help is in the name of the Lord! Who made heaven and earth! May you be blessed by Almighty God, the Father and the Son and the Holy Spirit!"

When the Pope left the balcony he was carried in the *Sedia Gestatoria,* the gold and dark red portable throne—Pope John once said, "The first time I was lifted high in the Sedia, I thought only of my father"—back to the Sistine Chapel, where once again he received the homage of the cardinals. After the ceremony he told them that he had seen them watching the *Urbi et Orbi* blessing from various vantage points in windows and on the roofs. "You risked excommunication in leaving the conclave area without our permission," he said smiling broadly. "But we will use our influence to get you off."

Pope John then asked the cardinals to remain in the conclave another night instead of leaving immediately as was customary. He probably had a dual purpose: to caution them again against revealing the secrets of his election to outsiders, and to give himself an opportunity to talk with them intimately and in private about the future.

From the Sistine Chapel he went to the temporary quarters that had been hastily prepared for him in the apartment of the Secretary of State which had not been used since the death of the last Cardinal-Secretary, Luigi Cardinal Maglione in 1944, whom Pope Pius XII had never replaced. The great ornate rooms were decidedly dank and musty from fourteen years of disuse. While the new Pope was receiving and conferring with his immediate staff and various cardinals, there was a great hullabaloo of cleaning and freshening things, opening windows and making beds; a group of electricians worked feverishly to install telephones.

The Sisters of Marta fixed supper for the Supreme Pontiff; he ate alone according to custom. After a few days of these solitary meals, Pope John announced, "I have gone all through the Old Testament and the Holy Gospel and I can't find a single word in them that says the Pope must eat alone. So I am not going to do it anymore."

After supper and more conferences with the cardinals, the Holy Father was left alone at last with Monsignor Capovilla. "Now what is there we must do?" the secretary asked.

"We are behind in our office. We must read our breviary."

He sat up most of that night writing his first public message with the help of Monsignor Capovilla, the Latinist Monsignor Bacci, and Monsignor Angelo Dell' Acqua. He was up again at dawn and when someone asked how he had slept he said, "Very well, as always."

At ten o'clock the Pope went again to the Sistine Chapel to receive the third submission of the cardinals. As Cardinal Tien-Ken-Sin was brought up in a wheel chair, Pope John jumped up from the throne and walked down the steps to embrace him lovingly. When the ceremony ended, Pope John read the public message he had prepared over the radio from his throne in the Sistine Chapel. It was broadcast by the Vatican radio in thirty-six languages. The message was typical in its emphasis on unity, peace, and forgiveness. After greeting prelates, religious, and Catholics all over the world, he said:

"In a special way our thoughts go to the bishops, priests, sisters, and all the faithful who dwell in those nations . . . where men dare to trample the sacred rights of the Church . . . We wish them all to know that we share their sorrows, hardships and distress and that we beg God, the Giver of all good things, that some day He may put an end to such inhuman persecution. . . . May He enlighten the minds of the rulers of these nations with His divine light. May He grant pardon to persecutors. May all enjoy lawful freedom most speedily and may He bestow on them better and happier times.

"With fervent fatherly love we embrace the Universal Church, the Eastern and the Western alike. And to all who are separated from this Apostolic See, where Peter lives in his successors . . . to these we open our heart most lovingly and extend our open arms. Ardently desiring their return to the house of the common Father . . . we pray that all may come willingly and gladly . . . No strange house will they find, but their own. . . ."

The Pope then launched a most eloquent plea for peace and disarmament, quoting the Gospels and the Church Fathers on the beauty and necessity of peace. This peace did not mean surrender to evil; he added a quotation from Cicero, "The name of peace is sweet, and peace itself is beneficial, but there is a very great difference between peace and slavery. Peace is tranquil liberty . . ."

Most of the cardinals thought they had elected an interim Pope, a Pope of conciliation, one who would drift along without making drastic changes. They did not know Roncalli well; most of his years in the Church had been spent in missions to far countries and he had seen comparatively little of his colleagues. The French cardinals, of course, knew him intimately; it is thought that they had backed him all the way. *They* were not surprised.

Although he was almost seventy-seven years old Pope John was an extraordinarily vigorous man. This writer, who talked with him shortly after his election, was amazed to feel no sense of the frailty of age; one gets an impression of great strength of body and mind, youthful enthusiasm, and irrepressible gaiety.

As Pope John's vigor manifested itself, the historically inclined were reminded of another "interim" Pope, Sixtus V, who entered the conclave of 1585 A.D. tottering along on a cane, barely able to speak. When his election was announced this "old man" threw away his cane, regaining a youthful vigor and became one of the greatest figures of the Catholic reform.

Since God willed that John be Pope, he would play his role with all the energy of his nature. He would act in accordance with his favorite maxim: "See everything; disregard much; correct a little." And he would do it gaily. If "a sad priest was a bad priest," so also would be a sad Pope.

Things began to happen fast around the Vatican. As *Time* put it, "He did not tiptoe into his reign; he stomped in boldly like the owner of the place, throwing windows open and moving furniture about." His first official act was to send for the editor of *L' Osservatore Romano,* and tell him to announce that he was appointing Monsignor Domenico Tardini, who had been Pro-Secretary of State for Extraordinary (Foreign) Affairs, to the overall post of Pro-Secretary of State, which Pope Pius XII had filled himself.

Tardini was the sort of man with whom Pope John liked to work. A stout, energetic, bullet-headed peasant, he had a brilliant mind, enormous good will, and no pretentiousness whatever. His favorite recreation was playing football with the boys of the Villa Nazareth, a school he had founded for bright young orphans and boys from poor families who could not get the education they deserved at home. He called them "my boys," and even after he became a cardinal they called him, "our Monsignor."

That first day Pope John also filled another post left vacant by his predecessor: the post of Major Domo of the Supreme Pontiff to which he appointed Monsignor Federico di Vignale. Cardinal Masella was confirmed as Chamberlain, and Monsignor Mario Nasalli Rocca di Corneliano was appointed Maestro di Camera, while four new private chamberlains were added to assist him. In all the bustle, Pope John found time to offer Monsignor Capovilla an honorary post. With his eyes misting behind his thick horn-rimmed glasses, the young secretary declined, saying he thought he should go back to Venice, and the Venetian chauffeur, Guido Gusso, thought he also would go home. Pope John is reported to have said, "Well, if you two go, I'll go back to Venice, too."

Of course they stayed.

Having established his new entourage, the Pope inspected the closed papal apartments and gave directions as to what he wanted done—he moved in the next day. In addition, he saw many visitors with appointments and a few who just happened by. He decided that his coronation would not be on Sunday, November 9, as was expected, but on Tuesday, November 4. He had both a sentimental and a practical motive for choosing the earlier date. First, because it was the feast of one of his favorite saints, Charles Borromeo. Secondly, so the foreign cardinals, who had been away from their Sees so long, could get home, and everybody, including himself, could get back to work as soon as possible. Pope John's first day was quite full.

He continued this pace during the next four days. The cardinals and many others connected with the Holy See grew quite accustomed to answering their telephones and hearing a strong familiar voice say, *"Pronto. Il Papa qui parla."* One of these was Archbishop Giovanni Urbani, whom the Pope appointed Patriarch of Venice over the telephone with the instruction that he "take good care of our beloved Venetians."

Other items in the next few days included restoring the
weekly "cabinet" meetings with the Curia cardinals, and sched-
uling long, intimate talks with all the foreign cardinals, especially with Cardinal Wyszynski. The new Pope also announced
his hope of traveling abroad—a hope that remained unfulfilled.

One day Pope John drove in his car to the replica of the
Grotto of Lourdes in the Vatican gardens and spent a long time
on his knees before the statue of the Virgin. When he got up
and looked around, he noticed the Vatican radio station nearby
and went to look it over. At the unexpected appearance of the
white-clad man smiling under his round broad-brimmed hat
the staff almost collapsed. However, Pope John soon changed
nervousness to laughter as he talked and joked with the broad-
casters from twenty nations about their countries. To the Span-
iard he told the story of how a Jesuit Superior in Spain had
insisted on making soup for him with his own hands. "As a
theologian he was brilliant," the Pope said. "As a cook"—he
pulled his face into a lugubrious moue—"I was sick for two
days."

The Pope also sent for Count Giuseppe della Torre, the
editor of the *L' Osservatore Romano,* and gave him a few suggestions on editorial style. "We would like to see less antique
formality in your references to us," Pope John said. "Instead
of phrases like, 'The Supreme Pontiff,' or 'the illuminated Holy
Father,' or 'We gathered from the august lips,' please simply
say, 'The Pope or the Pontiff did so and so.' "

Another decision concerned the Pope's Coat of Arms. He
decided on the same escutcheon he had used as Cardinal-Patriarch—The Roncalli Tower and the Lion of St. Mark which
would now be surmounted by the Triple Tiara and the Keys
of Peter. When the heralds brought him their design the Pope's
only suggestion was, "Please don't make my lion look so cross."

It has been noted that the Pope stopped taking his meals
alone within a week. Pius XII had eaten little and cared even
less about the quality of his food. Pope John was no gourmet,
but he liked his food cooked with a certain artistry. Good food

was one of the many things the Lord had provided for the
enjoyment of His children; there was no sense in ruining it.

The first four days of Pope John's reign were indeed busy.
The fifth day came swiftly, the day of his coronation.

Riding in the *Sedia Gestatoria* on the shoulders of twelve
strong bearers, Pope John XXIII entered the Basilica of St.
Peter's to the sonance of silver trumpets, the voices of the Choir
singing *Tu es Petrus,* and the wild cheering of fifty thousand
people. The Basilica had never seemed more splendid or more
beautiful to him, but he had never seen it from that vantage
point before. St. Peter's was ablaze with color and light; the
marble and gold pillars were hung with rich red damask; the
lights of a thousand chandeliers sparkled brilliantly, their size
diminishing with distance until those at the top of the great
dome seemed no more than the minute sparks of fireflies. Near
the end of the long aisle, the bronze statue of St. Peter was
dressed in the brilliant regalia and the Triple Tiara of the Supreme Pontiff which he had never worn in life. And as far as
the Pope could see, in every distant columned recess, were
upturned faces stirred by the emotion of love for him and all
that he represented.

Swaying slightly, the throne-chair moved slowly up the
long, long aisle toward the great bronze baldachin with its
twisted columns and ornate canopy rising almost one hundred
feet over St. Peter's tomb. Six masters of ceremony walked
ahead with the burning braziers into which were tossed balls
of flax that flared brightly and died to ashes as they intoned
three times, *"Pater Sancte, sic transit gloria mundi"* to remind
the new Pope of the transitory character of earthly glory. Meanwhile the shouts of *"Viva il Papa"* became almost hysterical.
Although he was accustomed to the Italian custom of cheering
the Pope in church, John was troubled. Cheering a sinful man
in the House of the Lord did not seem fitting.

As he neared the apse around which the cardinals and
bishops made a great splash of scarlet and purple, Pope John

scanned the tribunes where the special envoys from fifty nations and other important personages sat. He was looking for some very special people; they were there in the place of honor, three gnarled old men, uneasy in Sunday black, and between them a plump old lady with thick glasses. As Giuseppe, Saverio, Alfredo, and Assunta Roncalli met his eyes, the Pope's face burst into the jolliest possible smile and he leaned forward to give them a special blessing.

At the Chapel of the Blessed Sacrament, the bearers slid the great throne-chair expertly to the ground, and the Pope stepped out. He took off his tall golden miter, and before Christ present in the Sacrament, he knelt, a humble "servant of the servants of God."

After his adoration of the Eucharist, he mounted a throne in the Chapel of St. Gregory, and again received the obeisance of the cardinals and bishops, this time allowing them to kiss his foot according to tradition. Then, while the choristers chanted *Tierce*, the Pope was robed for the Mass in buskins, amice, alb, cincture, stole, lace tunic, dalmatic, and the chasuble, around which was draped the white, silken fanon with its golden cross. He put on the golden miter and, after ceremonially washing his hands, the white gloves embroidered with jewels and over them his episcopal ring. Then he went to the High Altar and kneeling made the humble confession of sin with which parish priest or pope begins the Mass: ". . . I have sinned exceedingly in thought, word and deed, through my fault, through my most grievous fault . . ."

The long beautiful Sacrifice of the Mass proceeded with the Pope intoning his recitations in a strong vibrant voice. While he read the Epistle, Monsignor Staffa sang it in Latin and then Don Pietro Tamburi of the Greek Pontifical College sang it in Greek as a special gesture to the Eastern Church.

After the singing of the Gospels ("Thou art Peter and upon this rock I will build my Church." Matt. 16:18), Pope John said in Greek, "Peace to you all!" Then, departing from custom, he read a sermon in Latin. As he had done in Venice,

he begged the faithful to regard him mainly as a priest and a
pastor remembering that he was, above all, Bishop of Rome—
"We have at heart in a very special manner our task as Shepherd
of the entire flock." He gently chided them for cheering him
in Church and begged them to refrain in the future. Then he
welcomed the separated brethren. He spoke of St. Charles
Borromeo, the Shepherd of Milan, as his priestly model, on
whose feast day he had deliberately chosen to be crowned.
Finally, in the same strong voice, but a voice charged with emotion, he begged them all to "Keep praying for us that our faith
fail not."

The Mass continued. The silver trumpets rang out again;
all the guards and noble knights stood at attention and all others
knelt as the Pope whispered the words that change bread and
wine into the Body and Blood of Christ, lifting the Host and
then the Chalice for all to see. Then after the Canon and the
Our Father, he went to his throne and received the Host from
Monsignor Staffa and the Chalice of the Precious Blood from
Cardinal Wendel.

What tremendous emotions, what ecstasy of devotion surged
through him as he fulfilled his ultimate priestly function can
only inadequately be imagined. But one may be sure that he
thought of the young priest offering the Holy Sacrifice for the
first time in this same Church. And it is certain that his spirit
was as pleasing to God as it had been on that day more than
half a century past.

The Coronation ceremony took nearly four hours; the
Coronation itself took four minutes. Preceded by the three-
barred Cross and followed by the cardinals in procession, amid
the cheers people could not repress, Pope John was carried in
the *Sedia Gestatoria* back down the aisle and up the great flight
of stairs to the Hall of Benediction. At his instruction a platform had been built on the balcony to raise the papal throne
above the balustrade so that the great crowd waiting in the

Square could see. A red and gold banner with the Pope's new coat of arms was draped over the balustrade.

At 12:40 P.M. the three-barred Papal Cross, glittering and flashing in the sunlight, appeared, followed by the participants in the ceremony. A few minutes later the Holy Father came out on the balcony, and took his place on the carved and gilded throne. He stilled the tremendous din of cheering with a single gesture. A choir of six voices, amplified electronically so they sounded throughout the Square and the streets of the city, sang "A Crown of Gold Upon His Head" in Latin. Cardinal Tisserant intoned the Our Father, and said the prescribed Coronation prayer. Then Cardinal Ottaviani lifted the tall golden miter from the Pope's head. It was exactly 12:50 P.M.

Cardinal Canali came forward holding high the great Triple Tiara, shaped like a tall silver dome circled by three bands of gold set with precious, sparkling jewels. Pope John bent his head in humility, and the Cardinal standing on tiptoe placed the crown on his head, saying in a tremendous voice, "Receive the tiara adorned with three crowns and know that you are the Father of princes and of kings, Pontiff of the whole world and Vicar on Earth of Our Lord Jesus Christ to whom be honor and glory for ever and ever!"

Stepping from his throne to the edge of the balcony Pope John XXIII gave his second blessing to the City and the World.

Medieval Episcopal Throne—St. John Lateran

CHAPTER THIRTEEN

A GREAT BEGINNING

The innovations made by Pope John in the first days of his pontificate were minor matters. After his coronation he made several very important moves, and he also continued to do many lesser things that were considered unconventional—for a Supreme Pontiff.

On November 6, two days after he was crowned, Pope John held what might be considered the first papal press conference. Of course, the announcement merely stated that the Supreme Pontiff had received in audience some five hundred journalists who were in Rome to cover his Coronation. The journalists did not question him. Nevertheless, granting this audience showed the importance Pope John rightly attached to the press as an instrument for the propagation of the Faith and exalting the Church in the eyes of the world.

In his address to the reporters Pope John chided them gently. "During the last few nights," he said, "when it was difficult for us to get to sleep—a sleep made necessary by the arduousness of the last few days during which we were, so to speak, making our novitiate in universal fatherhood—we looked over many newspapers, not, of course, in order to satisfy self-

love, but because of our interest in what the world says about
the papacy. . . . Well, this was the constantly recurring theme:
every one of you was trying to guess the secrets of the conclave.
One journal pretended to give a complete account. Of course,
there were not two lines in it that were true." With a mischievous smile the Pope continued, "Even though the powers
of journalists to see through things are well known to be re-
markably good, silence might have been the best policy . . ."
And he added that they should emulate the words of Alessandro
Manzoni, "Truth is holy and I have never betrayed it."

Pope John chided the reporters again on the occasion of
his visit to the children in the Gesu Bambino (Baby Jesus)
Hospital on Christmas Day. The constant flicker of photographers' flash bulbs annoyed him and upset the children. "There
are fourteen recognized works of mercy," he pointed out to the
reporters. "But we should probably add a fifteenth: that of
enduring annoying people. I am very fond of photographers
but by these words I mean I want a little peace." Then with
a twinkle he won them back by adding, "But now I don't want
to make you practice the fifteenth work of mercy by listening
to a long speech. So I'll be brief."

On November 14, Pope John received a deputation of
Italian businessmen to whom he talked in a very businesslike
manner. He told them he appreciated their initiative and hard
work, and complimented them on the good effect they were
having on economic conditions. "But," he said, "there comes
to mind the necessity of reflecting in your affairs the spiritual
values that vivify even material things. Business combinations
. . . can succeed with a splendid effect if they are guided by
faith and Christian principles. Today, for example, we are
about to renew the ancient custom . . . of receiving the cardinals who come to us to render an account of their responsibilities in the affairs of the Church. You see we also use the
word affairs in the ecclesiastical and spiritual realm. Though it
usually is employed about material things it can be adapted to
a higher, more general meaning."

Later, Pope John received the cardinals and took a vigorous look at the material affairs of the Church. The working capital of the Holy See is probably less than five hundred million dollars. This, of course, does not include its inalienable assets such as churches and the Apostolic Palace and its priceless works of art. The revenues of the Church are not nearly as great as is supposed. In fact, they are comparatively small enough to require the most rigorous economy in the administration of its vicarate of over five hundred million souls.

Pope John promptly reorganized the financial administration of the Holy See. He put some of the older cardinals, who had been responsible, in less demanding posts, and gave fiscal responsibility to a triumvirate consisting of Cardinals Tardini, Cicognani and di Jorio. The latter was already head of the Institute for Religious Works, which, curiously, is the name of the Bank of Vatican City.

Pope John kept several of his predecessor's appointees on his small personal staff. Among them were two old friends whom he found at the Vatican, Monsignor Dell' Acqua and Monsignor Ryan, both of whom had been with him in Turkey. The exuberant Irishman, of whom he had grown so fond, became a key member of his staff. Because the Pope spoke no English, he relied heavily on Ryan to write his brief speeches in that language and also to translate his more formal allocutions into English. Dell' Acqua also became a close adviser, and the Pope saw a great deal of him. Cardinal Canali, who had crowned him was also often with him in those days. When a visitor asked the Pope how he liked Rome after Venice, John replied with a twinkle. "It's not so different. I'm still surrounded by Acqua and Canali (water and canals)."

A little later some nuns from Bergamo were brought in to replace the Bavarians who had been in charge of the kitchen under Pope Pius XII. Thus John was assured of some of the home dishes he loved.

In June, 1959, Pope John raised the pay of the employees of the Holy See by from 25 per cent to 40 per cent. It was a long-needed reform; they had been getting starvation wages even for Italy. It is said that this fact was drawn to his attention when he went in to talk to an electrician who was working to get the telephones installed. "How are things going?" asked the Pope.

"Badly, badly, Your Eminence," said the man. He looked so tired and thin that John took time to ask him about his family and his work; the electrician poured out his tale of struggle against poverty.

"We'll have to do something about this," was the comforting assurance. "For just between you and me, I'm not Your Eminence; I'm the Pope."

The Vatican employees who were being paid the least received the biggest advances in wages, and extra allowances were made realistically according to the number of children in a man's family. Those lowest on the scale now received the equivalent of about $112.00 a month, $16.00 for a wife and $20.00 for each child; this was a very decent wage by Roman standards. Buying their supplies in the tax-free shops of Vatican City and the accommodations that were provided for many of them in low-rent apartments owned by the Holy See also helped.

The fact that pay rates were not increased as much in the higher brackets caused some muttering about "brains not being paid as well as brawn." Pope John's reply, according to Cardinal Tardini, was, "One man's learning calls for reward, but another man's need can be even more urgent—a dozen mouths to feed."

In reply to the objection that the Vatican finances could not stand the extra expense and that the only means of meeting it was to cut down on the Holy See's direct charitable contributions, the Pope said, "Then we'll have to cut them. For this raise is simple justice, and justice comes before charity."

Pope John did not altogether forget the higher echelons. The cardinals of the Curia had been getting about $565.00 a month plus $96.00 for housing. With this salary they were expected to maintain a household consonant with their dignity

The new Pope in his new robes as he appeared after his election.

Nana

Left: Pope John strolls on the terrace of his summer residence, Castel Gondolfo. Another one of the Pope's projects was the redecoration of the Castel, which is situated in the Italian mountain country that John has always loved. Also, he had the stone tower of St. John, which for many years stood useless, completely redone so that it now contains a small but charming apartment—situated in the middle of the Vatican Gardens and overlooking the Aurelian Way *(below).* Pope John also had decided to have his Vatican quarters redecorated.

Giordani

The Pope leaves the *Propaganda Fide College,* where special Mass was celebrated on his eighty-first birthday, November 25, 1962.

Nana

Above: During a planned tour of the Queen of Heaven Prison, Pope John suddenly detours into a cell block he was not expected to visit. *Below:* Rapt in his prayers during the Mass, John kneels beside Bishop Van Lierde (*right*), author of *The Holy See at Work*.

Felicia

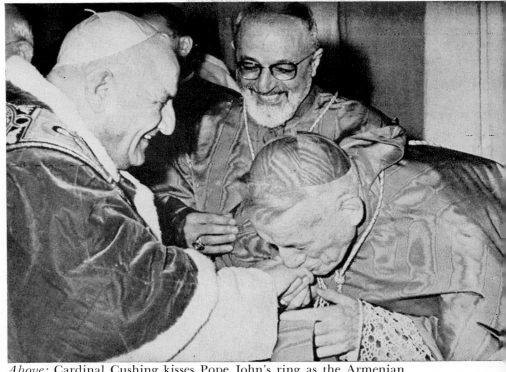

Above: Cardinal Cushing kisses Pope John's ring as the Armenian Cardinal Agagianian looks on. *Below:* The Pope welcomes American prelates at the Ecumenical Council in 1962—from left to right, Bishops McEntegart and Sheen, and Cardinals Ritter and Meyer.

Felicia

Pope John studied English so that he could talk more easily with American clergymen and laymen. Here he has paused in his conversations for formal portraits with American Cardinals MacIntyre (*left*) and Spellman (*right*).

Felicia

Right: Pope John talks with American Cardinal Meyer. *Below:* Auxiliary Bishop of New York Fulton J. Sheen (author of *These are the Sacraments*) who is Director of the Society for the Propagation of the Faith, uses a globe to explain a point during a meeting with the Pope.

United Press International

Left: With his Secretary of State, Domenico Cardinal Tardini, the Pope strolls about the Vatican Garden. Tardini came from a peasant family, as did John, and the two became very close. After Tardini's death (June 30, 1961) John said he was his "closest and strongest helper." And when the Cardinal died the Pope needed his helper, for the Ecumenical Council was about to begin. *Below:* Stefan Cardinal Wyszynski, the only cardinal who came to the Council from behind the Iron Curtain, as he was met by the Pope. He and Cardinal Wyszynski discussed the problems of the Polish Church.

Wide World

Left: With Britain's Queen Elizabeth II the Pope walks through the Vatican's Clementine Hall after her audience on May 5, 1961. A few months before the Pope held a history-making conference with the Archbishop of Canterbury. *Below:* In the Apostolic Palace, Prince Rainier and Princess Grace of Monaco listen to an address by the Pope, on June 18, 1959. *Right:* The Pope addresses President Eisenhower, with his son John and daughter-in-law, on December 6, 1959.

Religious News Service

Left: The Pope presides at the elevation of Father Vincent Palotti to the dignity of the altar. *Below:* St. Peter's is crowded for the opening of ceremonies for the beatification of Mother Seton, first American-born saint.

Giordani

Religious News Service

As Pope, John behaved just as he did in Venice, refusing to abide by restrictions or customs which made no sense to him. By attending *Murder in the Cathedral* he became the first pope to have gone to the theatre in more than two hundred years. He often left the Vatican alone and unguarded to visit with the people of Rome. *Left:* After visiting the Church of Santa Sabina a car returns him to Vatican City. *Below:* The Pope visits the Church of the Ascension of Jesus Christ.

Religious News Service

On October 4, 1962, Pope John became the first pope to travel by train in ninety-nine years. He is shown here as he departs on his astounding four hundred-mile pilgrimage to the shrines of Loreto and Assisi to pray for the success of the Second Vatican Council.

Left: From his portable throne, as he is carried to St. Peter's in the procession opening the Second Vatican Council, Pope John blesses the crowd. *Right:* Inside St. Peter's John prays for the Council's success.

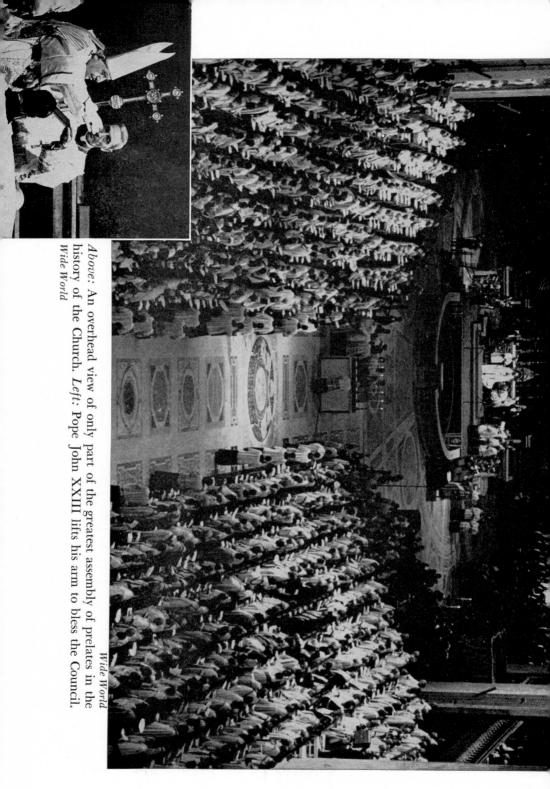

Above: An overhead view of only part of the greatest assembly of prelates in the history of the Church. *Left:* Pope John XXIII lifts his arm to bless the Council.

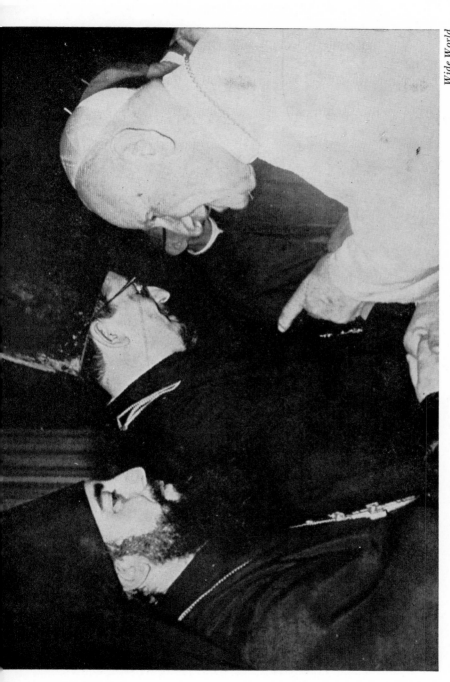

Pope John greets Vladimir Koteliarov (*left*) and Vitali Borovoi, Russian Orthodox observers at the Council.

Pope John XXIII wrote eight encyclicals. Here he is signing his last, the much-praised *Pacem in Terris* (April 12, 1963).

as Princes of the Church and the reverence they must inspire. They had to have a proper residence, with a splendid throne-room for receiving visitors, an automobile for necessary trips and, of course, the elaborate and costly vestments of their office. Though many of them were provided with apartments in Vatican City, it was almost impossible to live in the required style on that amount of money. Although Pope John raised their salaries 15 per cent, it is still difficult. Cardinal-Archbishops living outside of Rome are, of course, supported by the revenues of their Archdioceses.

On November 17, 1958, Pope John received all the members of the Secretariat of State, who were presented to him by Monsignor Tardini. When the presentations were ended the Pope addressed them in his jovial fashion. After a greeting he said, "We find ourselves delayed and hampered by prefixes and suffixes and we are going to abolish as many as possible. We will begin by omitting the pro from Monsignor Tardini's title and simply call him 'Secretary of State for the Holy See.' "

A gasp of delight ran around the circle for this was the Pope's informal way of announcing that Tardini, who was immensely popular, had been promoted from Pro (Acting) Secretary of State to the full title and office. Even Tardini had no warning of it.

Right after lunch, while the reporters were still writing their stories of the morning's announcement, the Pope gave them an even bigger scoop. He announced that a consistory would be held on December 15 to create new cardinals. There was nothing very surprising in this. A consistory was long overdue; the Sacred College had dwindled to 52 members, twelve of whom were over eighty. The big news was that he would create twenty-three new cardinals making the total seventy-five, five more than the limit of seventy set by Pope Sixtus V in 1586.

He also reversed another canon of Sixtus V, that no one who was closely related to a cardinal should be so named, by announcing that Gaetano Cardinal Cicognani's brother, Archbishop Amleto Cicognani, the Apostolic Delegate to the United

States, would be made a cardinal. Pope John had been expected to revivify the Sacred College and bring it up to strength. This was beyond all anticipation!

The Pope paid special honor to Archbishop Montini by placing his name at the head of the list of new cardinals, thus making him his *prima creatura* (first creation). Although a Pontiff may not name his successor, it is said that Pope John would like to be followed by Montini.

Included in the long list of cardinals-elect were, of course, Monsignor di Jorio and Monsignor Tardini. The latter remarked, "I refused the Red Hat from Pope Pius XII because I wanted to be let alone. But there is no way of refusing this Pope."

Men from eight nations were included in the list, among them two from the United States, Archbishop Richard J. Cushing of Boston and Archbishop John O'Hara of Philadelphia. Most of the twenty-three were young, vigorous men who would be expected to give new force and direction to the "ever youthful Church."

To leap ahead of chronology, Pope John held two more consistories within the first seventeen months of his pontificate —Pius had held only three in nineteen years. At the second consistory held in December, 1959, he named eight more cardinals, several of whom he specially designated for work in the Ecumenical Council. Among these was the brilliant German priest, Father Augustin Bea, who had been confessor to Pope Pius XII.

Pope John had never met Bea (pronounced Bay-ah) until he became Pope. Then, on an inspection tour of the Holy Office, he was introduced to Father Bea as a key man there. A day or two later at the Institute for Bible Studies he was introduced to the head man there, Father Bea. Slightly confused, the Pope asked, "Are there two Father Beas around here?"

He soon developed a strong affection for the German, who was exactly his age. They could not have been more dissimilar physically. Bea, an enormously tall, thin man, had a long, thin face, a long upper lip, and merry eyes. Their characters, however, were much alike. One of the Protestant observers at the Ecumenical Council described Bea as "A jolly, loving man," a description that fits Pope John equally well.

Although born in Germany, Bea studied for the priesthood in Holland. When Eugenio Pacelli came to Bavaria as Nuncio, their friendship began. In 1924, Bea was chosen to head the newly organized Institute of Bible Studies in Rome. Later, Pope Pius XI sent him to represent the Holy See at a conference of Protestant Biblical Scholars in Germany. The Protestants expected the Catholic representative to be a bigoted amateur. Instead, his erudition earned so much respect that he was asked to deliver the closing address. This was the first opening—although slight—between Catholicism and German Protestantism.

As a friend to Pope Pius XII for nearly twenty years, Father Bea was closely in touch with the intricate problems of the Holy See. He was an all-around man. Pope John elevated him quickly to Cardinal because he realized that Bea's human qualities and his ability to win the respect of men of other faiths made him an ideal person to fill a key role in the future Council.

A third consistory, held only three months later, in March, 1960, brought the membership of the Sacred College to a total of eighty-five. Again Pope John innovated by naming Bishop Laurean Rugambwa of Rutabo, Tanganyika, the first Negro cardinal. Like all of the Pope's innovations, the increase in the membership of the Sacred College was not a whim, but an action based on common sense. The Church was growing larger and had need of more cardinals to carry on its work. The creation of cardinals in such far places as Africa and the Philippines bound the faithful there more closely to Rome.

On November 23, 1958, Pope John went to take possession of the Basilica of St. John Lateran, the official church of the Bishop of Rome. There was no parade, just a motorcade of six black limousines escorted by a few motorcycle policemen.

In the Pope's car rode Cardinals Tisserant, Pizzardo and Micara. Members of the Curia and all his personal staff followed.

First, Pope John went straight to the private chapel of the Lateran Palace to pray that he might be a good and worthy pastor to his personal flock. Then he received all the cardinals who were still in Rome in the great Audience Hall and welcomed the Mayor of Rome and other civic notables. After that, wearing the unusual conical miter of the Bishop of Rome, he was carried the short distance to the basilica in the *Sedia Gestatoria* through a crowd of sixty thousand wildly cheering people.

Inside the ancient church with its severely classical lines, lightened by brilliantly colored Romanesque mosaics, he was carried up the aisle, while silver trumpets blew and the people kept on cheering. Pope John tried to quiet them, but, as Monsignor James I. Tucek once remarked, "He could no more hush a Roman crowd than you could hush a thunderbolt."

The High Pontifical Mass followed, during which the Pope delivered a sermon in Italian. In it he again stressed his role as pastor and spoke happily of indications of a religious awakening of the world. The enormous world-wide interest in the death of Pope Pius XII and in his own election and Coronation were signs of this, he said, adding, "In any event they show that people are at least curious about religion."

He also referred to his own seventy-seventh birthday which was two days away, saying, "We have no right to look forward to a long road, but no one who trusts in God need fear any surprise, even death."

On his way back to Vatican City, Pope John detoured to visit the Basilica of San Clemente and say a special prayer at the Altar of San Cirillo asking that Saint's intercession on behalf of the Slavic Orthodox Christians and of Christians throughout the world.

That same week Pope John proved that he did not intend to play the dismal role of "the Prisoner of the Vatican." The day before, he had driven out to Castel Gandolfo, the Pope's summer residence in the hilly little town of the same name, and went through the high-ceilinged rooms of the ancient castle-villa whose rather somber, heavy furnishings and dark draperies contrasted with the superb views from the long windows of the golden green Campagna to the west, and the steep forested hills on the east, holding Lake Alban like a light blue sapphire in an emerald cup.

John gave directions for brightening up the papal suite, and then went out on the balcony to greet the villagers in the courtyard beneath. He promised them he would come to live there the next summer. On his way home, the Pope drove around the lovely lake on the steep, twisting mountain road stopping the car to savor an especially fine vista where he could see across the plain to the bright blue rim of the Tyrrhenian Sea.

Incidentally, John already had planned the redecoration of his suite in the Vatican. In the library, where Pope Pius XII had his desk, John kept the tall book cases which contained Pius XII's many reference books and dictionaries of different languages, but a new rose-colored carpet in which were woven the arms of St. Pius X was ordered for the floor, and a delicate, Venetian glass chandelier was hung from the ceiling. The walls were covered with maroon damask especially woven with the Pope's coat of arms; on one wall a colorful old tapestry was hung, showing Christ handing the Keys to St. Peter. A circle of new red leather arm chairs were arranged beneath the tapestry so the Pope could visit informally with his callers. He used the same big flat-topped desk as Pius. There was a large crucifix standing on it reminding him of the love of his Savior and two telephones to remind him of his worldly charge. Standing nearby was a large, lighted plastic globe showing the boundaries of all the dioceses in the world.

The other rooms, the high-ceilinged, narrow bedroom, the dressing-room and dining room, were similarly lightened to reflect John's cheerful disposition, but the beautiful little chapel was kept as it had always been.

A few days after he took possession of St. John Lateran, Pope John made another expedition beyond his temporal realm to visit the Apollinare, where he had studied for the priesthood. He made his way quickly through the ranks of awe-stricken young scholars down the long, familiar corridor. The damp, musty, boys'-school smell shucked half a century from his shoulders. He visited the Rector, his old friend Monsignor Pio Paschini, who lay sick in bed. After a pleasant visit with the old gentleman, the Pope returned to the students whose awe soon dissolved in laughter as he told them funny anecdotes of his student days, enlivening them with droll faces and such lively gestures that his white zucchetto kept slipping half off his head. Pope John has the rarest of comic gifts; he can be very funny without ever losing his dignity.

On another day John left the Vatican at the unheard of hour of 7:00 A.M. to go to the Urban College of the Propagation of the Faith, where he celebrated his first Mass outside of Vatican City as Pope. In his sermon he spoke to the future missionaries of the "uncontaminated glory of the Catholic priesthood," and rededicated his pontificate to concern for the mission territories.

The Pope paid another visit to a Roman seminary two weeks later when he went to the Pontifical Gregorian University, one of the greatest Catholic international institutions of learning. The students there were the intellectual elite of the Church, and they knew it—so Pope John quoted the first Patriarch of Venice, St. Laurence Giustiniani, to them that "One should arm oneself with humility and not permit oneself ambitious thoughts or impulses . . . or the desire for high pastoral office or beg in prayer for special missions and popular fame."

Pope John continued visiting outside of Vatican City to the surprised delight of the people of Rome and to the consternation of the Italian Government who feared—unnecessarily—for his safety, and wanted him always to follow a pre-determined route and to furnish security guards. On December 8, the Feast of the Immaculate Conception, he unexpectedly joined the peo-

ple of Rome in the Piazza di Spagna for the traditional ceremony of putting flowers at the foot of the column on which
stands a statue of the Blessed Virgin. John mingled almost unguarded with the crowd, and gave a little impromptu sermon.
Then he went to pray at the Basilica of St. Mary Major.

In addition, Pope John still liked to go for walks accompanied by only one attendant. He usually strolled in the Vatican
gardens; his favorite walk was to the replica of the Grotto of
Lourdes. Unlike Pope Pius XII he had no set time for these
excursions but went whenever his duties permitted. The civil
Governor of Vatican City asked him if he should close the
cupola of St. Peter's to the public when His Holiness was in
the gardens.

"Why should you?" John asked.

"Because people can look down and see you," the Governor
replied.

With his famous twinkle the Pope said, "Oh, we'll try to
conduct ourselves properly and not give rise to scandal."

But the Pope did not always stay in the gardens. Occasionally, he would stroll through the streets of Rome. On one such
day he was assailed by the lovely aroma of chestnut cakes in a
peddler's cart, and stopped for one. Then he looked embarrassed and said, "We have no money with us to pay you."

"Oh Your Holiness!" the peddler said. "Please take it as
a gift. Please take the whole cart!"

Pope John also astonished people by attending a performance in the Vatican of T. S. Eliot's reverently poetic play about
the death of Thomas à Becket, "Murder in the Cathedral." It
was probably the first time a Pope had witnessed a dramatic
performance in over two hundred years. He attended because
he felt that this was the kind of contribution the theatre should
be encouraged to make to the culture of our age. Besides, he
enjoyed it immensely.

On December 10, Pope John renewed Pope Pius XII's custom of holding large public audiences in the Vatican. This
writer was present on that occasion. The huge Hall of Audience

was filled with people from many nations and every strata of society. The crowd stretched back through several long salons through which the Pope was carried on his way to the throne at the far end of the Hall of Audience. As we waited we were in a solemn mood expecting an impressive but somber ceremony. When the Holy Father appeared, carried high on the *Sedia Gestatoria,* a ripple of cheering heralded his approach, and rose to a deafening din as he stepped down at the far end of the room. In places other than churches, Pope John likes expressions of affection and appreciation from the people. As he came in, beaming with happiness and love, and giving his blessing right and left so energetically that his white zucchetto kept slipping sideways, the whole mood of the crowd changed from sobriety to gaiety. An enormous sense of well-being, security, and innocent happiness filled us all, Catholics and Protestants alike.

When he had mounted to the throne, the Pope delivered a talk in Italian that was both inspiring and amusing, emphasizing his words by tapping the ground with his little red slippers and waving his arms. Then he spoke in excellent French and fairly fluent Spanish. After a pause, Pope John said almost shyly, "Now I will try to speak to my English and American children in English." He rolled his eyes toward heaven and waved his arms helplessly as if he had added, *"Molto difficile."* A crash of laughter sounded through the hall.

As Pope John left us we were all inspired by the renewed realization that religion should not be sad. As Pope John has said, "Christianity is peace, joy, love, and a life that is ever renewed."

The consistories installing the new cardinals were held from December 15 to 17, 1958, with all the solemn ceremonial and formal pageantry of ancient tradition. On such occasions Pope John can be an awe-inspiring figure of the dignity and sanctity befitting the Vicar of Christ on earth.

It was also typical, however, that he celebrated his first Christmas Mass with charming simplicity. The tribunes for the prelates were removed from St. Peter's and there were no reserved places. Surrounded by the people of his flock, he conducted the beautiful, joyous service celebrating the Nativity of our Savior.

Pope John continued his predecessor's custom of broadcasting a Christmas message to the world. In his first broadcast, he was careful to correct any impression of criticism of Pius XII that his many innovations might have given. In fact, he went so far as saying, "We already like to regard him as joined in heaven with God's saints, and from there continuing to dispense renewed strength to those Christians who survive him. . . ." The message itself was a call for unity and "a vigilant peace." Pope John quoted the words of Jesus according to St. John: "Them also must I bring . . . and there shall be one fold and one shepherd." And he added, "The birth of the Lord is an announcement of unity and of peace in all the world . . ." Pope John's Christmas wish to the world was, "May this be a constructive Christmas. May as many as hear this voice over the air waves, rising above the harmony of the bells to invite all to union and to prayer . . . may they wish to reinforce their good intentions for the sanctification of the New Year so that it may become for all the world a year of justice, of blessings, of goodness, and of peace."

On Christmas afternoon Pope John paid his visit to the Gesu Bambino Hospital for children. The next day, Friday, December 26, he astonished the Romans by going to visit the prisoners in the ironically-named Regina Coeli (Queen of Heaven) Prison. As he entered the high, gloomy rotunda from which the corridors to the triple-tiered cell blocks radiated, he was touched by the sight of an exquisite crêche made by the inmates. A thousand prisoners in loose, flapping, convict-striped uniforms were assembled there to greet him. Pope John addressed them as, "Dear Sons and Brothers," and told them that his own brother had once been arrested for hunting without a license, and that he understood how a man may break the law to steal for his hungry family. "In your first letter home," he said, "say that the Pope came to see you, that he was here among you. And in my Holy Mass and in my daily breviary I will have a special thought and intense affection for each of you and for all your dear ones."

The prisoners knew he meant it. They felt the strong current of his love and the dynamic power of his sheer goodness flowing into them, as they stood together singing *Adeste Fidelis*. The officials, unduly nervous as officials always are, had mapped out a course for the Pope's inspection tour marked by a red carpet. He soon veered off it, meandering down the dank and musty corridors while the prisoners knelt to kiss his ring. One old man with a long police record asked humbly if the Pope's message of hope was also for him. "I have made many mistakes, Holy Father," he said.

Bending over the kneeling man, John wiped his tears away; then he raised him and embraced him with a great bear-hug, saying, "I looked into your eyes with my eyes. I have put my heart near your heart."

When the Pope came to the cell block where the incorrigibles were confined he saw the grated doors placed there to keep them in. In his most commanding voice he ordered, "Open the gates. Do not bar them from me. They are all children of our Lord."

On January 20, 1959, the Pope got into his car with the apparent intention of driving as usual to the Vatican Gardens. Instead, the driver swung the car around St. Peter's Square and disappeared into the Roman traffic without benefit of an escort. Nobody knew where the Pope had gone; Vatican officials were frantic; the civil authorities of Rome and, in fact, the whole Italian Government were in a panic. What would the world say if something happened to the Pope?

Pope John knew that nothing would happen to him. He just wanted to see some old friends. Word had reached him that Father Joseph Bergeron of Canada, who managed a Home for old and retired Holy Cross priests, had wanted to see him, but had not asked for an audience because "A humble priest like me should not take up the Holy Father's time." The Pope's car beat its way through the traffic-clogged streets to the old priests' Home on Monte Mario. There, while the Vatican officials answered hundreds of telephone calls with the helpless words, "We don't know where he's gone," and security police rocketed around Rome searching fruitlessly, Pope John, having refused the big throne-like chair they offered him, sat in a rocker in a circle of twenty-two very happy old gentlemen, having a lovely time gossiping away the afternoon.

On Sunday, January 25, 1959, Pope John made an announcement that shook the whole Catholic world with excitement and sent tremors of interest throughout all Christendom even to the remote weary lands back of the Bamboo Curtain. He had talked the matter over with only one of his advisers, Cardinal Tardini. It was a stunning surprise. Dramatic as it was, it should not have amazed anyone, because it was completely in key with his character and was the culmination of his whole life's work—unifying Christians everywhere.

The Pope has since expressed the belief that his sudden decision was inspired by the Holy Spirit. "Suddenly and unexpectedly, we were struck by the idea of this, within the humbleness of our spirit," he said. "The certainty that it was heaven-sent emboldened us to put our humble intent into action." Later, in an unusually poetic phrase, he said that the idea "sprang up within us like the first flower of an early spring."

That Sunday morning Pope John drove out of Vatican City to the Monastery of St. Paul Outside-the-Walls, close to the tomb of the Apostle, to celebrate the Feast of the Conversion of St. Paul. After the celebration of the Mass, Pope John withdrew to a hall in the Monastery with the eighteen cardinals who had assisted at the Mass. There he spoke to them, intending his message for the whole world.

He said that it was his intention to "open our mind" concerning "some of the most notable aspects of the Apostolic Office" that had come to his attention during his first three months in Rome. He added that the first and most important thing was to correlate clearly the new Pontificate to contemporary spiritual needs. Realistically he said, "We are aware that the new Pope is being watched, in many quarters with friendship and devotion, in others with hostility or hesitation. . . ."

Everyone was waiting for some especially notable event that would foreshadow the course of his pontificate. He outlined some of the problems he faced as Bishop of Rome because of the tremendous growth of the city and the rapidly changing customs and material conditions of the times. But if the problems of the Bishop of Rome were difficult, he asked them to consider the enormity of those he faced in his responsibility for the spiritual government of the whole world. "If (the Pope) broadens his vision to cover the whole of his task," John said, "what a spectacle meets his gaze! A pleasing one on the one hand, where the Grace of Christ continues to multiply fruits and marvels of spiritual increase, of salvation and sanctity throughout the world; but, on the other hand, one evoking sorrow in the face of the abuse and compromise of the liberty of man, who does not recognize the opened heavens and withdraws from his faith in Christ, the Son of God, the Redeemer of the world and the founder of Holy Church . . ."

Does a solution to these tremendous problems of modern Rome and of the modern world exist? In a single sentence, Pope John gave his double-barreled answer, which unequivocally foreshadowed the course of his pontificate and set the stage for the crowning achievement of his work.

"Venerable Brothers and Dear Sons," he said, "though admittedly trembling with emotion, yet at the same time with a humble resoluteness of purpose, we pronounce before you the name and plan of this double consultation, a Diocesan Synod for Rome and an Ecumenical Council for the Universal Church."

It was indeed a daring and dramatic proposal. The Roman Synod, though unusual in that diocese, was in conformity with the custom of holding archdiocesan synods to consider the affairs of a particular area, but an ecumenical council was a gathering together of all the cardinals, archbishops, bishops and heads of religious orders from the whole world. There had not been such a meeting since the First Vatican Council of Pius IX over ninety years ago. The council before that was the Council of Trent which met in 1545, over four hundred years ago. In the whole history of the Church, only twenty ecumenical councils had been convened, and each had marked some great step in resolving a crisis defining dogma and clarifying Canon Law.

Pope John was returning to one of the most ancient customs of the Church to accomplish its reconciliation with the modern world. His hope for such a Council was expressed in his final words to the cardinals: "We earnestly pray for a good beginning, continuation, and successful outcome of these proposals, which involve hard work directed toward light, improvement, and joy for all Christian peoples, toward a renewed invitation to the faithful of the individual religious groups, for them also to follow us with friendly courtesy in this seeking after unity and grace which so many souls from every part of the earth eagerly desire."

Pope John ended with the salutation of St. Paul, as quoted by St. Leo the Great, "You are my crown . . . my joy, if your faith, which from the beginning of the Gospel was preached in the whole world, *remain in love and holiness.* Oh, what a salutation this is," John proclaimed, "entirely worthy of our spiritual family! Love and holiness—a salutation and a wish!

"The blessing of Almighty God, Father, Son and Holy Ghost. Amen."

Apartment of Pope John—St. John's Tower

CHAPTER FOURTEEN

A GREAT ENTERPRISE

The announcement of the Ecumenical Council sent such a surge of hope and zeal through the world as Pope John had not even anticipated. All Christians had begun to long for unity in the face of the growing threat of materialistic atheism. The Anglican, Protestant, and some Greek Orthodox churches had been working for unity among themselves, but since they excluded more than half the Christians in the world, they did not commend much hope. The announcement of a new Ecunemical Council to promote union among all Christian peoples loosed a tidal wave of enthusiasm. Unmindful of the theological difficulties involved in such a union, people everywhere greeted it with joy.

In fact, the response was so great that it badly frightened many of the Catholic hierarchy. They feared that because the Council aroused such great hopes it would be considered a failure if it fell short of fulfilling them. They knew that it could not possibly solve all the problems of unification and that the best that could be hoped for was a step in the right direction. Even Cardinal Tardini was appalled and began to back away from the idea, but Pope John was not. He took the popular reaction as a sign that he had done the right things. Of course, Pope John also recognized the impossibility of achieving perfect union immediately, and he agreed with his advisers in playing down the prospect of such an accomplishment and playing up the other great work which could be achieved by the Council. His simple, straightforward mind cut right to the heart of the matter: Christians everywhere no longer regarded others with suspicion but yearn for reconciliation.

With this in mind, Pope John made his favorite maxim the guidepost of the Council: "Stress that which unites rather than that which divides." He pointed out that there were strict limitations as to how far this work could be carried. The basic beliefs of the Church, as expressed in its formal creed and the infallible pronouncements of other ecumenical councils and other popes, could not be touched. But where unity could be reached without violating doctrine, as Vicar of Christ on earth, he was determined to achieve it.

Pope John described what he thought the Council's attitude toward the separated churches should be in these words, "We do not intend to conduct a trial of the past. We do not want to prove who was right or who was wrong. All we want to say is, 'Let us come together; let us make an end of our divisions.' " His instructions to Cardinal Bea, head of the Council's Secretariat for the Union of Christians, were, "In working for reunion it is necessary first to be very humble; second, to be patient and await God's hour; and third, to avoid any discussions that may impair the virtue of charity. We must leave aside, for the moment, those elements on which we differ."

There is no limit to the efforts he will exert personally to reconcile all Christians to the Universal Church. In fact, he is anxious to establish friendly relations with men of *every* religion; he has already changed phrases in the Liturgy which were offensive, referring to "perfidious Jews and infidels." *

---

* On Good Friday, 1963, the Cardinal who was the celebrant in St. Peter's said the old words from force of habit. Pope John stunned the worshippers by stopping him in midstream with the words, "Say it over the new way."

One of his first papal acts was to receive the Shah of Iran in audience, less than a month after his Coronation. The young Mohammedan ruler had asked to be received by the Vicar of Christ and was warmly welcomed. The crowd in St. Peter's Square gave him a warm welcoming cheer when he arrived in a black limousine which bore the Iranian standard that shows the prophet's crescent moon. This was not the first time a Roman crowd had cheered a Moslem ruler; when another Shah visited Rome, at a time of intense Italian anti-clericalism, they had shouted, "Long live the Shah! Down with the Pope!" John is said to have remarked to the Shah, "I'm glad that this time they are willing to cheer both of us."

Pope John received the Shah in his library. They sat chatting in the circle of chairs which had only recently been installed. The Pope said he was sorry not to have visited Iran although, when he was Apostolic Delegate to Turkey, he had been very close to Iran's borders. Then John added, "We are especially pleased by the benevolence Your Majesty has shown toward Christian institutions in Iran."

It was in fact a delightfully friendly meeting, characterized on both sides by the only kind of tact that is of value— that which comes from the heart. The Shah gave the Holy Father a superb Persian rug. Having pondered his return gift carefully, since the usual religious objects would not be appropriate, Pope John presented the Shah with a specially-designed gold medal and a book of fine reproductions of the paintings in the Sistine Chapel. When it was time for the Shah to leave, Pope John gave him his benediction which he had rephrased delicately to avoid offending the Mohammedan's religious principles: "May the most abundant favor of Almighty God be with you."

The Shah was followed by a stream of statesmen of diverse religions and political viewpoints. Devout de Gaulle of France had come; President Celal Bayer of Turkey, when visiting, received the Pope's blessing in Turkish. The Queen of England came, and the Prime Minister of Japan. Even pink-leaning Sukarno of Indonesia was received, as Pope John continued

to seek "that which unites" among all men. The situation sometimes required quick thinking, as it did when American Congressman Brooks Hayes arrived for a private audience. Either
because Hayes was upset by the ceremonial surroundings of
the Pope or because he did not want to sail under false colors,
the Congressman suddenly blurted out: "I'm a Baptist." Smiling, the Pope said, "Well, I'm John."

Another remarkable first, less remarkable from the Vatican's point of view than from that of America's more conservative Protestants, was the visit of the President of the United
States. A photographer caught them laughing uproariously, but
the joke remained a mystery for some time. It finally became
known that Pope John had made a slip in the English speech
he had so laboriously learned and had added in Italian: *"Era
di belli!"* (That was a beaut!), which was so close to being American slang that Ike understood it.

Perhaps his most important visitor from the point of view
of furthering Christian unity was Geoffrey Francis Fisher,
Archbishop of Canterbury. Fifty years ago it would have been
inconceivable for the Primate of the Anglican Church to call
on the head of an institution which was known in the bad old
days among the more fanatical of the English Protestants as
"The Scarlet Woman of Rome." In fact, even in these days it
was daring of both Pope and Primate. In England, it evoked a
few rumbles of discontent among the more conservative Anglican clergy and laity, and the Pope had to take great care to assure the faithful that he was not about to compromise any of
the basic tenets of the Church. To avoid difficulty for the Archbishop at home, the Vatican communiqué on his visit was deliberately non-committal and colorless. As a result the British press
described the meeting as "frigid." It was anything but that!

As the gaunt, gray Archbishop of Canterbury, clad in his
purple robes and wearing a pectoral cross similar to that which
a Catholic bishop wears, entered the Pope's library, on December 2, 1960, his first words were, "Your Holiness, we are making
history!" Pope John laughed, but agreed that they were indeed.

The Pope and the Archbishop then sat in easy chairs

talking intimately of their problems. Above their heads hung the tapestry that portrays Christ handing the Keys to Saint Peter, which emphasizes the most difficult point in reconciling the two churches—recognition of the primacy of the successor to the First Bishop of Rome. Tactfully, neither prelate mentioned it. No one knows exactly what they discussed, but it is certain that both men agreed on the desirability of reunion, if (an enormous IF) it could be brought about without violating the conscience of either faith.

Pope John's feeling about the Archbishop's visit was perhaps best expressed in the words of an editorial in the *Catholic American Journal:* "The beauty of such a deed of Christian courtesy is that its meaning can never be erased."

Although the Pope and the Archbishop probably dealt in generalities, Dr. Fisher's visit to Cardinal Bea had a concrete result. After a long discussion with the head of the Secretariat for Christian Unity, the Archbishop offered to do everything in his power to aid the Cardinal in his work. Later, a semi-official liaison was established between Rome and the Anglican Church through Canon Bernard C. Pawley who was sent to Rome to work with Cardinal Bea. Dr. Fisher's audience was purposely played down, "for fear of upsetting the applecart in England," but a "most reliable authority" stated that "the Holy See was most favorably impressed." Dr. Fisher was described as "a vivid human character, not a doctrinal one."

Another example of the Pope's flexibility was the celebration of a Catholic Eastern Rite Mass in St. Peter's on November 19, 1960. He presided at a Byzantine Mass; therefore, all the principal liturgical acts of honor and of jurisdiction were reserved to him. Throughout the ceremony he intoned the principal blessings in the Old Slavonic language; it was the first time in over a thousand years a Pope had done so.

It is difficult to imagine the enormous amount of preparation necessary for an ecumenical council. Such a gathering of the hierarchy of the Universal Church presupposes decisions on a diversity of matters, some of them momentous. It arouses enormous interest and hope, not only among the faithful, but among those Christians who belong to the separated sects. As Pope John said to the opening session of the Ante-Preparatory Commission of the Council, "We expect great things of this Council. . . ."

In another allocution the Pope said, "There is an uncertainty, you might even say a holy commotion, that goes with starting something new, and this in itself is an exercise in humility. But all this is soon transformed into a courageous feeling of confidence as each new ray of light makes the horizon grow brighter and gradually reveals the Lord's Hand intervening to enlighten us, and to encourage us to move ahead with a generous heart and a willing spirit." The divine inspiration and guidance which such a council invokes stems directly from the meeting of the apostles and disciples on the Jewish holyday known as Pentecost when the Holy Spirit descended upon the brethren in forked tongues of fire, bringing the gift of languages and inspiring the sacred work of the Universal Church.

And, at the Council held in Jerusalem in 52 A.D. by the still living apostles and disciples, they expressed their belief in its divine guidance in the beautiful opening phrase of the letter in which they announced the results of their deliberations: "The Holy Ghost and we have decided. . . ."

Of course, that was not a true ecumenical council in the accepted sense of the word, which means universal or worldwide. There were by then many thousands of Christians whose leaders or bishops were not present. Yet this began the tradition that the Pope may refer decisions of great import on matters of dogma, doctrine, and Canon Law to a council for deliberation, and that these deliberations in Council are guided by the Holy Spirit.

The first true ecumenical council in the official records of the Church was the Council of Nicea in 325 A.D. It was convoked by the Emperor Constantine, the first Christian Roman Emperor, with the assent of Pope St. Silvester, at Nicea in Bithynia near Byzantium. The Pope, who was ill, was represented by two delegates. The deliberations were conducted according to the parliamentary rules of the Roman Senate. The great achievement of this Council was the definition of the divinity of the Son and His equality to the Father, and the adoption of a test of faith based on a simple baptismal creed which provided a universal statement of faith in place of the earlier and varying baptismal formulas.

A history of all the nineteen ecumenical councils since then would fill many books, and indeed there are many books devoted to them. However, the two most recent ones must be mentioned—the Council of Trent (1545-63), and the First Vatican Council (1869-70). The Council of Trent worked intermittently under Paul III, Julius III, and Pius IV. This Council, as Henri Daniel-Rops says, "accomplished an enormous task . . . [It] affirmed the true doctrine rooted alike in scripture and tradition, which touches the whole field of belief. . . ." This Council began the period of Catholic Reform, which rooted out the abuses and laxities that had grown up in the Church and renewed its "ever youthful" purity and vigor.

The First Vatican Council was interrupted in 1870 by the fall of Rome to the secular troops of King Victor Emmanuel. One vitally important dogma it produced is that of the infallibility of the Pope *in matters of faith and morals*. After this act, some theologians thought there might never have to be another ecumenical council. However, Pope John decided that he needed the help of the Episcopate of the whole Church assembled in a council, which would invoke the Holy Spirit to guide its deliberations. Because the First Vatican Council was merely adjourned but not officially terminated, some people thought that the new Council might be considered a continuation of it. Pope John did not. He officially designated it the Second Vatican Council or Vatican II.

Intensive preparation was necessary lest the hopes of the world be destroyed. The first thing Pope John did was to establish a Preparatory Commission whose work was known as the ante-preparatory (or pre-preparatory) phase of the Council. This

Commission began by sending questionnaires to over thirty-five hundred bishops, heads of Orders, and Catholic universities, asking for their opinions as to what problems should be discussed by the Council. Their replies, literally millions of words, were studied, collated, condensed and finally published in fifteen huge volumes called the *Acta*. Archbishop Felici exclaimed, "They have sent us enough for ten councils!"

Organizing the logistics of the Council was, in itself, a huge job. It was to be by far the largest council ever held. The Council of Trent at its peak had only slightly over two hundred voting members; even at the First Vatican Council only some six hundred of the higher clergy were present. For Vatican II, preparations had to be made for an attendance of over thirty-five hundred.

Cardinals, patriarchs, primates, archbishops, and residential and titular bishops are entitled to vote in the Council. Abbots Primate and abbots and prelates directly charged with jurisdiction over a group of the faithful may vote, as can abbots who are superiors of monastic congregations, and superiors general of exempt male religious. Others invited to the Council included theologians and canonists, who have only the right of consultation. Pope John also invited a number of representatives of the separated churches, but they, of course, participated only as observers.

Vatican I was held in the right transept of St. Peter's in which temporary seats had been installed. The only appropriate place large enough to accommodate Vatican II is the longest nave in the world, the nave of St. Peter's. And, since each participating prelate brings from one to four secretaries and advisers, accommodations had to be found in Rome for an influx of at least 10,000 people, as well as for the large number of reporters, photographers, and so forth.

But logistics were only a minor detail. The Pre-Preparatory Committee also had to set up the commissions and secretariats for the preparatory work of the Council and allot them their tasks. The organization of this preparatory phase was as follows:

Committee	Chairman	Secretary
Central Committee	Pope John XXIII	Archbishop Felici (Italy)
Theological	Cardinal Ottaviani (Italy)	Father Tromp (Holland)
On Bishops and Dioceses	Cardinal Mimmi (Italy)	Bishop Gawlina (Poland)
For Discipline of Clergy and People	Cardinal Ciriaci (Italy)	Father Berutti (Italy)
On Religious	Cardinal Valeri (Italy)	Father Rousseau (Canada)
On Discipline of the Sacraments	Cardinal Masella (Italy)	Father Bigador (Spain)
On Liturgy	Cardinal G. Cicognani (Italy)	Father Bugnini (Italy)
Studies and Seminaries	Cardinal Pizzardo (Italy)	Father Mayer (Germany)
Oriental Churches	Cardinal A. Cicognani (Italy)	Father Welykyi (Ukraine)
Missions	Cardinal Agagianian (Armenia)	Bishop Mathew (England)
Lay Apostolate and Catholic Action	Cardinal Cento (Italy)	Msgr. Glorieux (France)
Ceremonial	Cardinal Tisserant (France)	Msgr. Nardone (Italy)
Secretariat for the Union of Christians	Cardinal Bea (Germany)	Msgr. Willebrands (Holland)
Secretariat for Communications and Entertainment Media	Archbishop O'Connor (U.S.A.)	Msgr. Deskur (Poland)
Administrative Secretariat	Cardinal di Jorio (Italy)	Msgr. Guerri (Italy)

Over five hundred people from fifty-nine countries have been involved in the work of these commissions, not all of them in Rome. As Pope John said on Christmas Day, 1961, "We gave them the arduous task of suggesting outlines for decrees concerning faith and morals from among which we would choose the ones to be taken up in the general sessions of the Council. It gives us great joy to tell you that these preparations . . . to which cardinals, bishops, prelates, theologians, canon lawyers, and learned men have contributed their distinguished cooperative efforts are on the verge of being concluded. . . ."

They all worked—how they worked!—with dedicated ardor and the enthusiasm of new crusaders.

The cardinal chairmen of the commissions are generally the Prefects of the particular Congregations that have jurisdiction over the particular subject; for example, the Prefect of the Sacred Congregation of Religious was Chairman of the Committee for Religious. One exception is Archbishop O'Connor of the North American College, who is Chairman of the Secretariat for Communications and Entertainment Media. The Archbishop is not head of a Congregation, but rather he is in charge of the radio-television-press department of the Holy See.

The work of all the commissions is cleared through, and coordinated by, the Central Committee, which is composed of fifty-eight cardinals with the Pope as Chairman. Despite his many other obligations, Pope John has kept a firm guiding hand on its work. At odd moments he chose to drop in and take part in its deliberations. At first, its members were somewhat startled when the round, white-clad figure of the Vicar of Christ slipped unexpectedly through the door to take his place at the head of the Council table, but they soon became accustomed to it. Exhibiting his real humility and courtesy, John never asserted his authority unreasonably; at the same time his clear thinking and his pointed speaking cut right through obfuscations to the heart of the matter, and his quick wit lightened the atmosphere. They discovered that they enjoyed working with him.

The Pope frequently dropped in on meetings of the other commissions also. On these occasions he would gesture to the members to continue their business as he sat quietly in the background listening to the discussion.

During the three-and-a-half years of preparation for the Council, the Pope also clarified its purposes in a constant stream of official speeches, interviews, and informal commentary, including four major encyclicals which touched on its work. In each mention of the Council, the Pope pointed out, and the organization of the preparatory commissions plainly showed, that Christian unity was not officially the main purpose of the Council. In his encyclical *Ad Petri Cathedram*, Pope John wrote: "The chief end of the Council is to advance the growth of the Catholic Faith; the renewal of Christian life among the people; and the adaptation of Church discipline to the needs and conditions of our time. This event will furnish a wonderful spectacle of truth, unity, and charity. . . ."

As *The Sign* says, "It may come as a shock to many people to discover that the Catholic Church is determined to get down to brass tacks in a self-examination that will be more severe than the accusations of its most ardent critics, for while the Church proclaims herself to be a perfect society she knows her perfection comes from within, from Christ and the Holy Spirit. But, of course, the individual members of the Church—the Pope, bishops, and priests as well as the laity cannot claim perfection. . . ." The magazine goes on to say that, although subject to the authority of the Pope, the Council is basically democratic. Each bishop says exactly what is on his mind. They will attempt, with the help of the Holy Spirit, to reformulate the doctrines of the Church and to make dynamic applications of them to modern conditions.

This probably will include restatements of theological doctrine, and reconciliations of science and theology. Such vexed questions as evolution, birth control, psychiatry, and divorce were to be considered. Further interpretation of the Sacred Scriptures; a move to bring about greater participation of the laity; simplification of the Liturgy; a more liberal policy on the use of the language of the country rather than Latin; revision and updating of Canon Law—all these things and many more were put on the agenda, and some of them were ranked ahead of Christian unity by the officials. The Pope and the members of the commissions did not want to disappoint the Christian world by raising its hopes too high. They well knew that bringing the separated brethren back into the Church would be a long and difficult process. They did not want the faithful to feel that the Council was a failure if it did not bring about this miracle. If it produced one significant forward step toward Christian unity, it would be an enormous success.

Even though the movement toward unity was officially ranked behind other matters, there is no question but that it was the nearest to Pope John's heart. It was for this that he ardently prayed and for this he would gladly die. Therefore, the Council was pointed toward "our separated brothers" of whom Pope John said, "Whether they will it so or not, they are our brothers. They shall not cease to be our brothers until they cease to say 'Our Father.' "

Although Pope John's main interest naturally lay in the preparations for the Council, he did not neglect his pastorate during the years of preparation, despite the amount of work he personally put in on it. In fact, he has done more pastoral work than any recent Pope. During the first Lent of his papacy, he began going to the church designated in the Missal as the "station church" for that particular Sunday in Lent. It was the custom of the parishioners to go to church in procession that day. They could hardly believe their eyes the first time they saw the Supreme Pontiff get out of his black limousine and take his place at the head of the parade to lead them through the dirty, narrow streets of the old city to church.

He also revived the custom of the Pope having ashes placed on his forehead on Ash Wednesday as a token of his mortality. He walked barefoot in the processions of Holy Week, and washed the feet of thirteen seminarians on Holy Thursday as a sign of his humility.

When Lent was over, the Pope decided to continue his visits to parish churches. He visited the wretchedly poor slum districts which were strongholds of Communism. This gave the Italian Government nervous tremors, and they turned out the security police in force, although Pope John considered this foolishness. In a sense it was because Italian Communists are periodically often good Catholics, but there was always the risk that someone, driven insane by misfortune nourished by propaganda, might attack the Pope. Nothing ever happened. The people of these slum districts did their best to honor him, dressing up their dilapidated houses by hanging rugs or bright bedspreads from the windows, and standing in the rain in their best clothes to cheer him as he passed. Sometimes the crowds were so great that they broke through the police lines, not to harm him, but in their eagerness to show their love of the Holy Father.

Barrett McGurn reported one such visit to the small, new church that was the only solid building in a shanty town named Tiburtina Three. It was similar to the dump-heap colonies in the America of depression days. Its affluent people lived in tar paper and corrugated iron shacks, while those less fortunate made do with caves, or the walled-up arches of the crumbling Roman aqueduct. Even these dwellings were brightened with bedspreads or any other colorful thing their owners could find to hide the grime of indigence. In a cold drizzle he walked through the mud to the ugly little church, and took his place in the sanctuary while the priest celebrated the Mass. When the Pope finally rose to speak every member of the crowd shouted "Viva il Papa!" which resounded loudly in the splendid edifice. The Pope held up his fingers in admonition, and the sound stopped as instantaneously as a symphony orchestra on its conductor's signal. Smiling, he complimented them on their quick obedience. Gravely he reminded them, "In Church you must have two things, prayer and silence."

In another slum section Pope John drew howls of laughter by saying to the crowd which waited to greet him, "I really had to go some to get here. But this is a triumph!" Then

he wiped the smiles from their faces by saying in a strong
stern voice, "But beware of the enemy! You know whom I mean.
You know his last name and his first name. Beware!"

They knew whom he meant.

In the summers Pope John went to Castel Gandolfo where
he escaped from the heat of Rome but not from work. On Sun-
days he occasionally celebrated Mass in the big, old, yellow-
plastered church that stood on the square of the little town.
Sometimes he went for long excursions through the countryside to visit some church or religious house that especially interested him. One of his longest trips was to Roccantica in the
Sabine Hills, about fifty miles northeast of Rome. It was the
longest trip made by a Pope since 1857.

He left Castel Gandolfo on a lovely summer dawn, with
a red sun just bouncing up from behind the mountains to
change Lake Alban's midnight blue to flamingo pink and light
the plain of the Campagna in rose and gold. His objective was
the summer villa of the Seminario Romano, where he had
spent several happy holidays during his student days, and where
he celebrated his second Mass on August 12, 1904.

It is likely that he had never been more serenely happy
than on that lovely drive through the light green fields and
dark green hills, down whose steep roads the farmers walked
with their wives and children to their day's work in the fields,
just as he had walked long ago with his own family. He waved
gaily to them; they dropped to their knees and waved back
joyously.

He arrived at Roccantica in time to offer his morning Mass
in the chapel of the Seminary, and to talk to the seminarians,
asking them to pray for the success of the Council. He breakfasted with them. Afterward, he made a little speech to the
townsfolk who were beside themselves with excitement for no
Pope had come to Roccantica since Nicholas II had taken refuge
there from the rebellious people of Rome nine hundred years
before. On his way home the Pope made a detour to pray at
the tomb of his old friend and classmate, Monsignor Giuseppe
Belzedere, who had died the year before.

Pope John also found time during the forty-five strenuous months of preparation for the Council to do other things besides his regular pontifical duties, which included working with the Roman Synod and the Commission on Canon Law, holding two consistories for the creation of cardinals, consecrating of bishops, holding many special religious ceremonies, receiving hundreds of thousands of people at public and private audiences, making innumerable speeches, writing an untold number of letters of advice, comfort, and spiritual inspiration to prelates and people all over the world, and conferring with virtually every bishop who came to Rome from abroad. For the sake of history, he even squeezed in time to sit for his portrait. Of that experience he said, "Now I know how the martyrs felt being burned alive."

Pope John found a pleasant diversion in an addition he made to the Vatican. One day while walking in the garden with Monsignor Capovilla near the Shrine of Our Lady of Lourdes, he looked up at the stark, round, stone tower of St. John which was set on the highest point in the gardens. "It would be wonderful to have a little apartment there," he said. "A place where I could escape from formality to meditate and pray." "Why not?" asked Capovilla. "It should not be hard to arrange."

Pope John pursued the idea with his usual gusto. Count Enrico Galeazzi, the pontifical architect, was summoned. The count agreed that it could be easily done. Done it was, but not easily. The Tower of St. John dated from 852 A.D. It was one of twenty-one towers that studded the Leontine Wall, which had been built as a defense against the Saracen raiders. In those confused times, the Saracens harassed the coast of Italy right up to the ancient walls of Rome (which did not include the Vatican). The Tower was perfectly round, fifty-five feet in diameter, and had walls fifteen feet thick. Count Galeazzi found that it was in very bad shape. The undermined foundations had to be strengthened with concrete. Weak parts of the walls were reinforced with big blocks of rough-hewn stone cut from other ruined towers. Only then could the work begin.

The final result is charming. The ground floor of the tower

is an open circular hall with a staircase which winds around its interior walls. On one side is an enclosed shaft for the push-button elevator. Above this is a similar hall furnished as a reception room. On the third floor are a modern kitchen and laundry and general service areas. The Pope's quarters on the fourth floor consist of a small, round living room. Doors lead from it to the other rooms, none more than ten feet long to the farthest point of its curving outer wall. These include the bedroom of the Pope, his study, a little dining room, and a miniature chapel. They are furnished very simply, with the exception of the Chapel. It contains a masterpiece of oriental art—a teakwood altar given to the Pope by Chinese Catholics in 1959. Its tabernacle, with a two-tiered, upcurving roof like a Chinese pagoda, is made of teak and gold. The altar front piece is carved in an elaborate design of birds and dragons, and the golden candlesticks on either side also have a dragon design.

Since the tower tapers upward, the fifth floor is even smaller; it consists of quarters for attendants and a single guest room and bath. Above that is the battlemented terrace which commands a superb view of the ancient Aurelian Way and the cypress-covered hills beyond.

Pope John had not planned such an elaborate set-up. He was furious when he learned of its considerable cost, but he loved it dearly. Early in the morning, late at night, or at high noon—whenever he felt he could conscientiously get away from the imprisoning formality of the great gloomy Apostolic Palace for an hour or a day, and once even for a week—the guards would see his stocky figure stumping along, accompanied by his long lean shadow, Monsignor Capovilla.

People called it the finest apartment in Rome. Although Pope John thought it a wicked extravagance, *they* were glad he had a place which brought him serene happiness.

During the preparations for the Council, the Pope's burden was made heavier and his heart greatly saddened by the sudden death of Cardinal Tardini. The news was brought to him at

Castel Gandolfo before dawn on June 30, 1961. He dressed quickly and drove to the Vatican, where he went straight to the room where Tardini lay. For a long time John knelt, praying beside the still form of his friend and counselor.

At noon he announced the Cardinal's death from a balcony overlooking St. Peter's Square. He said, "Very early this morning the Angel of Death entered the Apostolic Palace and carried away with him the Cardinal Secretary of State, Domenico Tardini, who was the closest and strongest helper of the Pope in the government of the Holy Church. Think how our heart is afflicted. . . ." Many other hearts were afflicted by the death of the beloved cardinal, none more so than his boys at Villa Nazareth who literally adored "Our Monsignor." So forthright, so wise, and yet so irrepressibly boyish, he would be a hard man to replace.

Perhaps Pope John's most important works were the five major encyclicals he wrote between 1959 and 1963. In *Ad Petri Cathedram* the Pope dealt with "the seeking and promoting, under the impulse of charity, of truth, of unity and peace." Its far-ranging thought covered spiritual and worldly problems— from the truth of the Gospels leading to eternal life to the obligations of the press to truthfulness, including the moral obligations of radio, motion pictures, and television. In the section of unity, harmony, and peace, Pope John wrote wisely and profoundly on such subjects as the brotherhood of all men; union and agreement between nations; union and agreement between social classes; the problems of labor, stressing the duty of employers "to provide in some suitable way for workers to share more and more in the fruits of labor and feel themselves partners in the whole enterprise"; and on unity within the family. The long, final section was devoted to unity of the Church. In it, he developed his ideas on how true Christian unity might be brought about, and expressed again, as ever, his passionate hope and prayer for this great objective.

Another notable pronouncement was issued on May 15,

1961. It was called *Mater et Magistra* from its opening sentence: "Mother and Teacher of all nations—such is the Catholic Church in the mind of her Founder, Jesus Christ. . . ."

In *Mater et Magistra* the Pope dwelt on the attitude of the Church toward working people, enlarging its doctrine to include not only regard for their basic necessities, but also for the dignity of individuals and the proposition of simple justice which demands that all classes should participate in and benefit by the increasing productivity provided by modern technology. Former-farmer Roncalli also made some cogent suggestions about how the depressed position of agriculture in an increasingly industrialized world could be improved; he discussed the moral obligations of the prosperous nations toward undeveloped and impoverished countries.

Important as this pronouncement was it was completely overshadowed by the Pope's stunning encyclical, issued during the recess of the Ecumenical Council on April 12, 1963, *Pacem in Terris,* the first encyclical ever to be addressed not only to Catholics but "to *all* men of goodwill."

After considering the enormous difficulties of the times, Pope John solemnly set forth a new declaration of the Rights of Man which deserves to rank with the Magna Charta, the Bill of Rights, and all the greatest pronouncements in the history of the world.

Among the most important of the rights listed were those of every human being: "To life and the means that are necessary for proper development of life" including security. . . . To "respect for his person and good reputation" . . . To "freedom in searching for the truth, in communicating his opinions and, in the pursuit of art . . . and to be informed truthfully about public events . . ." To "share the benefits of culture . . . the right to . . . education."

"Every human being has the right to honor God according to the dictates of an upright conscience and therefore the right to worship God publicly and privately. . . ."

The Pope enumerated many other rights of an extremely

progressive nature, pointing out that every fundamental right demands a duty and an obligation. The section in which he outlined the obligations of human beings to each other, and of governments to those they govern, and vice versa was more profoundly emphatic than his "Bill of Rights."

Having treated at great length the relations among men, the Pope went on to the relations among states. He denied that a different moral code should govern these. He said, "Order between the political communities must be built on the unshakable and unchangeable rock of moral law made manifest in the natural order by the Creator himself . . . First, among these rules, is that of truth. . . ." Justice, implying more than recognition of the mutual rights of nations, large or small, requires the fulfillment of their respective duties.

In this connection Pope John said, "Justice, right reason, and humanity demand that the arms race should cease . . . that nuclear weapons should be banned . . . and that a general agreement should be reached about progressive disarmament and an effective method of control. . . ."

In an extraordinary excursion into political philosophy, Pope John pointed out that the complex, world-wide problems of our time could not be solved by nations acting alone. He proposed *"a public authority having world-wide power"* to be "set up by common accord not imposed by force . . ." to promote the universal common good. He expressed hope that the United Nations might become "ever more equal to its . . . noble tasks . . ." and that the day might come when every human being would find an effective safeguard of his "universal, inviolable, and inalienable rights . . ."

It is impossible to summarize this extraordinary, twenty-two-thousand-word document. Its impact on world thinking was tremendous. Men of goodwill in every country and of all religions—and none—praised it as embodying the best hopes of mankind. Because it was completely free of prejudice and dogmatism it was called "revolutionary." John himself thought of it as *evolutionary:* another step toward the brotherhood of all men everywhere.

The Ante-Preparatory Commission of the Ecumenical Council completed its work, and the full Commissions met for the first time on November 14, 1960. Two years later their work was nearing completion. On Christmas Day, 1961, Pope John formally convoked the Second Vatican Ecumenical Council for the year 1962.

Pope John then asked "each individual member of the faithful and the entire Christian people to pray for its success." He added, "To this chorus of prayers we also invite all Christians of churches separated from Rome that the Council may also be to their advantage. . . ."

Well it might be. The interest and good will which the Announcement of the Council inspired in the world outside the Church was in wonderful contrast to the reaction that the First Vatican Council had produced. At that time the Patriarch of the Greek Orthodox Church, who had been invited, sent an ungracious refusal, and all the Protestant churches viewed the proceedings with intense suspicion and hostility. In 1962, hardly a voice was raised that did not express good will and hope.

Before the Council opened, Pope John undertook an extraordinary pilgrimage, traveling almost five hundred miles by train to Loreto. No Pope had used a train for ninety-nine years; then the journey had been only twelve miles. It was centuries since a Pope had ventured so far from Rome. All the resources of modern communications were joined to bring it to as many people as possible, by Eurovision to all of Western Europe and by taped television, radio, and newspapers to the rest of the world.

The Vatican railroad station, unused since 1863, was hastily put in order. At six-thirty, Pope John boarded the special train which President Antonio Segni of Italy had lent him. With him went Monsignor Capovilla, six cardinals, twenty other prelates, and a number of laymen. There were also twelve Swiss Guardsmen in the full-dress uniforms. A whole regiment of reporters either rode the train or chased it across Italy in automobiles.

The train pulled slowly out of Vatican City. It stopped almost immediately at a station in Rome where Italian Prime Minister Amintore Fanfani got aboard. Then, preceded by a two-car pilot train, the special train roared off across Italy. In the meantime, President Segni had raced ahead to be on hand to welcome the Pope to Loreto. The honors paid him by the Government of Italy pleased John, especially because he remembered that when he had been a young priest the Church and the State were bitter enemies. In fact, all through that long, lovely day of summer-in-autumn he was as happy as a man could be. At every flag-draped station on the way, crowds of people, most of whom had never seen a Pope, were waiting to honor him, led by their mayor—whether he was Catholic, Socialist, or Communist—sporting his tri-color sash. The train would slow to a crawl and the Pope, standing in a big open window, would give them all his blessing.

At Loreto, more than fifty thousand people were packed into a town with a population of only seven thousand. The ceremonies in which the Pope placed crowns of gold upon Our Lady of Loreto and her Infant were so moving that many people wept happily, and the Pope himself was close to tears. There were even more people waiting at Assisi—it was the feast day of St. Francis.

As the homeward train slid smoothly through the Umbrian Hills in the red-gold light of an Italian summer evening, crowds still waited at the stations where they had waited all day, and from every hilltop *campanile* the church bells sent their greetings echoing down the narrow valleys.

It was after eleven o'clock when the train rumbled over the spur track from Italy into Vatican City. The long, lovely day was over. Pope John was very tired—as tired as a happy child on Christmas night.

Gardens—Vatican

CHAPTER FIFTEEN

THE COUNCIL

In 1869, Pope Pius XI said of ecumenical councils: "The first part belongs to the devil, the second to men, and in the third the Holy Spirit straightens everything out."

As the Second Vatican Council began its deliberations on October 13, 1962, two days after the formal opening, a number of conservative prelates must have thought, "How true! How true!" On that day the recommendations, made by the Curia and Preparatory Commissions, of the one hundred and sixty Fathers to be elected members of the ten permanent commissions of the Council were placed before the full membership of the Council assembled in St. Peter's. They were expected to accept this slate *in toto*.

Immediately the assembled Fathers indicated that they would not be a rubber stamp council. While the list of names was being read, notes were flying back and forth between the cardinals and bishops from France, Germany, Belgium, Holland, and supposedly conservative Spain. When the reading ended, Achille Cardinal Lienart of Lille, France, went to the microphone. Speaking extemporaneously in Latin, he said that since the Fathers had not been given sufficient information about the candidates or time to consult with each other concerning them, he would like to propose an adjournment.

There are ten presidents of the Council, each of whom presides in turn. It happened that Joseph Cardinal Frings of Germany, a leader of progressive thought, was presiding that day. Seeing that a majority of the Council favored it, he immediately accepted Cardinal Lienart's suggestion and declared the Council adjourned. The session had lasted about half an hour.

It was a startling surprise to the older members of the Curia, who had worked very conscientiously on the lists. It also wakened the outside world to a realization that the Council would not be a cut-and-dried affair of routine acceptance of proposals handed down from on high. The newspapers sensationally labeled it "The Revolt of the Bishops," which was an exaggeration. The non-Catholic observers were amazed and delighted. One of them said: "It showed that the Catholic Church was not the monolithic structure that so many of our people believed it to be, but instead had an area for free discussion and democratic decisions."

Pope John, watching the proceedings over closed circuit television in his Vatican apartment was as surprised as everyone else. At first, he may even have been dismayed, but when he evaluated the situation he was pleased. He had not called this Council merely to ratify preconceived edicts, but rather because he wanted the help of all the bishops of the Church, in their united wisdom and with the inspiration of the Holy Spirit, in working toward a great renewal of the Church.

The next meeting of the Council was postponed until Tuesday, October 16. During the three free days there was a tremendous ebullience among the twenty-five hundred bishops who had gathered for the Council. Meetings were held all over the city. Other lists of candidates were proposed and discussed. Compromises were agreed upon.

Meanwhile, Pope John, anxious to get on with the business of the Council, realized that the rule that all successful candidates must have an absolute majority of the votes was apt to result in deadlocks. Using his prerogative in favor of democracy, he unilaterally changed the rule by ordering that a plurality should be sufficient for election.

This was not all. The Pope heard that one North American bishop was sadly troubled as to whether he should vote for a candidate of his choice or one on the official slate. He told Capovilla to telephone the prelate. "Tell him," John said, "that a vote against the official list is not necessarily a vote against the Pope." On Tuesday and the days which followed, the matter was settled in a spirit of compromise, and a slate of candidates acceptable to all was ratified by large majorities.

According to the table of organization of the Council, after sixteen members of each Commission had been elected the Pope was to appoint eight more, making a total of twenty-four members on each commission. Pope John now realized that an even number might result in tie votes. Again in the interest of speeding things up, he appointed *nine* members making twenty-five. He chose his appointees with great care, considering their opinions and geographical origin to give all parts of the world a voice in the proceedings of the commissions. This was tremendously important, because they had the role of submitting all proposals to the Council. Even though these could be changed by vote of its members, there was, of course, a leverage in favor of the commissions' proposals.

As the Church is the first to recognize, although it is the chosen instrument of Jesus Christ and therefore infallible in its solemnly-proclaimed doctrine, the cardinals, bishops, and other prelates who staff it are fallible human beings. Therefore, no one expected the Council to run perfectly smoothly. As Pope John remarked to a group of Pakistani bishops: "Nobody around here knows how to run an ecumenical council. After all, none of us have ever been to one."

There were some very human mistakes. For example, seats were provided for twenty-two hundred voting members of the Council, and it is believed that over twenty-five hundred attended the opening session, although no one had an exact count. As a result over three hundred Fathers were relegated to the gallery originally intended for the non-Catholic observers.

Then the journalists, on whom Pope John depended to give the world inspiring news of the Council, became unhappy about the arrangements made for them. Approximately twelve hundred newsmen, speaking twenty different languages, had come from the ends of the earth to report the proceedings. The truth of the matter was that Vatican officials in charge of press relations had never experienced such a situation. Also, there were not enough of them to handle the situation. They were desperately overworked, and even the grumpiest journalists admitted they had done the best they could. In addition, there were not sufficient accommodations for the reporters. At the opening session, they were placed behind barriers in the north and south transepts of St. Peter's, where most of them could catch no more than a glimpse of the Pope's tall golden miter.

But the most frustrating thing for the newsmen was the lack of specific news. After the formal opening, they were quite properly barred from the sessions of the Council, for all the Fathers had to take the same dire oath of secrecy that the cardinals in conclave must take, and the non-Catholic observers were put on their honor not to reveal what went on—a precept which they observed as strictly as the members of the Council.

As a result, the reporters had very little to report. Each day an official communiqué was put out in several languages, but it was so cautiously worded that it meant very little. Starved for news and belabored by their editors at home, some of the journalists let their imaginations run wild.

Other difficulties of the Council included a general disorganization of procedure, poor accommodations for some of the poorer bishops, and transportation to the Council meetings, although the latter was handled reasonably well. Special buses ran to and from St. Peter's for the many who could not afford their own cars. Others used public transportation. It was quite a demotion for bishops who were treated with awe and respect in their own dioceses to be herded about in such a manner. As one American Bishop remarked: "We used to be shepherds, and now we're just a bunch of sheep." However, the Fathers took it very well. One of the great tourist sights of Rome became their departure from the sessions, which usually ran from nine o'clock until shortly after noon. Pope John often watched the scene from his window which overlooked the Square.

The crowd of tourists gathered behind barriers half way across the Square. Rows of buses waited by Bernini's colonnades. Private cars were parked wherever they could find space. The block-wide steps of the great basilica were grey and empty. Then from the doors came a trickle of "purple," the bright magenta hue worn by most of the bishops. The river of color flowed down the steps spreading out until they were completely covered by that glorious purple flood as water hyacinths spread out on the upper Nile. For a moment or two, it remained a splendid burst of color against the old stones between the flashing fountains. Then the vivid tide ebbed into the parked vehicles.

The bishops were as gay as boys let out of school. Some hurried to the buses which wheeled out into the traffic packed with chattering prelates. Others were met by friends whom they greeted by doffing their pompomed birettas to reveal the bright zuchettos beneath. Almost all of them talked gaily in a dozen languages, as if happy to be relieved of the formal Latin of the proceedings.

Pope John and Cardinal Tardini had decided long ago that Latin should be the language of the Council, not only because it emphasized the traditional unity of the Church but also because it was the one language that all the Fathers could understand. Tardini humorously gave the clinching argument when he said to the Pope, "Besides, they'll be less long-winded in Latin." John agreed.

Some of the Fathers did not agree. Nevertheless, it was **fascinating** to see the speech of the ancient Romans again be-.

come a living language in modern Rome. French-speaking bishops from Equatorial Africa used it to converse with such highly-literate colleagues as the British Archbishop of Westminster, and Japanese prelates spoke it to the Italian hierarchy. The most significant evidence of its vitality was the Latin advertisements in *L'Osservatore Romano* for such things as hearing aids and Hertz U-Drive-It cars: "HERTZ *Automobiles NOVISSIMAE LOCANTUR · Securitatem Hertz · Amplius Confert"*

However, Tardini's hope that the use of Latin would shorten the speeches was not justified. Like representatives in parliaments or in the United States Congress, most of the bishops spoke so that the people of their dioceses would know that they were being well represented. Once on their feet they seemed unable to stop, enchanted by the sonorous sound of their voices. The rule that no one could speak longer than ten minutes was badly breeched.

Pope John, sitting in front of the television set, often lost benignity as the Fathers droned on, repeating ideas already expressed by others. He was, in fact, possessed by a terrible urgency for the Council to get on with its business. Primarily, this was because he considered the swift and decisive renovation of the Church so vital. He was also frugally conscious of the enormous drain on the Vatican treasury. (Experts believe that the first session cost approximately eight million dollars, and that subsequent sessions will cost five millions dollars each.)

Another strong reason for his impatience was that he wanted so very much to live to see the Council's happy conclusion. For the first time in his life, John was aware of his aging body. Added to the natural discomforts of a man of his age, his magnificent digestion was failing him. At night he often suffered intense discomfort. The enormous load of work and worry which the Council had added to his usual duties was more than even his remarkable strength could stand.

On his eightieth birthday, in 1961, John had gently joked about discussions as to his possible successor, saying: "Those people who are planning who the next Pope will be may be disappointed. After all, my family is very long-lived. We usually die in our nineties." But on his eighty-first birthday, November 25, 1962, his tone was sadly different. "Any day is a good day to be born," he said, "and any day is a good day to die. I am now entering my eighty-second year. Whether I shall live to see the end of it or not I do not know. Nor does it give me much concern. . . ."

But he was concerned about being present to guide the Council to its conclusion. As the discussions continued, it became evident that it would take much longer than he had hoped. The Pope conferred with his advisers as to what should be done. He even considered keeping the Fathers in Rome throughout the winter instead of letting them go home in December as planned. In his charmingly naïve, or possibly mischievous, way he said, "What fun Christmas would be with all these bishops here!"

Second thoughts convinced the Pope of the impracticability of this Draconian solution. The idea of all those dioceses bereft of their spiritual leaders during that sacred season was not to be considered seriously. And the suffering it would entail among the bishops themselves weighed on his heart. Three of the Fathers had already died, perhaps from over-exertion. The penetrating cold and dampness of a Roman winter would surely wreak havoc in their ranks, especially among the many who came from tropical climates. Reluctantly the Pope returned to the original schedule of adjournment on December 8. Later, he even postponed the second session from May to September on the pleas of many bishops from far-off Sees; in order to give the newly-elected commissions time to work on the proposals to be put before the General Council in the hope that debate could be shortened, John also reduced the main topics from seventy to twenty. He hoped that the newly-elected members of the Commissions would be able to achieve compromise wordings that could be accepted by the Council Fathers with less discussion.

Although resigned to much delay, Pope John still kept push-

ing ahead for speed. Even when illness overtook him, he urged
them on from his sickbed.

The newspaper accounts of the Council put its differences
in political terms—"conservatives" and "liberals" were "bat-
tling" like delegates on a convention floor. In a witty speech to
the newsmen in Rome, American Bishop Fulton J. Sheen sati-
rized this by describing how the First Council of the Church in
Jerusalem in 52 A.D. might have been reported by the modern
press. Sheen had the Carthage paper headlining complaints
about the original lag in starting the work of the Church, "there
having been a ten-day delay between the Ascension and the Descent of the Holy Ghost upon the Apostles"; *The Roman Times*
might describe growing opposition to the Papal Authority of
Peter led by Bishops John and James; while the *Galilean Ex-
aminer* was reporting that the Council was split between the
"mysticals" led by Bishop John and the "modern criticism bloc"
led by (Doubting) Thomas. Sheen reeled off half a dozen head-
lines all of which a smart rewrite man could manufacture from
the story of the Council in the Acts of the Apostles.

The point was that the Ecumenical Council could not be
reported truthfully in political terms, because the Fathers were
not politicians out for personal gain or local advantage, but
were rather a group of men seeking a way to adapt eternal truths
to the understanding of modern men. As Sheen said, it was
composed of twenty-five hundred fallible men, "but add two
elements to those twenty-five hundred, namely the Holy Spirit
and the Vicar of Christ, and the twenty-five hundred fallibilities
come out as infallibility." Nevertheless, two groups of Fathers
with strong opposing views were certain to clash in the Council.
Let us call them the traditionalists and the non-traditionalists,
bishops more open to modern needs and problems, and remember that both were seeking only the best interests of the Church
and the greater glory of God.

The non-traditionalists were led by Cardinal Bea, head of

the Commission for the Promotion of Christian Unity [2]; they included the delegations from West Germany, France, Belgium, Holland, and Spain. The traditionalists included most of the Italian hierarchy, and Fathers from all over the world, including many from the United States. In fact, the American delegation was split almost equally between traditionalists and non-traditionalists. On the other hand, the African bishops formed a council within the Council, and were generally able to agree on a course of action. Their speeches were cleared through this council; when one of them rose to address the purple-clad phalanx of Fathers he could say, "I speak for Africa." This electrified the Council.

The chief spokesman for the traditionalists was Alfredo Cardinal Ottaviani, Secretary of the Sacred Supreme Congregation of the Holy Office. The reports of the Council proceedings sound as if it were divided into "good guys" and "bad guys"; the more dynamic being the "good guys," and the more staticly inclined the "bad guys." Since Ottaviani has been labeled the leader of the "bad guys," he should be better known. Alfredo Ottaviani was born in a crowded, poverty-stricken section of Rome. His father was a poor baker; like Angelo Roncalli, he got an education by winning scholarships in the Church schools. Also like Angelo Roncalli, he was a kindly man of simple tastes who when a young priest was on easy terms with all his poor neighbors in the Trastevere. After serving in the Vatican Secretariat of State with Pacelli, Ottaviani was made Assessor of the Holy Office in 1935. That job was equivalent to executive secretary. He was named Cardinal Pro-Secretary of the Holy Office in 1953, and Secretary in 1960. In effect, he has been "the mind" of the Holy Office for twenty-seven years.

Those who knew him long ago say that Cardinal Ottaviani was as progressive as the next priest until he entered the Holy

---

[2] Shortly after the Council opened, Pope John dramatically raised this body from a secretariat to the status of a full commission to emphasize its importance.

Office. What changed him was the responsibility of his position, because the Holy Office, which is headed by the Pope himself, ex-officio, has the sacred duty to defend and keep pure all teachings, writings, and other matters concerned with faith and morals. Thus, it is the guardian of truth and tradition. The man who heads it must in good conscience fight all innovations which may tamper with doctrine. This trust, plus the fact that he seldom left Rome, has made Cardinal Ottaviani seem over-rigid in his thinking.

Privately, Ottaviani loves to be with his many nieces and nephews and devotes his spare time to the orphanage which he founded. He never goes to parties and lives in a furnished apartment in the Holy Office building.

This mild, gentle man of seventy-three, with his almost unimpressive face, failing eyesight (due to cataracts), and firm sense of duty, has been cast in the role of a "bad guy"; but really he fulfills a most important role. He is the keeper of a sacred trust, the spokesman and preserver of tradition.

The first project to be discussed by the Council was reformation of the Liturgy. At first glance, there seemed to be little room for controversy in this highly technical subject which requires a profound knowledge of theology. Nevertheless, issue was sharply made by the Fathers over the question of whether portions of the Mass—and how much of it—might be said in the language of the people or must be in traditional Latin. This led to the discussion whether this decision should be left to national councils of bishops, which, of course, implied handing over to them authority held by the Curia.

Naturally the traditionalists fought it as a divisible and weakening proposal. The non-traditionalists favored it as a means of giving the faithful more sense of participation in the service, and as a gesture toward Christian unity. Speeches were made in halting Latin—by some Americans—defending the traditional language as an instrument of Catholic unity and precision. These were answered in stylish Latin by those who said,

"The Mass is not a law course; it is a prayer. The worshipers should be able to participate in the service."

A white-bearded figure in gold vestments, the eighty-four-year-old Patriarch Maximos IV Saigh of Antioch of the Melchites asserted his vigor and his independence by addressing the Council in French. He said that there was nothing sacred about Latin; his Church and other churches of the Eastern rite did not use it. Furthermore, neither Christ nor the Apostles spoke Latin, and it was not generally used in the Liturgy for the first two hundred years of the Church. To clinch the argument he quoted St. Paul's First Epistle to the Corinthians (14:13–16) "Therefore let him who speaks in a tongue pray that he may interpret . . . Else if thou givest praise with the spirit alone, how shall he who fills the place of the uninstructed say 'Amen' to thy thanksgiving? For he does not know what thou sayest."

But Archbishop Enrico Dante, the Vatican Prefect of Sacred Ceremonies, remarked sadly, "Everything has been ordained by tradition and now you want to change it all."

Then Cardinal Ottaviani arose to defend tradition in exquisite Latin. His speech ran beyond ten minutes. Dutch Cardinal Alfrink, presiding that day, warned him that his time was up, but Ottaviani ignored him, and kept on speaking—there was so much he wanted to say. When Ottaviani had been speaking for fifteen minutes, Alfrink reached over and pulled the cord of his microphone. The old cardinal's lips continued to move, but no sound reached his audience. A burst of applause, approving the president's act, brought a shock of realization to Ottaviani. Deeply hurt, he left the dead microphone and the Council and did not return for nearly a week.

Although Pope John wanted to avoid unnecessary delays, the discourtesy shown toward his old and honored friend by the applause was more than his tender heart could stand. He immediately issued a gentle, but public, warning to the Council against any further demonstrations of that kind.

On the other hand, perhaps to show that the Liturgy was not immutable, Pope John unilaterally made the first change in the Canon of the Mass in a thousand years. He ordained that the name of St. Joseph should be added after that of Mary. To the non-Catholic world, it seemed a small thing; it was, in fact, significant because it was the Pope's way of saying that the Liturgy *can* be changed. Pope John had long contemplated this because of his very special devotion to Mary's gentle spouse.

After over three weeks of discussion the Council approved, with amendments, the preamble and first section of the schema on Liturgy by a vote of 1922 to 11. It embodied liturgical reforms that allowed national or area councils of bishops to decide whether certain parts of the Mass should be said in the language of their people. This power had always belonged to the Curia; a great step had been taken toward decentralization.

The rest of the schema was sent back to the Commission for revision in line with the new preamble. The next schema or proposal concerned the Fonts of Revelation. This, as most expected, was a thorny subject.

At its center was the question: are the fonts of revelation two distinct ways in which God has spoken to man, or are they two different aspects of a single thing? Lurking behind this question was the argument which had been going on for a long time: should modern scientific methods and criticism be applied to the interpretation of Scripture?

To the ordinary layman, how the truth is revealed to man lies in the arcana of higher theology. Why, then, should it be a particular subject for heated controversy? Because it threatened the whole movement toward Christian unity, because it is one of the sharpest points of difference between Catholic and Anglican-Protestant theology. The traditional Catholics hold that the two sources of revelation—Holy Writ and oral tradition as passed down from the time of the Apostles—are quite separate; the Anglican and Protestant Churches recognize only Scripture.

The schema on the Fonts of Revelation was drawn up by the Preparatory Commission on Theology headed by Cardinal Ottaviani. He had chosen men of similar mind to be on it. As a result, the proposals they put before the Council represented the extreme, traditionalist viewpoint. They emphasized the separate nature of the two sources of revelation, totally ignoring the non-traditionalist viewpoint. In addition, they also backed the idea, as old as the Council of Trent, that the Bible should only be read under the guidance of a theologian. The non-traditionalists thought that, if accepted, the proposals would set back the cause of Christian unity a century or so, perhaps forever. They believed that scientific study of the Bible would clarify the Word of God.

As the debate opened in the Council, the non-traditionalists, led by Cardinals Lienart, Frings, Koenig, and Ritter of St. Louis, attacked the Schema on the grounds that it was old-fashioned, inflexible, and so abstruse that it was incomprehensible even to the average Catholic layman. They moved that, in parliamentary parlance, it be sent back to the Committee. The traditionalists, including Cardinals Ruffini, Siri, and McIntyre of Los Angeles, eloquently defended it on the grounds that it represented centuries of Catholic thinking; some of them suggested, however, that it might be modified in Council.

During the debate, Cardinal Bea, clothed in the new importance which the Pope had given him by raising the status of his Secretariat for Christian Unity to that of a commission, rose to speak. After politely praising the tremendous industry of the Theological Commission, he showed that it was misguided. He pointed out the tremendous damage that such an inflexible schema would do the cause for which he had labored so hard. Cardinal Bea said that the purpose of the Council must be to advance not enchain the movement toward Christian unity. With great emotion he said that the proposal before the Council "would close the door to intellectual Europe and the outstretched hands of friendship in the Old and New World."

His arguments really swayed the Council. Bishops and cardinals who were usually conservative began to have their doubts about the wisdom of voting for the schema. Knowing that the tide was running against him, Cardinal Ottaviani advanced the desperation argument that since the Pope had approved the schema on the Fonts of Revelation, it could not be rejected. Because everyone knew that Pope John would be the last man to throw an obstacle in the way of Christian unity, Ottaviani's argument was robbed of much force. In his opening address to the Council, Pope John had said that authentic doctrine should be studied and expounded, "through the methods of research and the literary forms of modern thought."

On November 20, the Secretary General, Archbishop Felici, at the request of Pope John, halted the debate and called for a vote. The rules of the Council were that all proposals must be ratified by two-thirds of the members present. Because the schema was already before the Council, under parliamentary procedure it required a two-thirds vote to reject it. Thirteen hundred and sixty-eight votes were cast to reject the schema; eight hundred and twenty-two votes were cast against rejection. The motion failed to get its two-thirds majority by only fifty-three votes. The schema would have to be fought out, paragraph by paragraph, in acrimonious debate.

Pope John had watched the progress of the debate on his private television set with intense anxiety. The arguments of Cardinal Bea, made to him privately as well as in the Council, had made a profound impression on him; he had not realized how strongly the Protestants felt on this matter. The thought that the Council he had called, instead of paving the way toward unity, might become a source of division began to trouble him.

When the opponents of the schema, though having a majority, fell short of the necessary two-thirds, the traditionalists had won the first round. Pope John had not attended any session of the Council except its formal opening, undoubtedly because he felt that his presence might embarrass free expression of opinion and exert an influence on the Fathers; he wanted the Council to reach its own decisions. The present situation, however, was different.

For one thing, Cardinal Ottaviani's suggestion that the Pope had approved the schema implied that Pope John favored the traditionalist view, and, thus, could influence the Fathers. For another, a clear majority of the Fathers were against it.

With real anguish the Pope considered the consequences of the vote—the haggling that would ensue as the Fathers debated the schema, section by section, and tried to amend and amend, and the interminable delay that would result. (The Romans were already making jokes about Vatican II outlasting Trent.) Meanwhile, the Pope knew, the separated brethren were watching the proceedings with anxious eyes. Even if it all came out right in the end, things would be said that would wound them or make them wary. The fine glow of their enthusiasm would be quenched, the spirit of brotherhood shaken. Pope John could not allow a parliamentary nuance to help the devil sow discord —not while he had the power to stop it. On November 21, the day after the vote, he again exercised the enormous authoritarian power of the Papacy in favor of democratic processes. At the morning session at which Cardinal Ruffini was presiding, Secretary General Felici dramatically announced that the Pope had withdrawn the schema on the Fonts of Revelation because its opponents had "a moral majority."

The Pope ordered the schema to be sent to a Special Joint Commission of which Cardinals Bea and Ottaviani would be joint Presidents. It would be composed of the Commission on Theology and the Commission for the Promotion of Christian Unity. This arrangement is reported to have been suggested by Cardinal Bea while the schema was being drawn up by the Preparatory Commission. It was rejected by Cardinal Ottaviani.

During the debate Laurean Cardinal Rugambwa of Tanganyika had asked the Pope to intervene, and to withdraw the schema. Similar appeals had been made by other Fathers, who pointed out that since changes in the schema would also require a two-thirds vote no important ones were likely to be made.

On November 24, the Pope named several Fathers who had taken an active part on both sides of the debate as additional members of the new Commission. Among them were Cardinals Lienart, Frings, Ruffini, and Meyer of Chicago. Pope John ardently hoped that the special Commission would be able to produce a new schema that, while conforming to Catholic dogma, would leave the door open to the separated brethren.

A very wise Catholic newsman in Rome said, "The importance of the Pope's action cannot be overestimated. Not only did it save the Council from parliamentary quirks, a vast waste of time, and bitter debate, but it also set the tone for the future. In one gesture, Pope John demonstrated that he wanted an open Council truly representative of the majority view, and that he would not stand for any steam-roller tactics."

A Protestant observer remarked, "Now I see why it can be a good thing to have a Pope!"

Pope John said, "Now my Council really begins."

The Pope's Window—Vatican
(from St. Peter's Square)

CHAPTER SIXTEEN

THE POPE AND
THE PROTESTANTS

Pope John had, in fact, completely won the hearts of the observers of whatever denomination, from the Quaker, Reverend Doctor Richard Ullman, through the varying shades of Protestantism to the High Church Anglicans, who do not consider themselves Protestants at all. In fact, the Anglican Dr. Frederick Grant, in a sermon at St. Paul's Episcopal Church in Rome on the Sunday after the Council opened, spoke of his church as "A bridge between Protestant and Catholic."

From the very first the observers were made to feel welcome. Most of them were met at Rome's Fiumicino Airport by Cardinal Bea's right-hand man, Monsignor Jan Willebrands of Holland. Those who needed financial assistance were accommodated in first-class pensions near St. Peter's at the expense of the Vatican. When, at the fifty-ninth second of the last minute, Archpriest Vitali Borovoi and Archimandrite Vladimir Kutlyarev arrived to represent the Patriarchal Church of Russia there was as much rejoicing at the Vatican as in heaven over a lost lamb.

In addition, the observers were admitted to all meetings of the Council and provided with copies of all the schemata. "When I heard *that*," an American Catholic Monsignor said, "I almost fell over."

263

To which Canon Pawley, who had probably arranged it, remarked, "If we didn't have the schemata, how could we understand what was going on?" Many wondered if the observers would understand even with the schemata. Most of them were classical scholars who were more familiar with Latin than many of the Fathers. For the "unlearned," a special translation of the proceedings was provided.

Soon after the Council opened, the Pope held an audience for the Observers, although audience is really too formal a word for what took place. Pope John came smiling into the room where the twenty-eight men representing seventeen different forms of Christian belief were seated in a circle. Ignoring the red and gold throne, he pulled up an ordinary chair and sat in it. As Congregationalist Doctor George H. Williams, put it, "Pope John is not setting himself up as someone above us. He is with us."

In his talk to the observers John made his intentions plain. Speaking of the papal power he said, "As far as it concerns my humble person, I don't like to claim any special inspiration. I am content with the sound doctrine that everything comes from God." Then in so warm a voice that every man there knew he was speaking from the heart, he told them of his emotions at the opening of the Council. "My eyes ranged over the multitude of sons and brothers," he said, "and suddenly as they rested on your group, on each of you personally, I drew extraordinary comfort from your presence. I will not say more about that right now, but will simply record the fact. *Benedictus Deus per singulos dies* (Blessed be God for each single day)."

"Yet, if you could read my heart," Pope John added emotionally, "perhaps you would understand more than words can say." It was easy for these men of many different creeds to read his heart, because it was obviously full of goodness and love.

As the Council got down to work in the secret sessions, great pains were taken to make the observers feel that the cry *"Exeunt Omnes,"* which warned all unauthorized persons to get out, did not apply to them. Each speaker would begin his address by saying, "Reverend Fathers and (bowing slightly in their direction) Honored Observers." Some of them even said, "And dear Observers."

Pope John's dramatic call for all Christians to work actively for Church unity produced a meeting without precedent in the annals of Christianity. Within twenty-four hours, Roman Catholic prelates and representatives of at least twelve other Christian denominations met secretly in a room in a hotel near the Vatican to explore the prospects for unity. There were Anglicans, Methodists, Congregationalists, Quakers, Lutherans, black-veiled, bearded priests of the Syrian Orthodox faith, Coptic Christians from Egypt, and Armenians. Seven members of the Commission for the Promotion of Christian Unity met with them. Cardinal Bea, feeling that his presence might hamper discussion, did not attend this first meeting, so Monsignor Willebrands led the Catholic group. *The Rome Daily American* commented: "Never before in modern times had so many Catholic churchmen sat down with so many representatives of so many different non-Catholic churches in a formal examination of joint aims."

As in the Council the people present at this meeting were honor bound to secrecy, but some news leaked out: the spirit of the conference was enthusiastically cooperative; they all agreed to meet again. And again. And again . . .

Pope John realized that the existing spirit of brotherhood did not mean that the enormous difficulties in the way of true unification would be quickly overcome. He was very much saddened, for example, that the Patriarch of Constantinople, who regarded himself as the Primate of the Greek Orthodox Churches, had refused to send an observer. The Patriarch insisted, "Unless our delegates sit as full members, it is *not* an ecumenical council."

The Pope, in fact, had been unrealistically optimistic about healing the thousand-year rift with the Greek Orthodox Church.

Because Rome recognizes the validity of the Orthodox sacraments, and almost the same Liturgy is used in the Catholic
churches of the Eastern Rite, he thought that the differences
between them could be compromised. He was deluded by his
own open-hearted nature; because he was not fond of theological
hair-splitting, his emphasis on that which unites glossed over
the very real divisions. The fact that Rome accepts the Eastern
Rite Catholics instead of being a bond of union is a sore point
with the Orthodox churches. They regard it as a form of sheep
stealing.

However, the main difference is the Catholic claim of papal
supremacy, something that all the Orthodox patriarchs ada-
mantly refuse to admit. They might be willing to regard the
Bishop of Rome as the first among equals, but not as the
supreme, infallible head of the Church.

This is, of course, a difficulty that Anglicans find. Though,
in their case, difficulties are numerous. Oddly enough, although
Dr. Grant had called the Church of England a "bridge," it is in
some respects further from the possibility of unity with Rome
than many of the Protestant churches. This, paradoxically,
is because England and Rome are more alike. Like the Catholics,
the Anglicans have a rigid set of beliefs (The Thirty-Nine Ar-
ticles of the Christian Faith), and an elaborate Liturgy. On the
other hand, the Free churches, as they like to be called, have a
more flexible attitude, although this does not necessarily mean
that they are ready to accept Catholic dogma.

Nevertheless, Pope John had reason for optimism. Much
progress had been made since the old days of hatreds and sus-
picions. For example, a reporter, who obviously was out of touch
with the times, described the observers at the opening ceremony
as watching the elaborate ritual "stony-faced." This comment
raised an uproar among them. Vehemently denying any lack
of sympathy, they said, on the contrary, that the solemnity of
their expressions was because they were so deeply moved.

A century ago they *would* have been stony-faced. That is
the enormous difference.

Pope John was right in his optimism; when people begin to manifest so much love and good will toward one another, something must come of it sooner or later. The Pope could take enormous pride in the fact that he has done more than any other single man to produce this happy circumstance. Of course, his humility would never allow it.

Yousuf Karsh of Ottawa tells a story that illustrates John's attitude about himself. When the famous photographer was taking the Pontiff's picture, Pope John wryly said to Karsh, "If the Lord knew I was going to be Pope, you'd think he would have made me more photogenic!"

It is not possible to dislike a man like that. The observers were very fond of him. Their attitude was well expressed by the Reverend Doctor Kissack who represented in Rome the Methodist Conference of Great Britain. Doctor Kissack was discussing the difference between the Protestant idea of the ministry and the Catholic conception of it. "The ideal of the ministry in the Protestant tradition," he said, "is quite different from Rome or the Anglicans. In our ministry, you identify yourself with the people of your congregation. The only thing you have they don't is, perhaps, a sense of divine inspiration. On the other hand the Catholic priest arrays himself in splendid vestments and appears before the Altar in the glory of light reflected from on high.

"The extraordinary thing about Pope John is that even with his sacramental view of the priesthood he succeeds in giving you the impression of being a man of like passions."

Then, in a sudden surge of tremendous affection, Doctor Kissack burst out, "In fact, the dear old Pope is just like one of us."

The Opening of the Ecumenical Council

CHAPTER SEVENTEEN

"THIS GRAND PROSPECT"

After the recall of the schema on the Fonts of Revelation, there were no more sharp disputes. Three more proposals were introduced—the schemata on the Communications Media, on the Oriental Churches, and on the Nature of the Church. Though there were sharp differences of opinion on all these proposals, especially the last, which also had been drawn up under the influence of Cardinal Ottaviani, the debates on them did not reach a critical point. There was not time to consider them in detail, and they were sent back to several commissions to be reshaped in the light of the majority opinion of the Council.

The Fathers had suddenly lost heart for heated argument because they were suddenly confronted by news that shocked them into a unanimity of anxiety. Pope John was ill—very ill, they feared. Ever since the Council opened, he had looked tired; his face had been tinged with gray instead of its normal rosy hue. But he had kept up a rigorous schedule—public audiences every Wednesday, special Masses and religious celebrations, a stream of private audiences with foreign prelates and VIPS in Rome for the Council, constant conferences with his advisers and members of various commissions, and many expeditions outside of Vatican City for special occasions, or to visit ailing cardinals and bishops; the Romans nicknamed him John-Out-side-the-Walls.

The first indication of trouble came on November 20, a day of special tension because of the vote on the Fonts of Revelation. It was an announcement by the Vatican that Dr. Antonio Gasbarrini of Bologna had been appointed personal physician to the Pope replacing Dr. Fillipo Rocchi who had died sometime before.

It was rather odd to choose a doctor from Bologna when there were so many in Rome, but Dr. Gasbarrini had a brilliant reputation throughout Italy for keeping closely in touch with the latest developments in medicine. Furthermore, Pope John liked him—liked his down-to-earth, straightforward approach, his sense of humor, and his friendly warmth. And, after all, Bologna was not very far from Rome. As his stand-in at the Vatican, Gasbarrini appointed Dr. Piero Mazzoni.

There was nothing too alarming in the Pope appointing a new doctor; it was just a straw in the wind. Only the few people closest to him knew what an ill wind it was. The truth was that the Pope's discomfort had certainly not been alleviated by his great activities. But more alarming was the fact that his famous digestion had broken down because of the nervous strain, the excitement, and the sheer exhaustion. The painful symptoms of stomach ulcer appeared. Dr. Gasbarrini put his patient on a special diet, and told him to get as much rest as possible.

As far as the diet went, Pope John was a very good patient; where rest was concerned, he was a very bad one. During the next week, he not only continued all his regular activities, but also made the tremendous decision to recall the schema on the Fonts of Revelation and set up the Joint Commission to redraw it. He held a long session with his advisers on the question of the other Fathers to be added to it.

On November 22, Pope John called for his car and went to the Spanish College to comfort Cardinal Pla y Daniel of Toledo who was sick. The fact that the Cardinal had a case of very infectious influenza did not give John even a moment's pause.

After visiting the Cardinal, the Pope made a little speech to the students, and on his way home detoured to the Roman Seminary for Juridical Studies—the new name for the old Apollinare—and, after greeting the students who were his successors there, went to say a prayer in the familiar old Church of St. Apollinaris, where the young aspirant to the priesthood had prayed so fervently long ago.

The next day, November 23, he held a special audience for the bishops of India. In a long speech he recalled his acquaintance with Nehru, whom he had met when he was Nuncio in Paris. He made public the messages he had exchanged with the Indian Prime Minister expressing his sympathy for Nehru in the face of Red Chinese aggression.

On his eighty-first birthday, November 25, Pope John was feeling very ill indeed. Nevertheless, he celebrated Mass in the chapel of the College for the Propagation of the Faith, and made a long speech to the cardinals, bishops, and seminarians from more than sixty mission countries who had gathered there to hear him. It was then that he made the gloomy prognostication about surviving his eighty-second year. But he was still looking ahead rather than backward; he ended his allocution by saying, "We are the wealthy heirs of the great lessons of the past, but we face a world which more than ever needs the grace of God in the evangelical sense. In our work it's more important that we look to the future than the past."

Thus, once again, the Pope disarmed a Protestant criticism of the attitude of the Church. Dr. Kissack voiced it when he said, "It seems to me that the Romans (Catholics) are too concerned with nostalgia. That is one great difference between the Catholics and the Free Churches. They cannot conceive of anything but nostalgia for lost unity, while the Protestants feel they are moving—slowly, but moving—*toward* this divine event."

So does Pope John.

That long exhausting day, which included a final speech to the crowds in St. Peter's Square who had gathered to wish him, *"Buon Natale!"* (Happy Birthday), finally brought down the strong body that Pope John had driven so hard. He felt so ill and weak on Monday that Dr. Mazzoni ordered the Pope to stay in bed.

The next day Pope John was worse. Despite Vatican reticence, all indications are that the ulcer began to hemorrhage. Badly frightened, Dr. Mazzoni sent for Gasbarrini. The situation was truly grave. For any man, the Pope's condition was serious; for a man in his eighties, it was critical. Even Dr. Gasbarrini lost his usual aplomb. Pope John was cheerfully resigned to whatever God willed, but he was still too optimistic to give up hope.

Poor Monsignor Capovilla was desperately worried. Shattered by his great love for the Pope and worried about the effect his illness would have on the Council and the world, he wore his thin body thinner still by spending every possible daytime moment and the long night hours in prayer.

The instinct of everyone in the Vatican was to keep the seriousness of the Pope's condition secret. They had succeeded in doing so on Monday. Then on Tuesday, November 27, they were faced by the fact that the usual Wednesday public audience would have to be cancelled. As men fearful of public reaction so often do under great strain, they foolishly tried to cover up with a false report—"The Pope is confined to bed with a bad cold."

The following day this was corrected with an even more vague announcement—the Pope was "indisposed." On November 29, *L'Osservatore Romano* came closer to the truth with the official report that the audiences had been interrupted, "because of the accentuations of symptoms of a gastropathy for which the Pope has been for some time under medical and dietary treatment, and which has provoked a fairly intense anemia."

These contradictory and ambiguous communiqués had exactly the opposite effect from the intended alleviation of public anxiety. Wild rumors were flying. The fact that the first report had been incorrect and that the third report used an obscure term, "gastropathy," which means stomach trouble without saying what kind, made everyone distrust them. Add to that the fact that Dr. Gasbarrini saw his patient twice on November 28 and that Dr. Mazzoni moved into the Vatican, and you have explosive fuel for sensational amateur diagnoses.

All sorts of alarming guesses appeared in the press . . . the Pope had cancer of the prostate gland, or of the stomach . . . he was positively going to be operated on for something on December 11 . . . he had leukemia . . . he was at death's door. The public reaction would have been very gratifying to a conceited man. The possibility of losing him brought home to the Fathers and to people everywhere of all faiths—and of none—how very much the world had need of him. And how much they loved him. It brought forth a tremendous outpouring of fervent prayers for his recovery, and an almost universal sense of impending irreplaceable loss.

Fortunately, the very day that public alarm reached a peak of panic, Pope John's grand constitution began its comeback. On November 29, the Pope felt well enough to treat himself to the pleasure of watching the televised performance of Beethoven's Ninth Symphony, given at St. Paul's Outside-the-Walls in honor of the Council, which he had planned to attend in person. The next day he was out of bed in the afternoon, and wanted to resume his full work schedule. Dr. Gasbarrini reported, "It is hard to restrain him."

When Archbishop Felici reported to the Council the Pope's improvement, the Fathers greeted the good news with a pandemonium of cheering. They had reason to cheer, because on the life of that one man probably hung the whole success of the Council. Besides, they loved him well. The Pope, watching them on his television set, was so affected by their expression of love and joy that tears ran down the deep lines of his smiling face.

On December 2, only five days after the first news of his illness became public, Pope John was well enough to sit by the open window of his room and, with loud speakers hooked up, recite the Angelus with the delighted crowd who had gathered in the Square to watch the bishops leave St. Peter's. On December 5, it was announced beforehand that he would bless the pilgrims from his window at noon. The Council Fathers adjourned early to be present, and that superb purple tide flowed down the steps and out over the pavement to mingle with the great crowd.

The Pope's window was thrown open at exactly noon, and again he recited the Angelus. As he ended, cardinals, bishops, priests, nuns, and people joined in an ecstatic demonstration of joy, punctuated by clanging bells, hooting horns, and the deep bray of the waiting buses.

Pope John let it go on for a little; then, as he held up his hand, the uproar stopped short. Smiling happily, he spoke to them. "My sons, Divine Providence is with us," he said. "As you see, from one day to the next there is progress. Not downward, but slowly upward. *Piano; Piano;* Sickness then convalescence." Then Pope John spread his arms over the crowd —the episcopal crimsons and purples, the blacks, grays, and browns. "What a spectacle we see before us today," he said exultantly. "The Church grouped together here in its full membership. *Ecco* its bishops! *Ecco* its priests! *Ecco* its Christian people! A whole family is present here—the family of Christ!"

On December 6, Archbishop Felici announced to the Council the Pope's directives, drawn up while he was still supposed to be resting, for the work of the Council throughout its recess. During that long interval, the Pope announced, it would be necessary to re-examine and perfect all the schemata in the light of the work of the Council so far, and the Pope's own statement at the opening session concerning its pastoral, rather than dogmatic, aims. This would be done by the commissions, assisted by special sub-commissions where proposals overlapped: "The Catholic Church, lifting high, by means of this Ecumenical Council, the torch of religious truth, intends to show herself as the loving Mother of all, benign, patient, full of goodness and mercy, so also to the brothers who are separated from her. To mankind, oppressed by so many difficulties, the Church says as Peter said to the poor who begged him for alms: 'I have neither gold nor silver, but what I have I give you; in the name of Christ of Nazareth arise and walk.' "

Detailed directions followed as to the principles which should be followed in revising the schemata and the methods of carrying out this work. Meanwhile a new commission was set up to coordinate all this activity and to make sure that the revised proposals *conformed to the aims of the Council.* In appointing Secretary of State Cardinal Cicognani president of this commission, Pope John made an excellent choice. A Monsignor, who works in the Secretariat of State described him as, "A very sweet, charming man; a diplomat who never pushes, but wins men to his way of thinking. In colloquial English, he's a gent."

As soon as the new proposals were ready, and given general approval by the Pope, they were ordered to be sent to all the Conciliar Fathers who would be asked to examine them, and to return them with their suggestions or objections within a time limit to be set later. The commissions would then again revise the schemata, taking the suggestions into account and carefully assessing pros and cons, and have them ready to be submitted to the Council when it reconvened on September 8.

Pope John hoped thus to avoid acrimonious disputes and speed things up by presenting proposals that were generally agreeable to the majority of the Council. Always the optimist, he spoke hopefully of concluding its business by Christmas, 1963.

On December 7, the day before the Council adjourned, Pope John paid a surprise visit to St. Peter's. His doctors were strongly against it, but he ordered his car, and drove the hundred yards or so to the side door of the Basilica. As the Pope walked in and seated himself on the throne, the Fathers cheered like a crowd at a football game. Even though it was in Church, they could not restrain their joy. This time, Pope John did not reprove them.

Instead he gave a little extemporaneous speech in Latin telling them: "Although we have not attended any meeting of the Council since its opening, we have been with you both in our prayers and by following your debates over television."

The next day, the Feast of the Immaculate Conception, Pope John went again to St. Peter's. He arrived at quarter-past ten, immediately after the Solemn Mass celebrated by Paolo Cardinal Marella, the Archpriest of St. Peter's. This time he came on foot, and walked the entire length of the nave between the tiered ranks of the Fathers. They thought he looked pale and much thinner, and noted how slowly he climbed to his throne on the dais. But when he put on his spectacles and began to read his address, his voice rang out with its old timbre, and his choppy gestures were as vigorous as ever.

"This Council," he told them, "in its reality, is an act of faith in God, of obedience to His laws, of sincere endeavor to correlate with the plan of redemption according to which the Word was made flesh of the Virgin Mary . . .

"Now that the bishops of the five continents are returning to their beloved dioceses . . . we should like to dwell a little on what has been done so far, and, encouraged and enlightened by this, to map out the future . . . The first session was like a slow and solemn introduction to the great work of the Council —a generous willingness to enter into the heart and substance of our Lord's plan. It was necessary for brothers, gathered together from afar around a common hearth, to make each other's closer acquaintance; it was necessary for them to look at each other squarely in order to understand what was in each other's hearts. They had need to describe their own experiences, reflecting the conditions of the apostolate under the most varied climates and circumstances, in order that there should be a thoughtful and profitable interchange of views on pastoral matters.

"In such a vast gathering it is understandable that a few days were needed to arrive at an agreement on a matter on which, in all charity, there existed, with good reason, sharply divergent views. But even this has a providential place in the triumph of truth, for it has shown all the world the holy liberty that the sons of God enjoy in the Church."

Pope John then noted the work done on the schema on the Sacred Liturgy and the introduction of the other proposals. He said, "A good beginning has been made."

Next, the Pope pointed out that the work of the Council, aided by modern communications, would continue during the recess, "which was certainly not the case during the recesses of previous councils," and he briefly described how the new commission headed by Cardinal Cicognani would function. He urged the bishops, in spite of the press of their pastoral duties, to cooperate so the next meeting in September would proceed "more surely, more steadily and with greater speed. . . ."

Then, Pope John turned his eyes toward the future saying, "The vision of this grand prospect, which reveals the whole course of the coming year, so rich in promise, arouses in the heart a more ardent hope for the realization of the goals for which we have convoked this Council . . ."

He spoke of the benefits he expected for the Catholic Church and then of his anticipation of "renewed attention on the part of all those countless children of ancient and glorious civilizations, which the light of Christianity does *not* wish to destroy, but in which she could—as has happened at other times —develop the richest seeds of religious vigor and human progress."

Emotionally he added, "Our heart casts its glance in that direction, Venerable Brethren, and we know also that your hearts have the same solicitude as our own."

After the Council finally ends, the task of putting the decisions into effect will begin. The entire Church will take part in this gigantic effort. . . . "In order that the acts of the Fathers may be seconded by the most joyful and faithful response . . . It will be a new Pentecost. . . ."

At the end of his address, Pope John expressed the confidence and exaltation with which the Council had inspired him: "In this hour of heartfelt joy it is as if the heavens are opened above our heads and the splendor of the heavenly court shines out upon us, filling us with superhuman certainty and a supernatural spirit of faith, joy, and profound peace.

"In this light we look forward to your return. We salute all of you, Venerable Brothers, 'with a holy Kiss,' while at the same time we call down upon you the most abundant blessings of our Lord of which the apostolic blessing is the pledge and the promise."

The second Vatican Council may well be renamed by historians, "The Council of Pope John XXIII." Inspired by the Holy Spirit, he called it without the counsel of his advisers; he guided its meticulous preliminary work; he inspired its opening session, and then he watched over its proceedings from his room in the Vatican, interfering only when the will and wisdom of the majority of the Fathers appeared to be thwarted by parliamentary technicalities.

But, although he delicately withdrew from asserting any influence by his presence, the influence was there. It pervaded that great assemblage, not by exhortation or diplomacy, but by the force of his character—his simple, earthy strength, his humility, his tolerance and humanity, his intelligence, his humor, his ardent faith and transparent purity, and, above all, by his sheer loving goodness.

Pseudo-sophisticates spend wasted time trying to find the secret of Pope John's diplomatic successes in some artful technique. They are on the wrong track. It is not an intellectual process—not a plan. It is the nature of the man. People always trust him because they know he wishes them well. A man of high intelligence, Pope John can deal with abstract problems in their place, but in human relations he is guided by his heart not his head.

A minor example was his audience in 1962, for the wife of the President of the United States. Beforehand, he asked Monsignor Capovilla what the protocol was for addressing her, and Capovilla answered, "The Americans call her simply Mrs. Kennedy, but since she is half French and you will be speaking that language, you might address her as Madame." The Pope tried it out, "Mrs. Kennedy—Madame Kennedy—Madame." But when she knelt in the doorway of his apartment, young and lovely with her sweet-shy expression, he opened his arms wide and said, "Jacqueline!"

He stands thus before the world, arms open wide. He called his Council to open the arms of the Church to all men who want her.

That is the spirit which pervades the Council, however sharply it may dispute on details. Many of its members had more of a parochial viewpoint before they came to Rome. Of course, almost all of them had been there before, but often only for brief visits. Their worlds were the small compasses of their own dioceses; their problems, local problems; their understanding of people, largely limited to their own flocks. The first great work of the Council was accomplished simply when it met, and by meeting exposed its members to a world-wide seminar, conducted not only in the Council but in private talks in the religious houses, hotels, and pensions, where the Fathers were quartered, and in the popular coffee bar set up in a hall of St. Peter's. These men from many nations educated each other. They learned things about other peoples, and gained understanding of foreign points of view. These were things Pope John had already learned through living in and visiting so many different countries, and through his understanding heart.

A very important thing the Fathers learned was not to be too much in awe of Rome. The Curia had been to many of them a distant, unpredictable body that must be blindly obeyed. They know now that it is a group of men like themselves—good men, dedicated men, but fallible men. The moment that the Council met, the Curia lost much of its imagined power. The Fathers learned that they themselves held the power, under the Pope. And they also learned from the Pope's example to think of exercising this new power with the utmost benevolence, understanding, and love toward all mankind.

As they do so, it in truth becomes the Council of Pope John XXIII.

Pope John XXIII gives his last Easter blessing—April 14, 1963.

"THAT THEY MAY BE ONE"

In His mysterious way, God called Pope John to Him before his work was done. At eleven minutes before eight on Monday evening, June 3, 1963, the most beloved pope of modern times, perhaps of all time, died. Though other pontiffs had won the love of their fellow Catholics, surely none had so touched the hearts of people of all faiths—and of no faith. For they knew he loved them no matter what they were or what they believed. And when he left them they were suddenly bereft.

Sudden it seemed to them, though not to John. For almost a year he had known that the small pain which almost imperceptibly sapped his magnificent stamina was a tumor that could not be removed because of his old age. Since nothing could be done, he splendidly ignored it, smiling, even laughing with enforced gaiety despite his secret, while he carried on his Master's business. During that year he drove himself beyond the capacity of a strong young man in his urgency to achieve his intense ambition—to bring unity to all who said "Our Father" and peace to all men everywhere.

The great opening days of the Ecumenical Council were both triumphant and tragic to him. Triumphant because never before in history had a council of the Church aroused such universal hope and well-wishing; tragic because he, almost alone, knew that, barring a miracle, he would not live to guide its ultimate conclusions.

Since that was not to be, when the Council adjourned for its essential period of study and reassessment, John threw himself, with a final surge of energy, into the writing of his magnificent encyclical *Pacem in Terris*—"Peace on Earth." Next to the Council itself, this message, in its profundity, charity and broad humanity, is the most important impulse toward world unity of this troubled era. It might have been the lifetime work of a dedicated theologian; John wrote it in less than three months. On April 12, 1963, smiling broadly, he signed it.

Of course, like all men who have a great goal to attain, he hoped that God might grant him the brief extension of time needed to finish the job. After his quick recovery from the first attack in November, 1962, it looked as though this wish might be granted.

But on May 25, 1963, a few days after personally receiving the new Balzan Prize for peace, he suffered another attack of internal bleeding and great pain. Even then he did not give up; that was never his habit. While people prayed for him in almost every language and every rite, he fought for his life with all the power of his strong peasant body and unshakable faith. And he seemed to be winning.

On Thursday morning, May 30, Pope John was so much better that his personal physician, Doctor Antonio Gasbarrini, said, "It is conceivable that the Pope may be able to bless the Sunday crowds in the Square from his window."

But as Friday, May 31, dawned, Doctor Piero Mazzoni, who was napping in a chair in the Pope's study, heard a loud cry from the bedroom. He rushed in to find the Pope in terrible pain. A glance told him that internal hemorrhaging had begun again. Soon he confirmed his fear that peritonitis had set in.

Though others might still hope, John realistically sensed that he must soon go. At 6:30 a.m. his faithful Capovilla, his

The effects of serious illness show on John's face in this portrait taken in his Vatican library the day after Easter Sunday, April 15.

Pope John blesses the crowds below his window in his last public appearance, on May 23, Ascension Day (photos by UPI).

voice breaking, said Mass in the next room. Then Pope John firmly asked for the Viaticum (the last sacrament). He received it from Bishop Peter van Lierde. Afterward he said "I am returning to the Lord." "I offer myself as a sacrifice on the altar, for the Church, for the Council and for peace," he told one visitor; to Dr. Gasbarrini he said, "My bags are packed and I am ready, very ready, to go." He asked Capovilla to send for his brothers and sister; but before they arrived he fell into a coma. The Vatican announced that he had entered the death agony.

They were wrong! At about two-thirty on Saturday morning Pope John suddenly rallied. Only the enormous strength of his great body made this seeming miracle possible. He recognized his brothers, Zaverio, Alfredo and Giuseppi, and his sister, Assunta, who were sitting by the bed, and blessed them. Then, amazingly, he grew stronger still and drank a cup of coffee. In firm tones he discussed the Council and expressed his wishes as to its future in very definite terms. He talked of old times and remembered the far places in which he had served. He spoke lovingly of people who had helped him, particularly remembering his dear Cardinal Tardini. Then he became unconscious again.

Throughout Saturday Pope John continued to rally from coma to full consciousness. Never once did his mind wander. Each time he revived he was completely lucid and "the most serene person in the room."

Though in great pain he seemed to enjoy the company of his family. It was the longest time they had spent together since he became Pope. He talked to them, prayed with them, blessed and embraced them. In the Bergamasch dialect he said, "Remember Papa? Remember Mama? I am going to see them. Let's pray for them." Nor did he forget to honor the places of his youth. He sent his special blessing to the people of Bergamo—oh those bells of Bergamo!

The last picture of John XXIII before his death, taken May 25 as he recorded a radio message.

On Sunday morning, against all probability, Pope John was still conscious. It was Pentecost. He followed the Mass said in the next room. Then he asked that the Epistle be read to him again: "And suddenly there came a noise from heaven, as of the rushing of a blast of wind, which filled the whole house where they were seated. And there appeared to them tongues, as though of fire, which parted and sat upon each one of them. And they were all filled with the Holy Spirit, and began to speak in foreign tongues, according as the Spirit gave them to utter ... each one heard them speaking his own language ... Parthians and Medes and Elamites, dwellers in Mesopotamia, Judea and Cappadocia, in Pontus and Asia, in Phrygia and Pamphylia, in Egypt and the parts of Africa about Cyrene ..."

All that day, too, the cardinals came to the room where the Pope lay in his narrow bed, half raised by four pillows. Some he recognized and some he did not. In the late afternoon the doc-

Pope John's body, clad in his robes and with his Bishop's miter on his head, is borne across the crowded square to St. Peter's Basilica.

tors asked that the visits be stopped. Only the Pope's family remained around his bed. His eighty-three-year-old confessor, Bishop Alfredo Cavagna, sat near the foot of the bed reading his breviary. Capovilla knelt in a corner praying and weeping. John saw him, and, pitying him, indicated that he wished to speak. When Capovilla knelt beside his bed the Pope said, "When this is all over be sure to go and see your mother."

On Monday morning the Pope was still, incredibly, alive. He seemed to follow the Mass said by Cardinal Cicognani in the next room though he was too weak to swallow the wafer. At noon he lost consciousness for the last time. His family sat around the bed.

Shortly after seven that evening all those who were with the Pope recited the Rosary together. Out in the warm golden sunshine of St. Peter's Square Cardinal Traglia, pro-vicar-general of the city of Rome, celebrated Mass before seventy-five thousand people. Almost as the Mass ended, while the choir was singing *Veni Creator Spiritu,* Pope John died.

Even in death Pope John broke all precedents. By his orders the long and elaborate ceremonies of past days were cut short. On Tuesday his body, clothed in white Papal vestments, lay in a simple bier in his apartment while those cardinals who were in Rome, the diplomatic corps, high officials, and his closest friends filed by. At six o'clock his body was carried in state down the royal stairway and across the square to St. Peter's. From eight o'clock Wednesday morning until six o'clock Thursday evening the sad crowds filed through the great basilica, where the council hall, with its banks of empty seats, still awaited the reconvening of the Ecumenical Council. High Requiem Mass was celebrated while the long lines of devout

Pope John's body is given absolution by Archbishop Felici (right) inside St. Peter's Basilica.

weeping people, John's people, moved slowly by. At six o'clock the doors were closed and half an hour later the body of the good Pope John was solemnly interred in the crypt beneath the High Altar. Later, it would be removed to the Basilica of St. John Lateran, where the Pope had wished to rest.

While John was ill messages of tribute from all the world had begun to pour into the Vatican. Some of those which had been shown to the Pope before he died genuinely amazed him. Such unlikely persons as Fidel Castro and Nikita Khrushchev sent messages of praise and sorrow. Perhaps one of the most fitting tributes of all was paid Pope John by the leader of the Church of England, Dr. Arthur M. Ramsey, Archbishop of Canterbury, speaking in Canterbury Cathedral the Sunday before the Pope died:

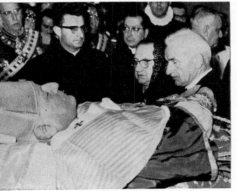

Assunta and Giuseppe Roncalli bid their brother a last farewell.

"The hearts of Christian people everywhere go out to one man, a great Christian of our time, Pope John . . ."

"He is one, in the words of the Bible, who 'is a good man and full of the Holy Ghost and of Faith.' He is one of whom the Holy Spirit, like tongues of fire, has given vision, the vision of the unity of all Christians

The coffin of Pope John XXIII in the crypt under St. Peters.

and a warmth of love for humanity far and near.

"He is one who lives and dies very near to God, and self is burnt away as the fire of divine charity fills him. May God keep him in death as in life, and God grant him a heavenly reward and the fulfillment of all his prayers for peace and unity on earth."

These words, from the head of a church separated from Rome, would have meant much to John, who, during his last days and even during his last hours, kept repeating over and over the prayer for unity, *Ut unum sint,* taken from Christ's own words at the Last Supper as they appear in the Gospel of St. John. One verse from that Gospel sums up all that need be said about Angelo Guiseppe Roncalli of Sotto il Monte, Bergamo, who became Pope John XXIII, Bishop of Rome and Vicar of Jesus Christ, Successor of St. Peter, Prince of the Apostles, Supreme Pontiff of the Universal Church, Patriarch of the West, Primate of Italy, Archbishop and Metropolitan of the Roman Province, Sovereign of Vatican City and maker of history:

"And I am no more in the world; and they are in the world, and I come to thee. Holy Father, keep them in thy name, which thou has given me, that they may be one, as we."

INDEX

281